Ezekiel

EZEKIEL

*A Focused Commentary
for Preaching and Teaching*

John W. Hilber

CASCADE *Books* · Eugene, Oregon

EZEKIEL
A Focused Commentary for Preaching and Teaching

Copyright © 2019 John W. Hilber. All rights reserved. Except for brief quotations in critical publications or reviews, no part of this book may be reproduced in any manner without prior written permission from the publisher. Write: Permissions, Wipf and Stock Publishers, 199 W. 8th Ave., Suite 3, Eugene, OR 97401.

Cascade Books
An Imprint of Wipf and Stock Publishers
199 W. 8th Ave., Suite 3
Eugene, OR 97401

www.wipfandstock.com

PAPERBACK ISBN: 978-1-4982-9421-8
HARDCOVER ISBN: 978-1-4982-9423-2
EBOOK ISBN: 978-1-4982-9422-5

Cataloging-in-Publication data:

Names: Hilber, John W. (John Walter), author.
Title: Ezekiel : a focused commentary for preaching and teaching / John W. Hilber.
Description: Eugene, OR: Cascade Books, 2018. | Includes bibliographical references.
Identifiers: ISBN: 978-1-4982-9421-8 (paperback). | ISBN: 978-1-4982-9423-2 (hardcover). | ISBN: 978-1-4982-9422-5 (ebook).
Subjects: LCSH: Bible—Ezekiel—Commentaries.
Classification: BS1545.3 H47 2019 (print). | BS1545.3 (epub).

Manufactured in the U.S.A.   JULY 30, 2019

Scripture quotations that head verse divisions and those marked (NIV) are taken from the Holy Bible, New International Version®, NIV®. Copyright © 1973, 1978, 1984, 2011 by Biblica, Inc.™ Used by permission of Zondervan. All rights reserved worldwide. www.zondervan.com.

Scripture quotations marked (ESV) are taken from The Holy Bible, English Standard Version® (ESV®) Copyright © 2001 by Crossway, a publishing ministry of Good News Publishers. All rights reserved. ESV Text Edition: 2016.

Scripture quotations marked (NASB) are taken from the New American Standard Bible® (NASB), copyright © 1960, 1962, 1963, 1968, 1971, 1972, 1973, 1975, 1977, 1995 by The Lockman Foundation. Used by permission. www.Lockman.org.

Scripture quotations marked (NET) are taken from the NET Bible® copyright ©1996–2016 by Biblical Studies Press, L.L.C. Used by permission. http://netbible.com All rights reserved.

Scripture quotations marked (NJPS) are taken from the TANAKH: The Holy Scriptures: the new JPS translation according to the traditional Hebrew text, copyright © 1985. Used by permission. All rights reserved.

Scripture quotations marked (NKJV) are taken the New King James Version®. Copyright © 1982 by Thomas Nelson. Used by permission. All rights reserved.

Scripture quotations marked (NLT) are taken from the Holy Bible, New Living Translation, copyright © 1996, 2004, 2015 by Tyndale House Foundation. Used by permission of Tyndale House Publishers, Inc., Carol Stream, Illinois 60188. All rights reserved.

Scripture quotations marked (NRSV) are taken from the New Revised Standard Version Bible, copyright © 1989 National Council of the Churches of Christ in the United States of America. Used by permission. All rights reserved worldwide.

Unless indicated, other translations are my own.

For Charlotte,
my wise and faithful ally

CONTENTS

List of Special Topics | xi
List of Figures | xii
Preface and Acknowledgments | xiii
Abbreviations | xv

Introduction | 1
The God of Glory Calls (1:1–28) | 10
Embracing the Word (2:1—3:15) | 17
Responsibility to Respond (3:16–27) | 24
Failing to Live as Light (4:1—5:17) | 30
Our Grievous Idols (6:1–14) | 36
The Impotence of Materialism (7:1–27) | 42
Rebellion in God's Face (8:1–18) | 48
Mercy for the Broken of Heart (9:1–11) | 55
God's Parting Judgment (10:1–22) | 61
Hope amidst Judgment (11:1–25) | 67
A Word against False Hope (12:1–28) | 73
Speaking Presumptuously in God's Name (13:1–23) | 79
Sin and Hindered Prayer (14:1–11) | 85
No Righteousness by Association (14:12—15:8) | 91
God's Relentless Love (16:1–63) | 98
The Sovereign LORD of Destinies (17:1–24) | 105
The Individual Responsibility to Repent (18:1–32) | 111
A Lament over Fallen Leaders (19:1–14) | 117
Divine Pursuit of a Purified People (20:1–44) | 124
Sovereign Determination of Judgment (20:45—21:32) | 131
Exposing Sin in the Furnace of God's Anger (22:1–31) | 137
An Allegory of Political Prostitution (23:1–49) | 143

A Real Cause for Mourning (24:1-27) | 149
Judgment on a Vindictive Spirit (25:1-17) | 155
The Sinking of Tyre's Wealth (26:1—27:36) | 161
The Corruption of Tyre's Pride (28:1-26) | 167
Leaning on Unreliable Allies (29:1—30:26) | 175
A Great Fall (31:1—32:32) | 183
No Privileged Status (33:1-33) | 190
Two Kinds of Shepherds (34:1-31) | 198
Reclaiming and Renewing the Land (35:1—36:15) | 206
Spiritual Transformation for God's Honor (36:16—38) | 213
A Whole Covenant Package (37:1-28) | 220
The Permanence of God's Care (38:1—39:29) | 228
Return of God's Glory (40:1—43:12) | 241
Return to Order in Worship and the Land (43:13—48:35) | 253

Bibliography | 265

SPECIAL TOPICS

Cherubim | 11
Prophetic Signs in the Ancient Near East | 31
High Places and Sacred Trees | 37
Tammuz | 51
The Remnant | 58
Divine Abandonment in Mesopotamian Religion | 64
Divination | 76
True and False Prophecy | 81
Daniel of Judah or Dan'el of Ugarit? | 93
Offensive Sexual Imagery | 100
Hostages in Exile | 107
The Last Kings of Judah | 119
Is the "King of Tyre" Satan? | 170
Failed Prophecy? | 178
Sheol | 186
Modern Israel in the Land | 211
Transformation of Heart in the Old Testament | 217
Ezekiel 37 and Future Hope | 224
Literal or Literalism? | 234
A Future Temple? | 244
Atonement | 254

FIGURES

Fig. 1 Ezekiel's Temple Vision | 247
Fig. 2 Mari Panel Depicting Sacred Precincts | 249

PREFACE AND ACKNOWLEDGMENTS

WHEN WRESTLING WITH THE task of preaching and teaching, it is essential to attend to the main point and key themes that drive the main point of each passage. No one likes their words to be taken out of context, and this holds true for the biblical authors. The primary goal of this commentary is to focus attention on what mattered most to Ezekiel and to craft a direction and scope of application that the prophet himself would recognize were he to preach to God's people today. A discussion of the interpretive model behind this can be found in the Bridge to Application section of the Introduction.

The English-speaking world is blessed with an abundance of good Bible translations. However, as many people are aware, these translations do not always align. The preacher or teacher who cannot work directly with the Hebrew text has difficulty taking this into account in exposition. So, in addition to focusing on the most urgent interpretive issues of the text, another goal of this commentary is to explain in simple terms the reasons behind significant translation differences. The NIV text heads each verse-section of the commentary as the starting point for discussion. Other translations are brought into discussion where relevant.[1] Embedded in some verses in Ezekiel are particularly complicated or troubling biblical-theological issues. Hence, special topical discussions address these at appropriate locations throughout the commentary. Throughout the writing of the commentary, I continually asked myself—If I were teaching this passage, what would I most need to understand, and how is it relevant to modern times?

This commentary "began life" as part of the Teach the Text series for Baker Publishing, before the series was unfortunately discontinued. My

---

1. Unless otherwise noted, all translations are mine.

thanks to John H. Walton for casting the wonderful vision for that series and asking me to undertake Ezekiel. There are many good commentary series in print, but few offer the clear guidance and methodological consistency for bridging the gap between interpretation and application that Walton envisioned. I also thank Cascade Books for their willingness to pick up an "orphaned" commentary that was half-way complete at the time! My editor, K. C. Hanson, deserves praise for bringing better clarity in many places.

This is not a technical commentary. But the discerning reader will observe in the footnotes that I have benefited greatly from two technical commentaries in particular. Moshe Greenberg's Anchor Bible commentary and Daniel Block's commentary in the New International Commentary: Old Testament were my faithful companions throughout. Special thanks are in order to Stephen Cook, who graciously gave me prepublication access to his wonderful volume on Ezek 38—48, which completes the Anchor Bible commentary on Ezekiel. If the reader is interested in more comprehensive treatment of the many difficulties in the book of Ezekiel, he or she can do no better than consult these works, which are in many ways quite accessible for the average pastor or serious lay teacher. Often my foototes guide the reader to the appropriate pages of these commentaries. Finding help with questions on cultural background is often difficult, and so the reader is frequently directed in the footnotes to Daniel Bodi's treatment of Ezekiel in the *Zondervan Illustrated Bible Backgrounds Commentary*. This series makes an excellent companion for study, especially for its many visual aids and citations of ancient texts from the world of the Old Testament that enrich our understanding of the Bible. The electronic edition of this resource allows use of its rich visual images.

My thanks extend especially to my wife, Charlotte, who not only endured with patience countless evenings and weekends when her husband was occupied in Ezekiel's world, but who also lent her own judicious eye to reading and improving the manuscript.

John W. Hilber
All Saints' Day 2018

ABBREVIATIONS

ANET	*Ancient Near Eastern Texts*. 3rd ed. Edited by James B. Pritchard. Princeton: Princeton University Press, 1969
CAD	*The Assyrian Dictionary of the Oriental Institute of the University of Chicago*. Edited by Ignace J. Gelb et al. 21 vols. Chicago: Oriental Institute, 1956–2010
COS	*The Context of Scripture*. Edited by William W. Hallo and K. Lawson Younger Jr. 4 vols. Leiden: Brill, 1997–2017
ESV	English Standard Version
KJV	King James Version
NASB	New American Standard Bible
NJPS	Jewish Publication Society translation
NET	The NET Bible
NIV	New International Version
NKJV	New King James Version
NLT	New Living Translation
NRSV	New Revised Standard Version

INTRODUCTION

"Son of man, eat this scroll, then go and speak" (Ezek 3:1). The expectation that the prophet ingest God's Word before proclamation demonstrates to every teacher or preacher that the text must first enter the heart of the messenger. But properly "digesting" God's Word depends on correctly understanding the meaning of the text. The book of Ezekiel confronts the interpreter with a number of challenges; most notable are his visionary experiences and the high concentration of metaphor he uses in many of his oracles.[1] But even more difficult is the challenge of managing some of the most vociferous language in all the prophets. Ezekiel's blunt expressions do not make for delicate preaching material. Further complicating the practicality of teaching Ezekiel is its size—the second longest book in the Bible, barely surpassed only by the prophecies of Jeremiah.[2] It is not surprising that several of the best commentaries comprise several large volumes. Not many people in ministry are granted the time necessary to plow through these mammoth works, as beneficial as that would be. So this commentary attends especially to the needs of the teacher or preacher who works with limited time. For economy's sake, it addresses only the most difficult aspects of the text, providing discussion on crucial issues and focusing carefully on the central message for God's people. What pitfalls should be avoided in exposition, and in what direction would Ezekiel aim his arrows were he to address the church today?

---

1. Technically, "oracle" refers to the answer received from a deity in response to a specific question for advice, but the word has come to be used commonly to refer to any divine message.

2. Based on word count, Ezekiel is second in size only to Jeremiah among the latter prophets and larger even than Psalms.

The Life and Times of the Prophet Ezekiel

God's design from the beginning of creation was to bless his world (Gen 1:28). But his creatures rebelled (Gen 3:1–24; 6:5; 11:6), so beginning with Abraham, God called to himself a people through whom he might channel his blessing (Gen 12:1–3). Under Moses, God shaped the descendants of Abraham into a nation in order to form a missionary kingdom to the world (Exod 19:5–6). But they failed their calling in the land that God had given to them. They fought among themselves, split in civil war, overturned social justice with violence, and abandoned the God who called them. Like Adam and Eve, who were expelled from the garden, the northern kingdom (Israel) and the southern kingdom (Judah) were sent into exile (2 Kgs 17:7–23; 2 Chr 36:15–20).[3] Such were the final consequences of breaking the terms of the covenant between God and his people (Deut 28:63–64). But by God's grace, that is not the final word; and Ezekiel proclaims both the message of doom as well as the vision of restoration.

Ezekiel was born into a priestly family (Ezek 1:3) and was a young man when the Babylonians subjugated the kingdom of Judah. As was customary, the conquerors took youths from elite families into captivity in order to "socialize" them to be good servants of their overlord. The first such deportation was in 605 BC. Among these earliest political prisoners were the likes of Daniel (Dan 1:1–7). Ezekiel was likely part of a second wave of deportation. After Jehoiachin's rebellion against the Babylonian overlords in 598 BC, there was a punitive exile of Jerusalem's leaders (2 Kgs 24:12–16). Ezekiel's prophetic call came five years after this event while living among the exiles (Ezek 1:1–3). His oracles span 20 years of his life (see comments at Ezek 40:1). God addresses Ezekiel as "son of man," which stresses his human frailty in contrast to the sovereign sufficiency of God (see comments at Ezek 2:1). We do not know the exact location of the Kebar Canal, where Ezekiel lived among the exiles, but it was a primary irrigation canal branching off the Euphrates River.

Prophecy in the ancient Near East was treated with special care, because it was an authoritative word directly from a deity. This is true whether it was a word from the god Adad to the king of Mari, from the goddess Ishtar to the king of Assyria, or from Yahweh to his people Israel. These ancient cultures transmitted divine words with the same respect

---

3. For a summary of the cataclysmic events surrounding the final decades of the kingdom, see **Special Topic: The Last Kings of Judah** at Ezek 19:1–14.

given to royal, diplomatic correspondence, whether delivered orally or in writing. One dared not play fast and loose with it. So we have good reason to be confident that the words recorded in Ezekiel are the authoritative voice of God's prophet. If Ezekiel's oracles were not compiled by the prophet himself, his words were handled carefully and edited into book form under the guidance of inspired scribal editors (compare the process for wisdom literature presupposed in Prov 25:1).[4]

The Message of the Book as a Whole

One way to summarize the whole message of Ezekiel into one sentence is: *Yahweh, the God of glory, must judge his rebellious people, yet he will restore a repentant remnant to covenant blessing in the land, where they will enjoy his glorious presence forever.*[5] "Yahweh," was the revealed name of Israel's covenant God (Exod 3:13–15). It is usually translated "Lord" in our English versions (see discussion of "Sovereign Lord" at Ezek 2:3). Over sixty-five times in Ezekiel, the Lord declares, "then they will know that I am Yahweh." The intervention of Israel's God in history will once and for all make his name known and respected, not only in Israel but in all the earth. Of particular concern in Ezekiel is the glory of God, which cannot be present among a sinful people; so Ezekiel envisions the glory departing from the temple and from Jerusalem (Ezek 11:22–23; cf. Exod 33:3–5). In the oracles of judgment against the nations, God's glory is also of preeminent concern. This is demonstrated most clearly in the oracle against Tyre (Ezek 28:2, "because your heart is high you say, 'I am god'").

Ezekiel lived among a community of Jewish exiles who had not fully repented of the nation's corporate sins,[6] but they were nevertheless expecting an immanent return to their homeland. Their hope was rooted in an imbalanced theology that God would never abandon Jerusalem, the city of his temple (cf. Ps 48:8). They did not take seriously the warnings of the covenant. Much of Ezekiel's message was targeted at such presumptuous expectations. The people needed to understand that punishment for Judah's covenant rebellion had not run its course, especially because

---

4. For discussion and defense, see Hilber, "Culture of Prophecy and Writing," 219–41.

5. A earlier form of this statement has a pedigree stretching back through my professors, Elliot E. Johnson and Allen P. Ross, to Bruce K. Waltke.

6. The term "Jew" or "Jewish" is a common designation for the exilic community that perhaps more accurately could be called "Judean."

the people in exile and back in Jerusalem had not turned from their evil ways. Ezekiel's contemporary, the prophet Jeremiah, confronted this same problem from the vantage point of his residence back in Jerusalem (cf. Jer 29:1–23).

Nevertheless, Ezekiel envisions a day when God's glory will return to dwell among his people in a healed land (Ezek 43:5–7; 47:1–12). In preparation for that return, the people of Israel are restored spiritually as well as physically to full covenant blessing (Ezek 36–37). God will bring to fulfillment the covenant blessings promised to Abraham and Moses (Ezek 11:16–20; 16:60; 36:8–12; 37:11–14) as well as to David (Ezek 34:23–31; 37:24–28). The whole "covenant package" is assured in the final line of Ezekiel, "Yahweh is there" (cf. Exod 3:12–15; Lev 26:12). Much of the challenge in preaching Ezekiel is to translate these themes for Christian hope and living.

An overview of the book's structure is as follows:

1. Judgment against Israel (Ezek 1–24)

   After seeing a vision of the glory of God (chapters 1–3) and dramatically portraying the siege of Jerusalem (chapters 4–7), Ezekiel envisions the glory of God departing from the defiled temple (chapters 8–11). Then, a dramatic portrayal of exile (chapter 12) is followed by extensive explanation of the reasons for judgment (chapters 13–24).

2. Judgment against the Nations (Ezek 25–32)

   The nations, who would exult their own glory over that of the LORD will be humiliated in judgment, including: neighboring nations (chapter 25); Tyre (chapters 26–28); Egypt (chapters 29–32).

3. Renewal of Israel and Restoration to a Glorious Kingdom (Ezek 33–48)

   Through a new covenant, Yahweh will restore his people to new life, under new leadership, in a new kingdom in which his glory will again dwell forever. Ezekiel's messages turn to salvation (chapter 33); new leadership (chapter 34); restoration to the promised homeland (chapters 35:1—36:15); restoration spiritually (chapters 36:16—37:28); final deliverance from chaos (chapters 38—39); and restoration of worship in the blessing of God's presence (chapters 40—48).

Because Ezekiel's prophetic oracles are organized chronologically through the book, they present a story in a general way.[7] There is no elaborate plotline, but the chronological notices trace a progression of interactions between the prophet and his community, which has been traumatized by forced deportation. The narrative arc begins with the prophet's call and his confrontation with the exiled compatriots. He labors to convince them that their exile is justified because of sin, and furthermore, that the doom announced against Jerusalem is sure to come. This puts their trauma in theological perspective. This trauma is amplified when news arrives of the destruction of their homeland, recorded half-way through the book. From that point on, Ezekiel's task changes from confrontation to comfort.

Dividing the Book into Teachable Units

The immensity of the book of Ezekiel presents a challenge for a Sunday morning preaching series as well as for the length usually allowed for many seasonal Bible studies. While all Scripture is God's word, not all of it is equally important for constructing our faith nor as immediately relevant for Christian living. So it is necessary to be selective about what passages in Ezekiel to cover.

In addition to the difficulty of choosing which passages to preach, there is the challenge of assigning the boundaries of each selection. Breaking up the book into the best literary segments does not necessarily optimize the book for realistic teaching units. So, sometimes I have combined segments of the book that could easily be separated but are difficult to justify as stand-alone teaching or preaching units. In my comments on the context for each section, I explain my decision, and the reader can make his or her own judgment accordingly.

After a statement of Ezekiel's message, each passage is introduced by a contextual overview, placing the unit in the flow of the book. The bulk of the commentary focuses on the most important and difficult expressions used by the prophet. Then, a paragraph treats a central theological truth from the passage that bridges into discussion about teaching and applying the text to contemporary life.

---

7. Lyons, *Introduction to the Study of Ezekiel*, 79–80. The exception to proper chronological order is Ezek 29:17, where the concern for topic overrides the chronological need (see comments there).

If I were preaching through the book in an expository series, I would especially want to include the following units, which I judge to be particularly important for Ezekiel's message:

Ezek 1:1–28 / The God of Glory Calls

Ezek 4:1—5:17 / Failing to Live as Light

Ezek 7:1–27 / The Impotence of Materialism (or Ezek 26:1—27:36)

Ezek 8:1–18 / Rebellion in God's Face

Ezek 10:1–22 / God's Parting Judgment

Ezek 18:1–32 / The Individual Responsibility to Repent (or Ezek 33:1–33)

Ezek 20:1–44 / Divine Pursuit of a Purified People

Ezek 28:1–26 / The Corruption of Tyre's Pride

Ezek 34:1–31 / Two Kinds of Shepherds

Ezek 36:16–38 / Spiritual Transformation for God's Honor

Ezek 37:1–28 / A Whole Covenant Package

Ezek 40:1—43:12 / The Return of God's Glory

The reader is encouraged to read through Ezekiel and consider the main ideas stated at the beginning of each passage in the commentary as a guide to what other selections might be particularly relevant to a ministry context. Daniel Block has written an essay on "Preaching Ezekiel" that also offers very helpful guidance for understanding and delivering the message of the prophet.[8]

The Bridge to Application

We live in a world that has become broken due to human failure. Nevertheless, God has repeatedly intervened to redeem and restore his creation, decisively in the life and ministry of Jesus. But God was at work in Old Testament days as well, calling people into relationship with him, directing them in his ways, and establishing them as mission outposts in a world that naturally drifts into chaos. The Bible, both Old and New

---

8. Block, "Preaching Ezekiel," 157–78. This is reprinted also in Block, *By the River Chebar*, 1–24. This same volume contains a number of other essays on Ezekiel that the reader might find helpful.

Testaments, is the story of the reestablishment of God's kingdom on a planet in rebellion against him.

One can think of the Bible as the narrative of God's redemptive intervention, but a narrative that has not yet reached final conclusion in the outworking of history. It reveals to us the ways of God with humanity, it projects before us the world that God envisions to restore, and it invites us to participate cooperatively in this mission.[9] If I may use the metaphor of a motion picture, the Bible projects what God is doing in the world, and each passage is a frame in the whole moving story. We must step into roles within this story to advance God's program, not hinder it. As the instrument of God's Spirit, the Bible *does* something to us and *accomplishes* things by us.

When teaching or preaching the Old Testament, one must ask, What sort of world would God have us inhabit? What should that look like practically in our communities today? What is my responsibility to achieve this? Sometimes it means that we advocate for change in the relationships and social structures around us. Usually it also means that we come face to face with our own rebellion. But because many difficulties in life or society are intractable, sometimes all we can do is to rest in hope for God's personal intervention to redeem his world.

Answering the question, What is the prophet Ezekiel "doing" with this passage?, is a crucial step in aligning our interpretation and application with the scope of relevance the prophet had in view. Ezekiel chose his words carefully and efficiently to "hook" specific ideas in the mind of his audience. We want to attend to Ezekiel's message that best connects the prophet's words and the thought world of his audience. We could call that "contextual relevance," and it helps us guard against grasping for meanings of the text beyond what Ezekiel would have imagined.[10]

One of the most common mistakes in teaching the Old Testament is to use the passage only as a springboard or illustration for what ends up being an exposition from the New Testament. So the challenge of teaching Ezekiel is the same for all of the Old Testament—care must be taken to expound the meaning of the Old Testament text itself rather than

---

9. I am following here the model of application advocated by Kuruvilla, *Privilege the Text!*, especially 39–54.

10. Here I am influenced by a communication model called Relevance Theory. An accessible introduction can be found in Green, "Relevance Theory and Theological Interpretation," 75–90; or Green, "Relevance Theory and Biblical Interpretation," 266–73.

jump quickly into corresponding New Testament passages. New Testament texts can validate the message drawn from Ezekiel, but the message must be rooted in the meaning derived from Ezekiel itself. My use of the New Testament in this commentary is to validate the message of Ezekiel when necessary. This is done most often in passages where the message of Ezekiel strains Christian instincts about the life of believers who are in Christ. The use of the New Testament is also necessary to bring forward the message of Ezekiel to its consummation in our expectations of God's Old Testament promises in Jesus and the Holy Spirit.

Ancient Texts for Illustration

Illustrations are tools that clarify or drive home the point of a passage. They are not an end in themselves nor the framework upon which we hang the biblical message. In this commentary, I frequently quote ancient Near Eastern texts from the world of the Bible. Actually reading these texts to your audience can be effective in exposition; it helps clarify the cultural setting of the text in a way that informs meaning. The modern audience experiences more closely the impact that a particular passage would have had on the *original* audience. In my experience, people actually perk up when they hear these ancient voices from the past, voices they have never heard before that bring to concrete appreciation the life of the biblical world.

The Text and Translation of Ezekiel

My recommendation is always to consult three English translations when doing detailed Bible study. It is a good idea to choose at least one that is outside the translation tradition that you would normally consult. For example, the NIV, NASB, and NRSV offer a good mix. If there are no substantial differences, then it can be assumed the Hebrew text is reasonably clear and without significant difficulty. In these cases, the English versions offer a unified guide as to the meaning of the Hebrew text. However, when important differences do appear, it is due to one of three difficulties: (1) the Hebrew text has suffered in transmission over the ages, so there is discrepancy between manuscripts that witness to the original text; (2) there is a difficult grammatical expression that leaves some ambiguity as to meaning; (3) there is an unusual word meaning that remains unclear. One thing is sure, in this day of abundant English translations of the Bible, a variety of translations is present in any size of audience. This cannot be ignored. Our responsibility is to walk people through the differences, clarify when possible, and refrain from making dogmatic points on disputed readings.

It is helpful to remind people that the doctrine of inspiration does not extend to preservation of the text in the transmission process. Providentially, God has preserved for us an embarrassing overabundance of manuscript evidence for the New Testament and an adequate preservation of ancient manuscripts for the Old Testament. This includes Hebrew manuscripts as well as ancient translations, like the Old Greek that dates several hundred years before Christ. So I have endeavored to offer some explanation where significant differences appear between some of the most commonly used, modern English versions.

THE GOD OF GLORY CALLS
1:1–28

Ezekiel's Message

The glorious God and King calls his people into submissive service.

Key Themes

- The King of Glory is ever present with his people.
- God's glory reveals his overpowering martial and royal splendor.
- The authority of God's call demands a response of willing submission.

Context in Ezekiel

Several times in Scripture, the call of a prophet begins with an inaugural vision of God's glorious presence. Moses received his call from God's presence in the burning bush (Exod 3:1–6), and Isaiah experienced an exceptional vision of God's holy presence while in the temple (Isa 6:1–5). Although Hosea and Jeremiah did not report a vision of God's glory, the substance of their prophetic call anticipates a central theme of their message (Hos 1:2–11; Jer 1:9–10). The visions served both to undergird the authority of the prophetic mission as well as shape the prophet's understanding of the nature of God as it applied to his message. For Ezekiel, the vision of God's glory commissions him with an authoritative message and leaves an indelible impression that even though Ezekiel and his fellow exiles are far removed from their homeland and the temple in

Jerusalem, God is with them even in exile and seeks to prepare them for future, kingdom work.

How eager Ezekiel was to comply with the LORD's call is disputed.[1] However, *reluctance* to carry out a painful task should not be confused with *resistance*. Moses, Jeremiah, and Ezekiel were reluctant, but Jonah was resistant. But unlike these others, Ezekiel offers no excuses. Even Isaiah's response, "Here I am," does not imply that he relished the seemingly fruitless ministry ahead of him (cf. Isa 6:11). When Isaiah asked God, "How long," he used a phrase that connotes lament (e.g., Pss 6:4; 74:10; 94:3; Zech 1:12). Should *anyone* be eager to deliver a message of judgment? The emphasis on the need for God's Spirit to fortify the prophet is not to overcome his resistance to the call but is to strengthen his weakness as a frail human in the face of a difficult task ("son of man"; see comments Ezek 2:1).

The glory of God is central to the message of the book of Ezekiel. Much of the first half of the book records Ezekiel's efforts to convince his fellow exiles that judgment on Jerusalem was both certain and imminent. An important validation of this is the prophet's vision that God's glory was departing from the temple, thereby allowing its destruction (Ezek 8–10). Conversely, the presence of God serves as a reminder to the exiles that God has not abandoned them. Not only does the glory appear to Ezekiel at the outset of his ministry *in Babylonian territory*, but God assures them that for the time of exile he is nevertheless a sanctuary to them (Ezek 11:16). The book of Ezekiel concludes with an encouraging vision of an ideal temple by which the LORD would be present in their midst (Ezek 48:35).

Special Topic: Cherubim

Ezekiel's vision of the glory of God strikes modern westerners as wildly bizarre. Indeed, Ezekiel's struggle to find language to describe what he saw suggests that he himself was overwhelmed. However, in several respects, what he saw conformed to his own sensibilities, since God appears to him in a way that accommodates Ezekiel's cultural expectations of features associated with deities on thrones.

The bulk of Ezekiel's description pertains to the four living creatures that carry the throne of God. A common feature in ancient Near Eastern

---

1. See Block, *Ezekiel 1–24*, 11–12.

palaces and temples was composite creatures that guarded the entrances and in some cases served as part of the throne itself. Egypt and Canaan are known for sphinxes, most often composed of a lion's body, sometimes with wings, and a human head. But in Mesopotamia, where Ezekiel was living, such guardian creatures had human heads, often on the bodies of winged bulls or lions, sometimes with wings on human bodies, as in the background to Ezekiel's vision. Horns on their heads indicate that they participated in the heavenly realm as lesser "deities" (we might call them "angelic"). These representations of supernatural guardians gave warning that one dare not approach the divine presence presumptuously. For a priest such as Ezekiel, the imagery would have been all the more familiar, being acquainted as he was with the winged cherubs guarding the Jerusalem temple and ark (footstool of God's throne; Pss 99:1; 132:7–8; cf. Gen 3:24) and "carrying" God as would a chariot (Ps 18:10; 1 Chr 28:18). The four *different* faces do not have exact parallel with any known archeological artifacts; however, figurines and descriptions of deities from the ancient world feature two or four faces, suggesting "all observing potency."[2]

Interpretive Highlights

1:1 *I was among the exiles*: The location of God's appearance is important to the message of the book. The Jews in exile felt cut off from life in the land of their ancestors; and in fact, their kin still living in Jerusalem and Judah evidently no longer regarded them as fellow heirs of the land promised to the Patriarchs (Ezek 11:15). Indeed, they were in exile as a result of God's judgment against Judah and enforcement of covenant sanctions (Deut 28:64–65; Jer 52:3). The word order in the Hebrew text of v. 3 stresses the word "there," highlighting the importance of God's presence in their midst to raise up a prophet to admonish and eventually to encourage these people.

1:4 *a windstorm . . . glowing metal*: Ezekiel's first impression was an approaching storm at the center of which was glowing metal. Some of this imagery recalls the manifestation of God's glory when he first appeared to Israel on Mt. Sinai (Exod 19:16; cf. Deut 33:1). Such displays were understood in the ancient Near East as the appearance of a divine warrior (Ps 18:8–14; Hab 3:3–9).[3] The word for "metal" is used only in

2. Bodi, "Ezekiel," 405–8.
3. For examples from ancient texts, see Hilber, "Psalms," 332–33.

Ezekiel (Ezek 1:4, 27; 8:2) and refers to a semi-precious stone or possibly amber, known for its brilliant reflection or refraction of light.[4]

1:10 *their faces*: After describing the four creatures generally (Ezek 1:4-9), Ezekiel proceeds to expand in detail. Each of the different kinds of faces suggests an important attribute of the creature: as for the human face, human nature is distinct in its capacity to image God in relationship and rule (Gen 1:26-28; Ps 8:6-8). In contrast to animals, a particular dignity and intellectual prowess is associated with it (Dan 4:16, 33-34, 36). This human face corresponds to their dominant form, humanlike in appearance (Ezek 1: 5). The lion was the most deadly and fearsome of beasts (Num 23:24; Judg 14:18; Prov 30:30; Amos 3:8). Oxen were associated with strength (Num 23:22; "wild ox"). But perhaps the point in Ezekiel's vision is the ox's status as greatest among the domesticated beasts (Deut 33:17; "bull" in NIV). This particular word for "ox" is mostly associated with the domesticated cattle (e.g., Deut 25:4; 1 Sam 12:3). This contrasts with the lion who presided over the wild domain. Eagles were revered for their swiftness (2 Sam 1:23; Jer 4:13) and enduring strength (Isa 40:31; Ezek 17:3) as well as being a terror of the sky (Job 9:26; Jer 49:22). These creatures in Ezekiel's vision were not to be trifled with, nor the God of glory whose throne they carried.

1:12 *Wherever the spirit would go*: The wings were positioned so as to touch tip to tip. This formed a square that could move in any compass direction with one of the creatures always facing forward (omni-directional). The "spirit" that impelled them was associated with their wheels (Ezek 1:20) yet was a property of the creatures themselves (Ezek 10:17). So while God on his throne would determine the direction, the driving force energizing life was within the creatures, not identical with God's Spirit.[5] The word translated "spirit" can refer to an energizing force that vitalizes or gives direction, not necessarily a personal agent such as God or another supernatural being (e.g., Gen 45:27; Num 14:24; Hos 4:12). However, as Block argues, the energizing power of life derives ultimately from God in Ezekiel's theology.[6]

1:13 *burning coals of fire*: Fire both destroys and purifies, depending on the application of it. It corresponds to the weapons of a divine warrior (Ps 18:13, translated "bolts of lightning" in NIV), but it also refers

---

4. See Bodi, "Ezekiel," 405; Greenberg, *Ezekiel 1-20*, 43.
5. Taylor, *Ezekiel*, 56.
6. Block, *Ezekiel 1-24*, 101.

to coals from the sacrificial altar used in the atonement ritual and so part of purification (Lev 16:12; cf. Isa 6:4–5).

1:15 *a wheel on the ground beside each creature:* The wheels appear to be *functionally* similar to casters, capable of omnidirectional movement (cf. Ezek 1:16–17). Corresponding to this, the eyes probably signify complete situational awareness, the impact of which was frightening ("awesome," NIV). Overall, one has the impression of a war chariot that is lightning swift, maneuverable, and responsive to any and all situations—formidable equipment of a divine warrior (2 Sam 22:11; Ps 18:10).

1:22–25 *a vault . . . a voice:* Similar to the vision of God's glory experienced by the elders of Israel (Exod 24:10), Ezekiel observes the floor of heaven above the creatures.[7] However, the primary emphasis on this section is the movement and sound of the creatures' wings that prepares for the vision of God himself. As for the four wings possessed by each creature (mentioned earlier; Ezek 1:11), two covered its body. A similar use of wings by the seraphim in Isaiah's vision suggests that these creatures shielded their bodies in modest deference to the presence of God (Isa 6:2). What Ezekiel stresses here is the thunderous and frightening intensity of the sound of their movement (rushing waters, an army on the march), which corresponds in amplitude to the voice of God (v. 25) who addresses Ezekiel in the next moment. The repetition that the creatures stand still with lowered wings (vv. 24–25) prepares for the emergence of God's voice on the scene (mentioned between this repetition). The implication is that even these fabulous creatures still themselves when God is about to act (cf. the sun and moon become paralyzed by God's movement, Hab 3:11).

1:26 *a figure like that of a man:* Ezekiel's first impression when looking through the expanse is the vision of a throne; God's royal character dominates. As he gazes upon God himself, the intensified frequency of Ezekiel's use of the words "like," "figure," "appearance" is striking. It demonstrates his difficulty in finding words adequate to describe what he sees. Descriptions of radiant splendor were attached to divine images and kings in the ancient Near East;[8] but the concentration of simile used by Ezekiel is unparalleled. Such is the *"appearance of the likeness"* of the LORD's glory.

---

7. For the "firmament" or "vault" of heaven, see Walton, "Genesis," 12–13, 16–17.
8. Bodi, "Ezekiel," 408.

1:28 *I fell face down*: Overwhelmed by the sound of God's voice and the splendor of his appearance, Ezekiel falls prostrate before him. This posture often accompanies an appeal for mercy (cf. Gen 44:14; Num 16:22; Ezek 9:8), which is consistent with the fear of one who faces the danger of a divine encounter (Lev 9:24; Judg 13:20–22). It also expresses a submissive readiness for service (Gen 17:3; 18:3; 50:18; Ps 95:6–8). While in some instances a sense of inadequacy and reluctance characterized those called to God's service (e.g., Exod 4:1, 10; Jer 1:6), Ezekiel shows no resistance when commissioned in the next moment. His response can be understood as that of one too awestruck to contemplate anything but full submission (cf. Isa 6:8).

Theological Bridge to Application

The revelation that God is a glorious warrior-king is a central theological theme in the Bible. Already mentioned above are allusions to God's glorious appearance on Mt. Sinai at the inauguration of the Mosaic covenant (Exod 24:1–18), his terrifying and purifying presence at Isaiah's prophetic call (Isa 6:1–8), and his military prowess to defeat his enemies and deliver his people (Deut 33:2–3; Pss 18 [2 Sam 22]; 68; 97; Hab 3; cf. Dan 7:9–10). The psalmist attaches similar imagery (splendor of light, cosmic chariot, angelic servants) to God's power displayed in creation (Ps 104:1–4). A different aspect of God's glory can be seen in his gracious attributes (Exod 33:17—34:6); but here, Ezek 1 presses upon us God's terrifying majesty that is necessary for his cosmic kingship and his redeeming presence with his people. The gentle humanity of Jesus cloaks the splendor of his majesty (Matt 17:1–8; Mark 9:2–8; Luke 9:28–36) and for a time restrains his cosmic power to destroy his enemies in order to redeem his people at the coming of his presence (2 1:5–10; Rev 1:12–17; 19:11–21).

Focus of Application

In Ezek 1 we enter a very strange world of images that are rich with implications to the ancient audience but distant from the modern world. Rather than get entangled in validating the details of a concrete picture of this vision, it is more important to unpack the *meaning* of these images. In fact, a comparison of details between Ezek 1 and Rev 4 serves to warn against pressing for concrete referents in the vision. The crucial emphasis of Ezekiel's vision is the royal splendor and military prowess of the King of Glory.

God never "shows up" just to make an appearance. Such manifestations of his glory are associated in Scripture with formal prophetic calls, but also with God's call upon Israel in general (Exod 19:5-6, 14-16). The same God who was present with Israel in their exile "showed up" at Pentecost and is present with believers today. He has called his church into service under distressing circumstances; indeed, *in spite of those circumstances* (Matt 28:16-20; 1 Pet 2:9-10 [Peter's audience was a suffering church]). No matter the nature of one's situation, whether physical hardship, emotional distress, or entanglement in sin, God's sovereign (royal) and powerful (martial) presence is there to warn and to redeem.

While God's presence is always imminent, his course of action is not ours to direct. He was not at the beckon call of Ezekiel, nor is he at ours. The timing and nature of God's intervention is his to determine. Many of the promises of the book of Ezekiel to Israel have yet to be realized; and similarly, often in the life of believers today, God's tangible intervention awaits the resurrection and future kingdom. But when such Majesty calls us into service by his presence, how can we do otherwise than fall on our faces in willing submission?

EMBRACING THE WORD
2:1—3:15

Ezekiel's Message

We embrace with integrity the justice of God's word and should be unsurprised when others resist its uncomfortable truths.

Key Themes

- God's word contains both sweet and bitter news, which must be embraced with integrity before it can be proclaimed effectively.
- The nature of the human heart is naturally resistant to uncomfortable truths from God's word.
- The sovereign sufficiency of God more than matches resistance to his word.

Context in Ezekiel

Ezekiel 1:28 is a bridge from chapter 1 to chapter 2. It interprets the essential nature of the vision in chapter 1 ("This was . . . the glory of the LORD"), noting Ezekiel's response ("I fell facedown"), and introduces a voice from the storm. This in turn sets the scene for God to speak and formally commission Ezekiel as a prophet ("Son of man, stand on your feet . . . that I might send you," Ezek 2:1–3). The unit closes with the end of the vision, as the Spirit restores Ezekiel once again to conscious awareness of his geographical surroundings among exiles at the Kebar River (Ezek 1:1; 3:15).

Interpretive Highlights

2:1 *Son of man:* This phrase denotes essential human nature in contrast to divine nature, often stressing some inherent weakness (e.g., Num 23:19; Pss 8:4; 89:47; 90:3) that can be overcome through divine enablement (Ps 80:17). The vast majority of occurrences of this phrase (94 of the approximately 139 uses in the Old Testament) is when God addresses his prophet Ezekiel. As Taylor notes, God's opening words put Ezekiel "in his rightful place" before the majesty of God.[1] The special use of the phrase "son of man" in Dan 7:13 also stresses the essential human nature of this figure in contrast to the terrifying beasts described earlier in the passage. With a messianic identification of this Danielic figure in late, Second Temple Judaism, Jesus adopted it as his favorite expression for himself (cf. Mark 8:29–31; 13:36; 14:62), but messianic overtones belong to this later Jewish context and should not confuse the simpler usage of the phrase in Ezekiel.[2]

2:2 *the Spirit came into me:* As a mortal human who has been overwhelmed by such close encounter with divine glory, Ezekiel needs divine help to face and converse with his God. The Spirit of God is an extremely important agent in the book of Ezekiel, energizing not only the prophet (Ezek 2:2; 3:24) and transporting him in visionary experiences (Ezek 3:12; 8:3; 37:1) but ultimately accomplishing the spiritual renewal of the entire community of God's people (Ezek 11:19; 36:26–27; 37:14). Here, the Spirit enables him to receive his commission, as difficult an assignment as it will be (Ezek 2:3–4, 6; cf. Ezek 3:8–9).

2:3 *a rebellious nation:* Some translations emphasize the plural, "nations," of the Hebrew text (cf. ESV; NET), which is important to Ezekiel's eventual message of deliverance—God's plan encompasses both the northern and southern kingdoms (Ezek 37:15–27) that had been divided since the days of Rehoboam (1 Kgs 12:19).[3] Here, the stress is on the rebellious nature of *all* Israel. The word translated "rebellious" describes

---

1. Taylor, *Ezekiel*, 60.
2. See Bock, "Son of Man," 894–900.
3. Cf. Ezek 35:10. Further, see Alexander, "Ezekiel," 668, and comments at Ezek 4:4–5.

political revolt by a vassal nation against its overlord (Gen 14:4; 2 Kgs 18:7), and so it has the connotation of treason. It describes Israel's refusal to obey God's initial command to enter the promised land (Num 14:9), an illustration appropriate to the mention of "ancestors" in this verse. A similar tone reverberates from the word translated "revolt" (1 Kgs 12:19; 2 Kgs 1:1). The nation's obstinacy (v. 4) is a well-known characteristic of the ancestors ("stiff-necked"; Exod 32:9; 33:3, 5; 34:9; Deut 9:6, 13; 2 Chr 30:8). What is so pointed about God's comment here is that the combination of words translated "stubborn" is an idiom used outside of Ezek 2:4 and 3:7 for the hardening of Pharaoh's heart (Exod 7:13, 22; 8:15; 9:35). The language could not be more derogatory.

2:4 *the Sovereign LORD says:* Traditionally translated "LORD God," this form of the divine name combines the proper name for Israel's God, "Yahweh" (translated with lower case capitalization on "LORD") and the general word in the Old Testament for "lord." The latter term generally denotes a person of superior social rank, often as a term in respectful address (Gen 42:10; Num 11:28; 1 Sam 16:16; even within family, Gen 18:12; 31:35). It acknowledges authority (Gen 45:9), sometimes denoting ownership (1 Kgs 16:24). Hence, this divine name combines the proper name of Israel's God, Yahweh, with a term emphasizing his sovereign authority to which all must submit.

2:6 *Do not be afraid:* Ezekiel should take courage that he will prevail against all who oppose him. The metaphors of briars, thorns, and scorpions likely refer to severe social discomfort that Ezekiel will experience. Some interpret these terms as metaphors of protection.[4] However, the "fear not" formula used the second and third time in this verse seems to be connected with a reason one might fear ("at their words" . . . "a rebellious house"), so more likely these metaphors give reason why the prophet might be tempted to fear. Later in the commission, God assures Ezekiel that his fortitude will be adequate for the challenge (Ezek 3:8–9).

2:8 *Do not rebel . . . open . . . and eat:* In contrast to the rebellious nation, Ezekiel must willingly receive the message. The visionary experience of eating a scroll seems bizarre, yet the metaphor of consumption nicely describes what is involved when one responds receptively. His embracing it (metaphorically internalizing) was not merely a superficial acquiescence, rather he willingly acknowledged the rightness of God's judgments. We might say, he "took it to heart" (cf. Ezek 3:10; Jer 15:16).

---

4. See Block, *Ezekiel 1–24*, 121–22; and Bodi, "Ezekiel," 409.

This agreement is indicated by the description, "sweet as honey," which compares to the psalmists' delight in God's words (Pss 19:10; 119:103).

Normally, such language is sweet because it is gracious (Prov 16:24); however, the words of this message are "lament and mourning and woe" (filling *both* sides of the scroll). To describe such distressing content as "sweet" is paradoxical. It seems best to recognize the complexity of such an experience. On the one hand Ezekiel recognizes the validity of the message, in this case, the *justice* of God's judgment; but at the same time he responds with dismay at the *terrifying tragedy* about to unfold. This is consistent with what was noted above with respect to the complex nature of Ezekiel's call. He is *reluctant* but not *resistant*. He willingly submits yet not without misgivings. So at the end of the whole experience Ezekiel is left with bitter anger (see comments on Ezek 3:14–15). Obstinacy by people in the face of God is senseless and Ezekiel anguishes over their obstinacy.

3:5–6 *obscure speech and strange language:* The comparison of Israel to foreign peoples whose language Ezekiel does not share is to underscore the stubborn nature of Ezekiel's community. He would receive a better response from idolatrous foreigners with whom he has a language barrier than he will from his own people.

3:8–11 *I will make your forehead:* The change of imagery from "heart" to "forehead" ("face," ESV, NASB, NET) stresses the intimate nature of the confrontation ahead. The word translated "hardest stone" is used elsewhere in comparison to iron (Jer 17:1; a gem more akin to diamond, so ESV, NASB, NET). This enablement of Ezekiel befits his name, which means "God hardens."[5]

3:12 *the glory of the LORD arose:* Due to the difficulty of the Hebrew text at this point, there are two significantly different ways this phrase is translated; and the expositor must be aware. Traditionally, translators have rendered the Hebrew as a doxology, "Blessed be the glory of the LORD from its place" (NIV [1984]; cf. ESV; NASB; NKJV). This is awkward in both English and Hebrew; perhaps *too* awkward to make sense. This would suggest the Hebrew text became corrupted in transmission. The NIV (2011) is likely correct here (cf. NET; NLT margin; NRSV).[6] In either case, the passage brings the visionary experience to a close as the

---

5. Greenberg, *Ezekiel 1–20*, 69.

6. See Taylor, *Ezekiel*, 67; and for more detail Block, *Ezekiel 1–24*, 134–35.

living creatures resume their movement to carry away God's throne (cf. Ezek 1:24).

3:14–15 *I went in bitterness . . . anger of my spirit:* The question is, toward what is Ezekiel's anger directed? There are two possibilities: (1) Ezekiel was angry because of the inescapable hardship of his mission (Ezek 2:6; 3:8–10).[7] The following phrase, "and the strong hand of the LORD was upon me," might imply that such divine force was necessary to overcome his resistance. This would be similar, but for different reasons, to the reaction of Jonah (Jonah 4:1–9). (2) Ezekiel's feelings were caught up in the LORD's righteous anger toward the nation's sin and obstinacy (cf. Jer 6:10–11).[8] This is compatible with the observation that the message of God's judgment was sweet to him (Ezek 3:3). The choice depends largely on one's overall view of Ezekiel's attitude toward his call. Because Ezekiel's response is a reluctance due to the horrors of his message rather than resistance to the call, the second option is preferable (cf. Ezek 9:8; Rev 10:8–11).[9]

The phrase, "deeply distressed," translates a word used to describe devastation and desolation of objects or emotions (Gen 47:19; 2 Sam 13:20; Ezra 9:3). Ezekiel's feelings were complex; indignation coupled with dismay at the horrors to come (cf. Ezek 21:6). "Seven days" likely corresponds to the length of time for completion of mourning (Gen 50:10; Job 2:13).[10]

Theological Bridge to Application

The contrast between human inadequacy ("son of man") and divine enablement ("the Spirit came into me") underscores the important truth that God is sufficient to accomplish his agenda. Furthermore, human nature is naturally inclined to resist the message of truth; it is not just ancient Israel that is hard of heart. But Ezekiel's title for God, "Sovereign LORD," leaves no doubt who wins in any contest of wills.

---

7. Block, *Ezekiel 1–24*, 137. However, this need not mean that the prophet shared "some of the hardened disposition of his compatriots."

8. Taylor, *Ezekiel*, 68.

9. See discussion under Context in Ezekiel for Ezek 1:1–28.

10. Alexander, "Ezckiel," 671.

Focus of Application

The temptation in teaching this passage is to over emphasize analogies between the call-experience of Ezekiel *the priestly-prophet* (cf. Ezek 1:3) and that of ordinary believers today, who in a qualified sense are *priests* (mediators between God and the non-believing world; 1 Pet 2:9; Rev 1:6; 5:10; 20:6) as well as *"prophets."* The report of the Day of Pentecost (Acts 2:17–18) indicates that all believers function "prophetically" in a less technical sense, as ambassadors of the New Covenant who proclaim the gospel to the world (2 Cor 3:6; 5:18–20).[11] However, while it is true that there is a *limited* analogy between Ezekiel and us, that is not the primary thrust of this passage.

God directly addressed the prophet, commissioning him and speaking to his personal condition. However, when Ezekiel records in his prophetic book the experience of his encounter with God, he is not doing so to instruct his original audience about how they might receive divine callings or act prophetically. Rather, this section of Ezekiel does two things. First, it validates the authority of the prophet. That is the function of call narratives in the Old Testament, to show that the prophet is invested with divine authority (see discussion under Context at Ezek 1:1–28). Call narratives also function to teach us about God and prepare us to read further in the prophetic book something about the nature of its message. In Ezek 3, the call narrative warns the audience about the stubbornness of their heart. So, in answer to the question, What is God doing in this passage?, it is not setting forth a template for a prophetic call to be applied to us today. But it warns us all of the universal human inclination to resist God's truth and the necessity to receive the divine word for the truth that it proclaims. Neither the messenger nor the audience is at liberty to ignore the truth of God's word.

Today, as in the case of Ezekiel's generation, the message of the gospel is not one that the world naturally receives (John 15:18–25; Rom 1:18; 1 Cor 2:8; 2 Cor 4:1–4). Even for those who believe, it is a sweet and bitter message. We sincerely embrace the gospel with joyful hearts, yet know that for those who resist, it is a tragic message of death (2 Cor 2:14–17). The gospel contains both sweet and bitter news of the righteousness of God.

---

11. For democratization of the prophetic call to all New Testament believers, see Beale, *A New Testament Biblical Theology*, 603–4, 908–10.

This passage might raise the topic about Christians and social engagement; what should be the expectations of believers when God's truth conflicts with society at a moral level. Caution is in order. The New Testament calls upon Christians to live mindfully of the poor and powerless (e.g., Luke 18:22; 19:8; Gal 2:10; Jas 1:27); but focusing on the moral transformation of a post-Christian society is difficult to find biblical texts to support (in fact, contra-indicated in 1 Cor 5:12). On the other hand, accountability *within* the Christian community is encouraged (Gal 6:1; 2 Tim 3:16; 1 5:14), and at times bold confrontation is appropriate, because even the regenerate heart of a believer can harden to the word of truth (1 Cor 5:9–11; Gal 2:14; 1 Tim 5:20; 2 Tim 4:2).

RESPONSIBILITY TO RESPOND
3:16–27

Ezekiel's Message

Consequences of obedience or disobedience rest on the response of *individuals* to heed the warnings of God's word.

Key Themes

- God's warnings can apply to the righteous to encourage a consistent walk of obedience.
- The responsibility for discipline or judgment rests on the person who fails to respond.

Context in Ezekiel

This unit opens where the last left off: "at the end of seven days." The time had been sufficient for Ezekiel to recover somewhat from the dual trauma of encountering God's glorious presence and receiving such a grave commission. Now God moves Ezekiel from his general call as a prophet to his first active assignment—a "silent watchman" who conveys his message by *visual* signs (horrifying siege of Jerusalem in chapter 4 and the slaughter in chapter 5). One could argue for isolating Ezek 3:16–21 from what follows. But these verses, which expand upon Ezekiel's commission in Ezek 2:1—3:15, also introduce his assignment as a sign messenger, which begins in Ezek 3:22. Altogether, Ezek 3:16-27 leads into the following chapters 4 and 5, with Ezek 3:22-27 introducing his sign ministry.

Interpretive Highlights

3:17 *a watchman:* Cities posted watchmen atop walls to sound an alarm of news or approaching danger (2 Sam 18:24-27; 2 Kgs 9:17-20; cf. Ezek 33:1-6). So the image of "watchman" served as a fitting metaphor for the task of a prophet (Jer 6:17; Hos 9:8). In this immediate context, not only does Ezekiel warn his countrymen of the lethal danger of their sin, but as a watchman he also signals the siege in Ezek 4:1-3. Regarding Ezekiel's call to be a watchman, see also the parallel passage in Ezek 33:1-20 and the commentary there.

3:18-19 *you will surely die . . . saved yourself:* The death sentence announced to the wicked in these verses, and the similar warning to the righteous in vv. 20-21, should not be confused with matters of eternal life. This over reading of the text is tempting only because from a contemporary Christian perspective, the matter of *eternal* life and death is the dominant issue associated with the New Testament gospel. However, from the perspective of the Mosaic Covenant, life and death were most immediately associated with covenant blessings or curses in the promised land (Deut 30:1-20, esp. v. 15; cf. Deut 4:1-4; 11:26-27; 16:20; Lev 18:5). Similarly, the psalmists and sages spoke of wickedness leading to premature death (Pss 37:35-36; 55:23; Prov 10:16; 11:19). So, Ezekiel's warning would have been understood in the manner of Jeremiah's (Jer 21:8-10).[1]

For Ezekiel, failure as a watchman results in moral and legal culpability: "accountable for their blood." This is the expression for one who is held responsible for a capital crime and so forfeits life (Gen 9:5-6; 2 Sam 4:11-12).[2] The Hebrew phrase rendered "saved yourself" (NIV; cf. NASB) is often translated "saved your soul" (ESV; NKJV). This adds to the confusion, since in modern parlance, "soul" is associated with the immaterial component of human nature that survives physical death to enter the eternal state. However, in Old Testament usage, the word often translated "soul" primarily refers to the whole person (Exod 1:5; Num 6:6; Ps 35:9-10) or physical life (Gen 19:17; Lev 24:17). The authority to

---

1. Taylor, *Ezekiel*, 70-71; Greenberg, *Ezekiel 1-20*, 84.
2. Alexander, "Ezekiel," 672.

announce life and death to specific individuals is an exclusively prophetic task (e.g., Moses [Num 14:35; 26:65]; Samuel [1 Sam 2:33–34]; Nathan [2 Sam 12:13–14]; Elijah [2 Kgs 1:4]; Isaiah [2 Kgs 20:1, 5]; Jeremiah [Jer 38:17–18]).[3] For further discussion on personal responsibility, see the parallel passage in Ezek 18:1–32 and the commentary there.

3:20 *stumbling block:* The threat of death not only applies to the wicked, but even the righteous person who turns to wickedness will experience the Lord's severity. The word translated "stumbling block" refers to an object over which one trips to their harm (Lev 19:14). So, it lends itself metaphorically, as here, to something that results in death (cf. Jer 6:21) and might be translated as "calamity."[4] Recall what was said above, that this language does not pertain to matters of eternal life.

3:22–23 *The hand of the Lord ... the glory:* A repetition of Ezekiel's initial, visionary experience accompanies the more detailed instruction for his task. Anticipated rejection by the people, both of his message and of him personally (Ezek 3:25–26), required special emboldening (Ezek 3:9).

3:24–25 *shut yourself inside ... you will be bound:* The difficulty here is envisioning exactly what would happen. Would the prophet sequester himself, or would his opponents bind him to isolate him from the public? Alternatively, perhaps those binding him were associates cooperating with his sign acts (cf. Ezek 4:8). It is also possible that the binding here is metaphorical, that is, public resistance forced a strategy of reclusion. In any event, while Jeremiah found himself confined by rebellious leadership (Jer 20:1–2 [cf. Jer 29:26]; Jer 37:21; 38:6), in Ezekiel's case he seems to have regular access to public space, such as in the dramatic performance of his signs. As Block notes, "public apathy toward his message seems to have been a more serious problem than malevolence toward his person."[5] But also, Ezekiel's compatriots frequently sought him in his home (Ezek 8:1; 14:1; 20:1; 33:30–33). So, although it is impossible to be sure exactly what took place, the binding complements the constrained nature of Ezekiel's proclamation. This is expressed in the next verse by the command to silence. Together with the exotic nature of his prophetic signs, his reclusive habit had a magnetic social effect similar to "playing hard to get."

---

3. Greenberg, *Ezekiel 1–20*, 94.
4. Greenberg, *Ezekiel 1–20*, 85; Block, *Ezekiel 1–24*, 146–47.
5. Block, *Ezekiel 1–24*, 155.

3:26–27a *you will be silent:* One need not entertain that Ezekiel's silence was due to some pathological condition that kept him from being able to speak. In Job 29:10 the image of the tongue stuck to the roof of the mouth refers to *voluntary* speechlessness. The prophet was so controlled by the Spirit of God that he would speak out only when compelled by the Spirit, a command that lasted seven years (Ezek 24:27; 33:21–22).[6] As Taylor states, "From that moment onwards, Ezekiel was to be known as nothing more than the mouthpiece of Yahweh."[7]

Some interpret the phrase "you must not be for them a man who rebukes" as a prohibition against functioning as an *intercessor*.[8] In this interpretation, the key word that refers to "one who rebukes" (as in Prov 25:12; Job 32:12) actually refers to a "defender" in a legal context (as in Job's contention with God; Job 13:3; 40:2). In other words, this would refer to Ezekiel's instinct to *defend* his people. This is consistent with the view held by some interpreters that Ezekiel is resistant to proclaiming a message of doom. Therefore, God must command him not to intercede on behalf of those judged. However, if one concludes in the previous call narrative that Ezekiel's anger (Ezek 3:14) arose in *agreement* with God's assessment of sin and judgment, then this interpretation is contextually unlikely (cf. his intercession at Ezek 9:8). Furthermore, this interpretation depends on questionable support from word usage in Job, the only place where it might even possibly carry this meaning. More likely, Job is acting as the *accuser* of God, who has afflicted him unjustly.[9] Ezekiel's divinely imposed silence, then, is an ironic twist to his call as watchman. He is not to warn unless bid to do so by God. While this silence is not called a "sign" in the text, it functions this way: a signature that Ezekiel's ministry is completely domination by the will of God. This reinforces the authority of his message when he is impelled to speak.

3:27b *Whoever will listen:* This almost proverbial expression summarizes a point stressed in the previous unit (Ezek 3:7, 11)—as watchman, the prophet is responsible to issue the warning, but the choice of response is in the hands of each individual. In Ezek 2:1—3:15, the emphasis is on the call of Ezekiel to speak by divine enablement, regardless of the results, which would generally not be positive. In Ezek 3:16–27,

6. For detailed discussion, see Block, *Ezekiel 1–24*, 155–56.
7. Taylor, *Ezekiel*, 74.
8. See Alexander, "Ezekiel," 674; and Block, *Ezekiel 1–24*, 156–58.
9. Allen, *Ezekiel 1–19*, 62, notes that the noun form of this word means "rebuke" elsewhere in Ezekiel. Cf. Greenberg, *Ezekiel 1–20*, 102.

this theme continues, as stated in the phrase, "for they are a rebellious house"; but the emphasis here is the responsibility of Ezekiel to comply with his commission with unfailing obedience to God's Spirit, who must control all aspects of his ministry.

Theological Bridge to Application

The concept of divine retribution must be understood within its Old Testament context before considering how it might apply today, for God does not work in exactly the same way now as then. Due to the nature of the Mosaic Covenant, life in Old Testament times was more "contractual" in terms of the results of disobedience or obedience. As noted above, psalms and wisdom teach that this applied to some extent at the individual level, although wisdom traditions, like the story of Job, also taught that retribution was not as formulaic or rigidly experienced as often thought. In general, retribution for obedience or disobedience was experienced more at a national level than individual. The circumstances of Ezekiel's time were perhaps unusual in that the nation was already experiencing maximum covenant sanctions in exile, so the instructions to Ezekiel brought new focus to bear on the destiny of individuals living under the national curse. These qualifications and distinctions are important to understand before considering any analogy for Christians today. God relates to national Israel at a contractual level in the Old Covenant. His relationship to believers today is not governed by such covenant stipulations.

Focus of Application

If a key theme of the previous unit (Ezek 2:1—3:15) stresses the eagerness with which God's people must embrace the truth to be proclaimed, the thrust of this unit spotlights the responsibility of those who resist. Applying Ezek 3:16–21 is difficult, because the *unique* obligation placed upon Ezekiel with the threat of death differs from the general commission for believers today to proclaim the gospel. Ezekiel's commission was unique to him and his situation. It has been preached, wrongly, that the "blood of unbelievers" is on the hands of Christians who fail to present the gospel. The Apostle Paul received a commission similar to Ezekiel (1 Cor 9:16); but the personal burden placed on prophets and apostles does not extend to variously gifted Christians. Recall the axiom of application: What is

God doing through the prophetic message, delivered first and foremost to Ezekiel's contemporaries? God is not urging Ezekiel's audience to imitate the prophet. If not the original audience, then he is not urging us to do so either. This does not give us liberty to be lax in our evangelistic boldness; it is just to say that encouragement for evangelism is a different message to be rooted in a different text (e.g., Isa Mark 8:38; Luke 9:26; Rom 1:16; Rev 2:10, 13). Rather, the prophet's written message to his compatriots warns them about the dire consequences of not responding to God's message. That is the lesson to which we must give ear.

Although the New Covenant does not have stipulations pertaining to blessings and curses as did the Mosaic Covenant, the concept of temporal discipline for wayward Christians can be found in such passages as 1 Cor 5:4–5; 11:30–32; Rev 3:19. James 5:19–20 is especially relevant as it uses the same metaphor, saving the "soul," as used in Ezekiel for physical life and death (cf. Jas 5:14–15; cf. 1 John 5:16–17). Of course, *complete rejection of the gospel* entails not just physical but eternal death as well (John 3:36; 1 John 5:12). God holds people responsible for what they have heard and for the actions they need to take, with potentially serious consequences. Whatever an individual's response, he or she bears the responsibility for the choice, as Jesus warned in correspondence to Ezekiel's truth, "Whoever has ears to hear, let them hear" (Mark 4:9).

FAILING TO LIVE AS LIGHT
4:1—5:17

Ezekiel's Message

God's people live in a manner that displays God at work among them, and when they fail to live distinctly, it incurs God's displeasure.

Key Themes

- God's people bring conviction through the quality of their lives as much as through the spoken word.
- When believers fail to live up even to the ethical standards of the world, it undermines the kingdom purpose and angers God.
- The execution of judgment vindicates God's zeal to accomplish his purposes.

Context in Ezekiel

Ezekiel's ministry as a silent watchman was introduced in Ezek 3:16–27. The next two chapters offer a glimpse of how he effectively communicates his message of God's judgment in symbolic drama more than through words. Ezekiel offers two signs: (1) Sign of Siege (Ezek 4:1–16—building the model [vv. 1–3]; enduring punishment [vv. 4–8]; famine rations [vv. 9–16]); and (2) Sign of the Razor (Ezek 5:1–17—cutting hair [vv. 1–4]; interpretation [vv. 5–12]; summary of signs [vv. 13–17]). The two chapters, Ezek 4 and 5, are linked by the theme of famine (Ezek 4:16–17 and 5:16–17). Both chapters together comprise a unified segment on Ezekiel's message through symbolic action (see also Ezek 12:6, 11).

Special Topic: Prophetic Signs in the Ancient Near East

Biblical prophets and their families served as dramatic illustrations of their message, a sort of living visual aid. For example, Hosea's marriage and family illustrated covenantal faithlessness of the nation and the Lord's contrasting faithfulness (Hos 1–3). Similarly, Isaiah's children were named in ways that signified what God was doing with his people (Isa 7:3; 8:1–3), and Isaiah himself dramatized a judgment of exile when he walked naked (Isa 20:3–4). Jeremiah enacted his message of hope for restoration when he purchased land that was falling into Babylonian hands (Jer 32:6–15; cf. Jer 13:1–7; 18:1–4). But Israelite prophets were not unique in this regard. A graphic example of this is when a non-Israelite prophet living in the Mesopotamian city of Saggaratum ate a lamb in the city gate to illustrate a warning from the god Dagan: "[The governor gave him] a lamb and he devoured it raw in front of the city gate. He assembled the elders in front of the gate of Saggaratum and said: 'A devouring will take place! . . . Whoever commits an act of violence shall be expelled from the city . . .'"[1]

Prophetic speech was the primary vehicle for communicating God's message to his people, but visual aids add a sharpness through dramatic effect. The old adage is true that actions speak louder than words, both the ancient prophet's and our own.

Interpretive Highlights

4:1–3 *block of clay . . . a sign:* The first seven years of Ezekiel's ministry is spent convincing his fellow exiles that the Lord's holy city, Jerusalem, will fall catastrophically to Babylonian invasion. Consistent with the relative verbal silence of Ezekiel, he uses drama to illustrate his message. Clay maps of cities were familiar to the culture of Babylon in which the exiles lived.[2] But the meaning of the iron pan is unclear. It could represent the

---

1. Mari letter ARM 26 206 lines 10–22 (Nissinen et al., *Prophets and Prophecy*, 38).

2. See Bodi, "Ezekiel," 412–14, for illustration and discussion of clay models and

fortifications of the city against siege. Alternatively, since the prophet himself symbolized the LORD's hostile posture toward the city, it may connote the immovable barrier between the people and their God (cf. Lam 3:44; Isa 59:2).[3] In the Old Testament, a "sign" denotes a visual experience that symbolizes (Exod 13:9; Deut 6:8) or confirms a message (Exod 3:12; Deut 4:34), sometimes concerning future events (1 Sam 14:10; 2 Kgs 20:8; Isa 20:3; Jer 44:29).

4:4-8 *Then lie on your . . . side:* Accompanying the sign of military siege (cf. Ezek 4:7-8), Ezekiel lies on his respective sides, symbolizing 40 years for the period of exile and 390 years for the period of sin that contributed to this judgment. In this division of time, the text is not differentiating the northern kingdom, Israel, from the southern kingdom, Judah, for the passage refers twice in this immediate context to Judah/Jerusalem (Ezek 4:13; 5:4-5). In other instances in Ezekiel where the terms "Israel" and "Judah" occur together, they are interchangeable (e.g., Ezek 8:1 with 14:1; 20:1), especially in other contexts of sign-acts (e.g., Ezek 6:11; 12:6; 21:12; 24:21).[4] The history and fate of the original nation of twelve tribes was bound up with that of Judah (see comments at Ezek 2:3).

This method of numeric symbolism is illustrated in reverse in Num 14:33-34 (years for days instead of days for years as in Ezekiel). The specific span of years referred to by the numbers 390 and 40 is difficult to determine, since the math does not correspond *exactly* to any obvious periods. The forty-year period is likely a round number (schematic "40") for the years from 586 BC, when Jerusalem was destroyed, to 539 BC, when the change from Babylonian to Persian Empires marked the end of exile. The 390 years could be the approximate span of time from the building of Solomon's temple (c. 970 BC) to its destruction (586 BC). One might recall that even in Solomon's reign idolatry had taken hold (cf. 1 Kgs 11:4-5). So Ezekiel portrays the entire history of the temple period as one that was marred by sin. In spite of uncertainty in our interpretation, the point of Ezekiel's sign is clear: the nation has sinned and judgment is coming.

The idea to "bear sin" does not mean that Ezekiel plays a substitutionary role on behalf of the nation (like Isaiah's suffering servant; Isa 52:12—53:12), since the nation indeed paid for the consequences of

---

siege technology.

3. Greenberg, *Ezekiel 1-20*, 104.

4. Block, *Ezekiel 1-24*, 176. For the view that the 390 years and 40 years are Israel's and Judah's guilt respectively, see Taylor, *Ezekiel*, 78-80.

its sin during exile (cf. Isa 40:2). Rather, as a prophet he represents the people and so serves as an appropriate symbol identified with the people (cf. Hosea). The word translated "sin" can refer to the wrongful action itself (Hos 9:9; Jer 36:3, both "wickedness" in NIV), the guilt incurred (Num 15:31; Jer 50:20), or the punishment (Gen 4:13; Ezek 21:25, both "punishment" in NIV). Ezekiel's action symbolizes the period of guilt (390 years) and punishment (40 years). The practical details of how this sign was acted out are impossible to determine. Perhaps a time each day was set aside for performance.[5] Being bound probably signifies that the message is unalterable.[6]

4:9-17 *Take wheat ... they ... will waste away:* These foods hardly constitute a normal diet (insufficient grains supplemented with beans to make bread). Rather, as Ezek 4:16 and 5:10 make clear, these are rations in a city under siege. Human waste rendered things unclean (cf. Deut 23:12-14; although animal dung was common fuel), and so Israel would become unclean among the nations where they would eat unclean food (Hos 9:3; cf. Josh 22:19; Amos 7:17). The LORD relented of the indignity regarding human waste and substituted animal waste; but the symbol of siege remained.

5:1-4 *a third:* In the second symbol act, shaving with a sword, Ezekiel illustrates three destinies of the inhabitants of Jerusalem. During siege, the city experienced unprecedented acts of cannibalism (Ezek 5:10; cf. covenant curse in Lev 26:29; Deut 28:53-57; Lam 2:20). Subsequent burning of hairs tucked in Ezekiel's garment reinforces the fate of the last third (Ezek 5:12 summarizes with only three groups).

5:7 *more unruly than the nations:* God's plan for Israel was that the nation would live in such a manner as to offer light to the nations and so attract them into relationship with the LORD (Deut 4:6-8; Isa 2:1-4; 42:6-7). The irony is that Israel's behavior showed nothing distinct but in fact surpassed the nations in idolatry, wickedness, and injustice. This lies at the foundation of God's accusation and judgment and therefore lies at the heart of the message to teach from this passage today.

In the description of judgment in this paragraph, there is a translation difficulty that the teacher might wish to be aware of. The phrase rendered in the NIV, "I will shave," appears in other translations as "I will withdraw" (ESV; NASB; NET). The word means to "reduce" (Exod

---

5. For helpful discussion, see Block, *Ezekiel 1-24*, 168-69; and Wright, *Ezekiel*, 79-80.

6. Block, *Ezekiel 1-24*, 180-81.

5:8; Deut 4:2), and in contexts of hair it can mean to "shave" (Isa 15:2; Jer 48:37), so the NIV makes good sense in the context of Ezek 5 (cf. NJPS).

5:13 *spoken in my zeal:* The judgment of God for Israel's failure to be distinct points to a very important attribute, his jealousy for his people. The word translated "zeal" often denotes the jealousy experienced by someone in an exclusive relationship (Num 5:14; Song 8:6) or passion for the interest of another (2 Kgs 10:16; Ps 69:9). As such, it describes God's feelings toward the people with whom he is in covenant, both to exclude all rivals (Ezek 8:3–5; 16:38) and to execute his kingdom program on their behalf (Zech 1:14–15; Isa 59:17). In the context of Ezek 5, God's jealousy results in judgment in order that his people might know his demand of exclusive devotion. In fulfillment of the jealousy promised in Deut 29:20, God will defend the covenant relationship with severe sanctions, alluded to in Ezek 5:14–17 (cf. Lev 26:32–33; Deut 32:22–24).

Theological Bridge to Application

The covenant relationship takes central place in the announcement of judgment in this passage. The covenant will surface again both in contexts of judgment (Ezek 16:61–62; 17:18–19) and restoration (Ezek 34:25; 37:26), especially in the important covenant theme of God's presence (Ezek 48:35). God has a purpose for Israel, his covenant people (a means of blessing for the nations), and it is the perversion of this kingdom plan that stirs God's zeal to protect the covenant through judgment. God judges even his covenant people when they fail to fulfill his purposes for them corporately. God's jealous nature is not of the immature sort that often characterizes human zeal. Rather, his jealousy for his people and his kingdom guards his covenant relationships and his purpose for human history.

Focus of Application

The nation Israel was called into covenant relationship with God to bring the blessings of Abraham to the nations (Gen 12:3; Exod 19:5–6, "a kingdom of priests"). One aspect of this involved living distinctly by God's standards and so attract others to him (Deut 4:6–8; 1 Kgs 8:41–43; Isa 2:1–4; 42:6–7).[7] At the foundation of Ezekiel's accusation against Judah

---

7. For an excellent discussion of this, written for a popular audience, see Wright,

is the nation's failure in this regard; indeed, their behavior exceeded the surrounding nations in wickedness.

Similar to Israel, the community of believers today is called to bear witness to the ways of God through their style of living (Matt 5:13–16; Titus 2:10; 1 Pet 2:15–16). Simply living righteously is a reminder to people that there is a God to whom one must give account, which often provokes conviction and sometimes anger in others (1 Pet 3:13–17; 4:1–5). Steadfastness in such faith is a sign of destruction for those who oppose God (Phil 1:27–28). But conversely, when Christians fail to show by their lives the distinct beauty of God's kingdom, they betray the covenant into which they are called and incur God's displeasure. It is tragically the case, particularly in the United States, that Christians have become so syncretized to the culture around them that the distinction is hardly noticeable, whether it is failure to love one another, consumerism, or grasping for social and political power. Whatever the nature of judgment for believers, it stands as a strong warning to live as citizens of God's kingdom (Rom 14:10; 2 Cor 5:10; 1 Pet 4:17). Although the warning to teachers in Jas 3:1 pertains primarily to one's speech, it implicitly gathers in the whole of one's life (Jas 3:2). God's displeasure, even if it is not eternal wrath, is a consequence to be avoided. For discussion of temporal discipline of Christians, see the application section to Ezek 3:16–27.

The Mission of God's People.

OUR GRIEVOUS IDOLS
Ezekiel 6:1–14

Ezekiel's Message

Idolatry grieves the heart of God and warrants our remorse.

Key Themes

- Human creations that replace the true God are diverse and abundant.
- Idolatry grieves the heart of God and should evoke remorse in us.
- Idolatry stirs God to judgment.

Context in Ezekiel

The opening formula in Ezek 6:1, "The word of the Lord came to me," identifies this as a new unit separated from chapter 5. The oracle ends with the formula, "they will know that I am the Lord" (Ezek 6:14). The rhetorical aim of this passage is similar to the last (cf. Ezek 5:13, 16), that Ezekiel's audience would know that the Lord is in sovereign control (cf. Ezek 5:5, 8) and acts to hold Israel accountable to the covenant. But a new emphasis in chapter 6 is the profusion of idolatry that grieves God and should stir remorse in the heart of his people.

Special Topic: High Places and Sacred Trees

Before the centralization of worship at the Jerusalem temple, various other locations were used for worship of Yahweh. Some of these shrines are called "high places" (1 Sam 9:11–35; 10:5 1 Kgs 3:2–4). After the building of the central sanctuary, sacrifice at locations other than the Jerusalem temple was no longer legitimate. The only exceptions were special cases, such as Elijah's altar (1 Kgs 18). But continuation of the practice became inseparably linked with the worship of other gods (1 Kgs 11:7; 2 Kgs 23:1–20; cf. Judg 6:24–26 even before temple construction). Such unorthodox shrines are condemned (Lev 26:30; Deut 12:2; Ps 78:58). As the name suggests, high places included hilltop shrines where images of various gods and goddesses were set up (1 Kgs 14:23). But "high places" were not the hills themselves, since they were also located in valleys (Jer 7:31; 32:35) and at city gates (2 Kgs 23:8). Probably, hilltops were fitting locations because of the relative proximity to the heavens. Some featured altars for offering sacrifices (1 Kgs 12:31–33; 22:43) or burning incense (2 Kgs 17:11; 23:8); although the word translated "incense altars" in Ezek 6:4 may refer rather to a building or tent-like structure often found at these places (cf. 2 Chr 34:4).[1] The standing stones, which represent the presence of deities, were the focal point. Another feature associated with worship at high places was the sacred tree. Perhaps symbolizing the fertility of life, lush trees were viewed as logical places by which to place representations of deities (1 Kgs 14:23; 2 Kgs 17:10; Jer 17:2).[2]

Interpretive Highlights

6:3 *mountains of Israel:* The bulk of the population of Israel and Judah lived along the central mountain spine that ran north-south through the country. In particular, Jerusalem was nestled among three high spots, one of which was the temple mount itself overlooking the city. By a figure of speech called metonymy, the reference to "mountains" can substitute for the *population* living there, against whom Ezekiel preaches. But considering that Ezekiel's accusation in this passage names the "high places," the image is particularly appropriate.

---

1. Block, *Ezekiel 1–24*, 225–26.
2. For more discussion, see Petter, "High Places," 413–18.

6:3 *your high places:* These shrines (see **Special Topic: High Places and Sacred Trees**) facilitated the proliferation and diversity of idol worship. The stress on "every" hill, "all" mountaintops, "every" tree, and "all" idols in Ezek 6:13 underscores this reality. Second Kings 23:5 names a plethora of gods worshipped at high places (Baal, sun god, moon god, and other astral deities). This diversity of objects represented the diversity of gods that drew away Israel's affection for their covenant God.

6:4 *idols:* There are over a dozen Hebrew words in the Old Testament that are translated "idol" by our English versions. A number of these Hebrew words are actually derogatory terms that normally denote concepts such as "emptiness" (*shawe'*; Jer 18:15), "vanity" (*hebel*; Jer 2:5; Ps 31:6), or "abomination" (*to'ebah*; Deut 32:16; Ezek 5:11). As such, they are pointedly critical. The word translated "idols" in this verse (*gillulim*) makes a play on words with another Hebrew term for "dung" (*galal*; 1 Kgs 14:10; and *gel*; Ezek 4:12, 15). This is Ezekiel's favorite word for "idols" (39 times), leaving a graphic impression of what he thinks of them. Not only are idols useless, they are repugnant and disgusting. The image is not only visual but connotes stench as well.

6:5 *dead bodies . . . in front of their idols:* The result of God's intervention to destroy idolatry includes the slaughter of idolaters, described here in the language of covenant curse (Lev 26:30). Dead things contaminate and defile holy space, like a temple or shrine (Lev 21:11–12; 22:8). So in ironic fashion, the idols and cultic objects would be defiled by the dead bodies of those who worshipped them (cf. 2 Kgs 23:6, 14–16, 20).

6:8 *some of you will escape:* Speaking of the inhabitants of Jerusalem who will experience the impending slaughter, Ezekiel emphasizes the totality of destruction, for even those who *think* they have escaped will meet untimely deaths (cf. v. 12 and discussion on Ezek 5:1–4). Ezekiel cannot be speaking in absolute terms, since others will be captured and taken to Babylon (v. 9). He speaks hyperbolically.

6:9 *how I have been grieved:* This statement is an astonishing testimony to the personal and relational nature of God. The word translated "grieved" often means to "be broken" (e.g., Eli's neck, 1 Sam 4:18; an animal's leg, Exod 22:10; cf. ESV); thus, it is a good metaphor for emotional turmoil. Furthermore, the redemptive outcome of judgment is that God's idolatrous people will "loath" themselves for their behavior, a word used of the psalmist's contempt for sinners (Pss 119:158; 139:21) or Job's self-disgust (Job 10:1).

6:10 *you will know that I am the* LORD: Four times in this passage Ezekiel declares that judgment must occur in order for Israel to truly understand that the LORD (God's proper name, Yahweh) is their covenant God (cf. Exod 3:14–15; 6:2–5; 10:12). The irony is that Israel needed to learn once again the fundamentals of their faith, this time in the way their Egyptian oppressors came to "know" Israel's God in the exodus plagues (Exod 7:5, 17; 8:22; 14:4). The phrase "in vain" could mean that God's threat would prove true and so vindicate his prophet.[3] But frequently, it stresses that an action had no result (e.g., Prov 1:17; Mal 1:10); and so, here, God's judgment accomplishes his purpose (cf. Ezek 14:23). This second understanding fits the immediate context better.

6:11 *Strike your hands:* Body motions such as this express an outburst of emotion. The cause might be joy (2 Kgs 11:12; Ps 47:1), even if over another's calamity (Ezek 25:6; Nah 3:19), or anger (Num 24:10). Considering that this expression is provoked by sin and judgment, it appropriately marks God's expectation for Ezekiel's response (cf. Ezek 3:14).

6:14 *Diblah:* The location is unknown. Therefore, some translations (ESV; NET; NRSV) assume a confusion of the first letter in Hebrew and render it "Riblah," after the known site (2 Kgs 23:33). The form of the letters "*d*" and "*r*" in Hebrew are easily confused. Either way, the point remains the same regarding the desolating result of divine judgment.

Theological Bridge to Application

While it is true that God transcends his creation and is not dependent on it in any way, the Bible unabashedly describes God's personal interaction with human creatures in startling ways. Not only does sin anger God, but our actions can grieve him (v. 9; cf. Isa 63:10; Eph 4:30). This is consistent with what was described earlier in Ezekiel as God's jealousy to defend the boundaries of the covenantal relationship (see comments at Ezek 5:13). A covenant is not simply a legal contract but is also an interpersonal relationship. So when God's people betray the covenant, its effect on the relationship is similar to adultery (cf. "adulterous hearts" in v. 9).

---

3. Greenberg, *Ezekiel 1–20*, 134–35.

Focus of Application

Aside from the certainty and totality of judgment, which is common to many chapters in Ezekiel, there are three other themes one might stress in the teaching of this passage: the diverse nature of idolatry, the impact on the heart of God, and the appropriate response of the human heart in repentance over idolatry.

As to the nature of idolatry, there is a technical distinction between worshipping other gods and worshipping the true God through idol statues. This distinction is reflected in the differing emphasis between the first and second commandments of Exod 20: 3–4. At times, Israel worshipped the true God in conjunction with an image, thus violating the second commandment. For example, Aaron's and Jeroboam's calves were likely pedestals upon which to imagine Yahweh standing (Exod 32:1–6 [note the object of worship in v. 5 is Yahweh]; 1 Kgs 12:25–33). More often, however, Scripture condemns Israel for directly worshipping other gods in violation of the first commandment. This invariably manifested itself in the worship of these deities thought to be present in idols (whether statues, pillars, or sacred trees). This frequent connection between worshipping a false god and doing so through an illicit object is part of the reason why the Jewish tradition combines the first and second commandments of the Christian tradition as a single, second commandment. The first commandment in Judaism is the statement about redemption from Egypt (Exod 20:2). Prohibition against other gods and worship through idols were practically inseparable in the ancient world. The accusation in Ezek 6 stresses the diverse ways by which Israel betrayed her allegiance to god through pursuit of these idols.

The nature of idolatry in some majority world countries today is very similar both conceptually and ritually to that of the ancient Near East. But in the developed, western world, beliefs and practices that constitute "rivals" of the one true God are usually more abstract. Our cultural equivalents that often violate the first commandment are many: educational credentials; career goals; political control; children or perhaps *their* accomplishments; human lovers or even "love" in the abstract; celebrities on stage, screen, or the sports arena; body image or personal magnetism (in short, ourselves)—these easily become alternative absolutes that compete for our loyalty and affection toward the true God. The distinction between a rival *person* and a representative *idol image* is blurred.

It is easy to think of our God as the "unmoved mover," but Scripture paints a different picture of him as a very personal God whose response to betrayal is similar to our own experience—brokenness and pain. Accepting this does not entail that God's being is somehow diminished in perfection or that his sovereign control of the universe is threatened. Rather, it recognizes his deep, personal attributes whereby he was capable of entering fully into human experience (cf. Jesus).

Appreciation of this personal, divine character, is prerequisite to an appropriate repentance of our own idolatry, because remorse comes in part through admission of the pain caused to another. An honest appraisal of the pain we cause our God leads to an appropriate sense of shame for what we have done. We quickly move our hearts to the grace of the gospel, realizing there is no condemnation. However, deep abhorrence of our attitudes and actions is part of balanced, self-examination. One who would truly "know" the Lord, mentioned four times in this chapter, must understand not only the grace of God but also the demands of the covenant relationship and the effects of our attitudes and actions on God. Only after honest appraisal of the gravity of our idolatry should we move on to the good news: there is no condemnation (Rom 8:1).

THE IMPOTENCE OF MATERIALISM

Ezekiel 7:1–27

Ezekiel's Message

God's merciless judgment comes swiftly and unavoidably to those who seek security and pride in their own resources.

Key Themes

- There is a point after which turning to God for mercy is too late.
- The judgment of God comes at a time of his discretion.
- Materialism, like all idolatry, is useless to deliver from judgment.
- The inherent injustice of economic greed amplifies its culpability.

Context in Ezekiel

Similar to chapter 6, the limits of this unit are marked by the opening, "The word of the Lord came . . ." and the end, "Then they will know . . ." (Ezek 7:27). The chapter may be broken into smaller units, marked by the emphatic repetition of words that call the audience to attention: "end . . . end" (Ezek 7:2); "disaster . . . disaster" (Ezek 7:5); "see . . . see" (Ezek 7:10); "blown the trumpet . . . made all things ready" (Ezek 7:14); "full of bloodshed . . . full of violence" (Ezek 7:23).

Ezekiel develops his message of judgment with two new emphases in this passage. First, he stresses that merciless judgment is imminent, and second, he focuses his accusation on the arrogant yet useless economic greed of Israel's leadership that is linked with their idolatry.

Interpretive Highlights

7:2 *The end has come*: Like a series of exclamation points, the five-fold concentration of the word, "end," in the opening six verses punctuates this oracle with urgency. This language, first invoked by the prophet Amos concerning the northern kingdom (Amos 8:2), is now applied by Ezekiel to the southern kingdom. The irreversible nature of such judgment is stressed by the repetition of the phrase "has come" (8 times in the opening 7 verses). It is too late for repentance; judgment is already upon the city of Jerusalem, which is the primary referent throughout Ezekiel's judgment speeches (cf. "now," v. 3; "see, it comes," v. 10; "trumpet," v. 14).

7:3–4 *detestable practices*: This expression refers to a wide range of behavior that the Bible condemns as corrupt (variously translated with words related to "detestable" and "abominable" in the NIV). It includes the worship of foreign gods and the Canaanite practices associated with it (Deut 7:25; 20:18; 32:16), sexual immorality (Lev 18:22; 20:13; Ezek 22:11), falsehood (Prov 8:7), hypocritical prayer (Prov 28:9), and dishonesty in business dealings (Deut 25:16). All these things characterized Judah's behavior at the time of Ezekiel, but the prophet's emphasis in the context of this chapter is upon the financial materialism and injustice of the people (see below).

7:7 *the day is near*: Here Ezekiel draws upon another concept introduced by Amos. Perhaps related to ancient Near Eastern imagery for a king's decisive day of victory in battle, the expression "day of the LORD" (or more simply "that day"/"the day") became common in Old Testament texts to refer to any event when the LORD intervenes in war-like fashion for judgment and/or deliverance (see also discussion at Ezek 30:3). The shocking revelation in Amos is that such intervention would not necessarily be on behalf of God's covenant people (as in Isa 13:1, 6; Zeph 3:8) but could also entail his destruction of *them* (Amos 5:18–26; cf. Zeph 1:7–18; Joel 1:15; 2:1–11).

7:9 *the LORD who strikes you*: Rooted in Old Testament tradition are passages about the origin of compound names for God involving his covenant name "Yahweh" and a blessing he bestows ("The LORD Will Provide," Gen 22:14; "The LORD who Heals You," Exod 15:26; "The LORD is my Banner," Exod 17:15). In ironic fashion, in this context of judgment the LORD is known by the name of one who "strikes."

7:10–11 *the rod has budded:* This phrase probably alludes to the budding of Aaron's rod that put an "end" to the rebellion in Moses' generation (Num 17:8–12). Here, the literary allusion underscores the "end" in Ezekiel's day, when a "rod" arises to again challenge the arrogance of rebels. In v. 11, the allusion continues in reference to Aaron's rod as an instrument of judgment (Exod 7:9; 8:5). The Hebrew of this verse is difficult. Note that the NIV (compared with the ESV and NASB) clarifies, probably rightly, that the "rod" is directed toward the wicked.[1] This makes good sense with the parallel lines that follows, which stress the extermination of people and the wealth they have gained.

7:12–13 *buyer . . . seller:* In biblical law, both property and people (as bond-servants) could be exchanged for a price that was set according to a statute of limitations, after which the property must revert to its original owner and people set free (Exod 21:2; Lev 25:1–17; 27:22–25). In view of the imminent judgment, all parties of such transactions will be dead before anything is enjoyed or recovered.

7:15 *sword . . . famine . . . plague:* Ezekiel uses this triad (cf. Ezek 5:12; 6:11–12) to indicate that the major, lethal threats of a siege will successfully decimate the inhabitants of Jerusalem. Attempting to assign each threat to specific targets (inhabitants inside or outside the city) over reads the text, since the victims of each threat differ in the passages where the triad appears. The point is that few escape, and even these will suffer miserably (v. 16). A similar description features in a Mesopotamian text that describes the progressive decimation of the population of a city: "Anyone who has not died in battle will die in an epidemic. Anyone who has not died in the epidemic, the enemy will carry off as spoil. Anyone whom the enemy has not carried off, thieves will murder. Anyone whom thieves have not murdered, the king's weapon will overcome . . ." [and on for another seven rounds].[2]

7:17 *wet with urine:* The figure of speech here is unclear. Some translations (e.g., ESV, NASB, NJPS) render the second half of v. 17 in a way that closely parallels the image of "limp" hands in the first half of the

---

1. For alternatives, see Block, *Ezekiel 1–24*, 255–56.
2. Erra and Ishum (*COS* 1.113: 413). See also Bodi, "Ezekiel," 419.

verse. So, "knees turn to water," that is, they have no supporting strength. On the other hand, the NIV (cf. NET) reflects an understanding that this is a euphemism in which the Hebrew idiom, "knees running with water," refers to urine coming down the legs. Either translation is possible, but the NIV translation is more likely, given this particular combination of words. While the word picture differs, the same grammatical idiom expresses the idea of eyes running with tears (Jer 9:17; Lam 1:16).[3] An Assyrian text expresses the same imagery of soldiers fleeing in battle and passing urine in their fear: "Their hearts throbbed like the pursued young of pigeons, they passed their urine hotly."[4]

7:19–20 *caused them to stumble:* The sense in which the wealthy stumble is clarified by reference to "idols" made with their gold and silver. Merely making such objects constitutes illicit worship (see chapter 6), but here Ezekiel mocks the impotence of religious belief behind idolatry—these objects and the gods they represent cannot truly save (cf. Isa 46:6–7; Jer 2:25; 11:12; esp. Zeph 1:18).

7:22 *desecrate the place I treasure:* In the days of Jeremiah, there was a false sense of security among the leaders of Jerusalem that God would never allow foreign armies to harm the holy city of his temple (Jer 7:4). Ezekiel, as well, warns that this is a false hope. In the logic of this context, if God is willing to suffer the loss of the gold and silver treasures of his own temple, how much more at risk is the opulence of the wealthy inhabitants of Jerusalem.

7:23 *full of bloodshed:* Amplifying the culpability of the wealthy is the social atrocity by which they amassed such wealth (cf. Ezek 22:6, 27). The Old Testament testifies to some who gained material success by virtue and hard work (Boaz in the book of Ruth; cf. Prov 10:4; 21:5); but frequently, the means of financial gain in Israelite society was through injustice and physical violence (Ahab seizing Naboth's vineyard [1 Kgs 21:1–16]; cf. Isa 1:21–23; Amos 2:6–8; Mic 7:3; Hab 1:2–4; Zeph 1:8–9). It is this aspect of materialism, the disregard for human welfare, that lies deeper in Ezekiel's accusation against not only idolatry but the broader range of misconduct (Ezek 7:3–4).

---

3. For technical discussion, see Greenberg, *Ezekiel 1–20*, 152.

4. Grayson, *Royal Inscriptions*, 184 (no. 22, vi 29–31). See also Greenberg, *Ezekiel 1–20*, 152. The quotations of this line in Block, *Ezekiel 1–24*, 281 and Bodi, "Ezekiel," 419 incorrectly cite *CAD* 8, 103, which should be *CAD* 16, 103. The latter translates the text "they passed hot urine."

7:26 *they will go searching*: As it becomes apparent to the inhabitants of Jerusalem that disaster is looming, they will look beyond their trust in material self-sufficiency to human resources; but all of the customary leaders who might offer hope (cf. Jer 18:18; Mic 3:5–7) will also fail them.

Theological Bridge to Application

God is merciful and eager to relent of judgment (Exod 34:6; Jonah 2:9; 4:2). Before the call of Ezekiel, there was a time in Jerusalem's moral and social decay when the prophet Jeremiah offered hope if the city would repent (Jer 4:3–4; 7:1–3; cf. Zeph 2:1–3). However, in the ways of God, there comes a time when it is too late to turn to him (Ps 32:6; Isa 55:6). It is evident in Ezek 7 that the time had passed for Jerusalem, underscoring the terrible consequences of delay. There comes a point when God says, "Enough!"

Focus of Application

This chapter of Ezekiel presses upon each person the *urgency* of turning to God. There is a point after which turning to God for mercy is too late; and bargaining for time is a foolish gamble, since he sovereignly dictates the timing of his judgment. This principle applies to unbelievers, who might postpone coming to terms with their need for salvation. It also applies to people of faith, who live in relationship with God; yet both conspicuous and subtle sin stubbornly remain in the lifelong process of becoming more dependent on God and more like him in character. It is fortunate that God does not expose every dark corner of sin in our lives all at once; rather, his Spirit continually and with increasing subtlety sheds light on our outward behavior and inner thought world. What is demanded is a prompt response whenever there is conviction.

Ezekiel's accusations in this passage touch on several particulars. First, Ezek 7 carries forward from chapter 6 the theme of outward, more obvious expressions of idolatry. For Jerusalem, their worship of divine images was "detestable" (Ezek 7:3–4, 20); and North American, even christian, culture has its visual counterparts in the institutions and individuals we inappropriately celebrate. But second, at a deeper level, the making of idols was only a capacity that underlying material wealth made possible (Ezek 7: 19–20). Alongside wealth there is always the danger of materialism, which in turn fosters self-reliance in a way that undermines dependence on God.

Third, unjust, illicit, or unethical business and financial practices often exist at the foundation of wealthy gain. People, often those with less social capital, are literally robbed of their financial capital. The prophets, including Ezekiel (Ezek 7:23), use such language as "violence" and "bloodshed" to indict those who gain by the disadvantage of others. Sometimes this language is figurative, but in some cases real physical harm, even if indirect, is done to people who suffer from the actions of those more powerful than them. This application touches back to the detestable conduct denounced in Ezekiel's opening oracle. Ezekiel affirms that even the wicked know better than this and stand condemned by their own standard (Ezek 7:27).

Finally, when people realize that material resources no longer offer any hope, they often turn to and depend on human help. In modern society, this often takes the form of political, legal, or medical help, as our culture elevates professionals to divine status in terms of our expectations and hopes. There is a thin line between, on the one hand, the wise and godly pursuit of human assistance from professionals whom God has provided, and, on the other hand, placing one's final hope in such resources.

REBELLION IN GOD'S FACE
Ezekiel 8:1–18

Ezekiel's Message

Whether in secret denial of God or in open rebellion against him, human sin eventually provokes God to merciless judgment.

Key Themes

- There are degrees of sinful attitude that provoke corresponding degrees of anger in God.
- Denying God's knowledge of sin is illusory.
- Turning from God can manifest itself in bold rebellion.
- God regards violent injustice between human beings as more reprehensible than grotesque apostasy.

Context in Ezekiel

The date formula (Ezek 8:1) introduces a new major literary unit in the book (vision of the Lord's temple departure [Ezek 8:1—11:25]) and indicates that 14 months have transpired since Ezekiel's original visionary call.[1] In four scenes of increasing detestability (cf. Ezek 8:6, 13, 15), Ezekiel 8 demonstrates the blatant desecration of holiness by Jerusalem's leadership in the very presence of God, prompting his abandonment of

---

1. For literary design, see Block, *Ezekiel 1–24*, 272–73.

the temple (cf. Ezek 9:3; 10:3,18-19; 11:22-23). This effectively grants divine permission for the temple's destruction and sets the stage for Ezekiel's climactic vision of temple restoration and the return of God's presence (Ezek 40-48).

Interpretive Highlights

8:1 *elders of Judah*: Ezekiel had been confined to his house, except for his dramatic sign activity conducted outside (cf. chapters 4-5, 12), and he remained mute, speaking only the oracles God moved him to deliver (Ezek 3:24-27). As noted earlier, such eccentric behavior drew his neighboring Jewish leaders to him (cf. Ezek 14:1-3; 20:1). The visionary inclusion of the "seventy elders" at the Jerusalem temple (Ezek 8:11, see discussion there) signified representation of the whole nation. This could not have escaped the notice of his home audience as a warning to them as well.

8:2 *I saw a figure*: The parallels to Ezekiel's first vision build as his description unfolds (v. 4; see discussion of Ezek 1 and 10). From the description here, the figure who seizes Ezekiel is none other than the LORD himself (cf. Ezek 1:27).

8:3 *entrance of the north gate*: Ezekiel is not transported in body to Jerusalem, for when it is over, he reports that "the vision ... went up from me" (cf. Ezek 11:24). Rather, in a visionary trance he see activities of the temple from various vantage points. The Jerusalem temple-building itself was surrounded by two courtyards (inner and outer [cf. Ezek 10:5]; 2 Kgs 21:5; 23:12); and Ezekiel's first exposure to temple idolatry takes place at the northern gate leading from the outer to the inner courtyard.[2]

8:3-5 *idol that provokes to jealousy*: Commentators note that the unusual word translated "idol" only occurs elsewhere in Deut 4:16 and then again in 2 Chr 33:7, 15, where it describes Manasseh's image of Asherah that provoked God to anger (cf. 2 Kgs 21:6-7).[3] Ezekiel's vision could be of a representation of the Canaanite goddess, Asherah, or an image associated with some other deity.[4] Since Manasseh's image of Asherah was destroyed by Josiah (2 Kgs 23:6), some question the identification of

---

2. Greenberg, *Ezekiel 1-20*, 168.
3. For discussion of Asherah, see Curtis, "Canaanite Gods," 140-41.
4. Further, see Bodi, "Ezekiel," 420-21.

this object with the goddess Asherah.[5] However, another Asherah image may well have been produced after the failure of Josiah's reforms. Ezekiel's vision exposes the sorts of abominations that characterized temple worship in recent memory, which includes Manasseh's Asherah image. Why this particular idol especially provoked the LORD's jealousy is not clear.

8:6 *detestable:* For this important word, see comments at Ezek 7:3–4.

8:7 *entrance to the court:* The second scene portrays activity inside a chamber in the gatehouse of the north gate in the previous scene.[6] The necessity to dig through the wall in this visionary experience suggests that the activities inside were conducted in secret.

8:10 *portrayed all over the walls:* The exact nature of this worship activity is impossible to identify. Ezekiel's language alludes to unclean animals (Lev 7:21; 11:41) and prohibited images (Deut 4:16–18). Offering incense denotes prayer, perhaps to composite (human/animal) deities in Egyptian religion or animal motifs used in Babylonian wall decorations.[7]

8:11 *seventy elders . . . Jaazaniah:* Elders served as lay leaders in the Jerusalem council (cf. Ezek 7:26), perhaps rising to prominence after the deportation of high level officials (including Ezekiel himself) in 598 BC. Their number, seventy, stands in ironic contrast to another gathering of 70 elders to worship with Moses during the covenant-making ceremonies on Mt. Sinai (Exod 24:1, 9–11) and the legitimation of a similar group who shared in a measure of Moses' spirit (Num 11:24–25). The irony deepens if "Jaazaniah" is the son the same "Shaphan" who served under Josiah and whose other sons assisted Jeremiah (Jer 26:24; 29:3; 36:10–12, 25).[8]

8:12–13 *shrine of his own idol . . . the LORD does not see:* This first phrase is difficult (note ESV, "room of pictures"; NASB, "room of his carved images"). The word translated "idol" in the NIV refers to an object, either figurine or pictorial art, that represents a deity (Num 33:52; Lev 26:1). The word translated "shrine" denotes an interior chamber of a sort ("inner room," 1 Kgs 22:25; "bedroom," 2 Sam 4:7). Evidently, the chamber as a whole was covered with images (Ezek 8:10), yet each elder was assigned to a particular deity and participated in the rituals privately within his individual cubicle.

---

5. Block, *Ezekiel 1–24*, 281.
6. Greenberg, *Ezekiel 1–20*, 169.
7. Bodi, "Ezekiel," 421–22; Greenberg, *Ezekiel 1–20*, 169–70.
8. Block, *Ezekiel 1–24*, 291.

The religious rationalization of such behavior is the elders' conclusion that God has already abandoned Jerusalem—so why not turn to every other possible divine source for help? They imagined that the LORD is no longer present to take notice of such sacrilegious activity, even in his own temple complex. Ironically, the LORD had *not* yet abandoned his temple; but the activities of these elders were driving him away (Ezek 8:6).

8:14 *mourning the god Tammuz:* The gate location of this next scene is uncertain; but, judging from the reference to God's "house," it seems to be a move closer to the temple building itself. In contrast to the dark, inner chamber of the previous scene, worship of the Babylonian deity Tammuz occurred in the open court directly in view of God's temple. This reinforces the progressive detestability of each successive scene.

Special Topic: Tammuz

In Babylonian religion, the figure Tammuz appears as the ill-fated lover of the goddess, Ishtar, whose place he takes in the netherworld in order for her to return from death and inhabit life. He was associated with both newborn sheep and new growth of vegetation in the spring. In summer drought he was thought to be trapped in death's realm until ascending to life again the following spring. Mesopotamian texts mention annual rituals in which worshippers mourn his death. For example, a seventh-century BC Assyrian text ordains "weeping" in the month of Tammuz (June/July).[9] Similar practices in Canaanite religion accompanied the worship of Baal. For example, 1 Kgs 18:28 depicts mourning rites that imitated the god El's lament over Baal's death in Ugaritic myth. Probably related to this is later Greek worship of Adonis involving lamentation rituals by women.[10] With this custom, then, Israelite religion was participating fully in ancient Near Eastern beliefs about death, life, and fertility.

8:16 *backs toward the temple . . . faces toward the east:* The final scene takes place at God's front door, where "about twenty-five men" (a round number with no particular significance) worship the sun with backs turned against the LORD (cf. Jer 32:33-34). Astral deities, such as the sun, moon, planets, and stars, comprised the chief gods of ancient

---

9. Greenberg, *Ezekiel 1-20*, 171.
10. Block, *Ezekiel 1-24*, 295-96.

religion, and Jerusalem's idolatry fell in step (Jer 8:2; Zeph 1:5), especially in worshipping the sun (2 Kgs 21:5; 23:11).

8:17 violence . . . branch to their nose: As the four scenes of abominable worship reach a climax, the LORD denounces the sin of violence as more provocative to anger than idolatrous practices (cf. "filling land with violence," as at the time of the flood [Gen 6:11, 13]).[11] The assessment that violence and injustice are more reprehensible than religious apostasy is consistent with Ezek 7:23 and Ezek 9:9–10.

The significance of putting a branch to the nose is unclear. It is possible that it refers to a gesture of entreaty, for which there is an Assyrian relief depicting the king holding a branch (flower?) to his nose in worship; or possibly the branch alludes to the cedar branch, a symbol of life associated with Tammuz and Ishtar.[12] Alternatively, since the reference comes immediately after the accusation about violence, the phrase may denote a gesture of contempt or physical insult toward God commensurate with the severity of violence.[13] The line had been crossed beyond which there was no hope for mercy from God (Ezek 8:18; cf. chapter 7).

Theological Bridge to Application

Against the elders' claim that the LORD had departed and does not observe their activity (Ezek 8:13), stands the reality that the God of glory was indeed present. There are two important implications: First, God is longsuffering (Exod 34:6), as testified by his continued presence in his temple throughout years of such abominable idolatry. His *reluctant* departure in chapters 9 and 10 reinforce this observation. Second, denying God's knowledge of any human affair is illusory. Perhaps these men assumed that God was not present in his temple; nevertheless, they conducted their affairs in secret, just in case, in order to remain unobserved. Yet the walls and darkness were penetrated by his watchful eye. Even had the *glory* been absent, he would be present to know (cf. Pss 11:4–5; 139:2, 7).

---

11. For discussion of this idiom discussed by Greenberg, *Ezekiel 1–20*, 172 (1 Kgs 16:31; Isa 7:13).
12. Bodi, "Ezekiel," 423.
13. For discussion, see Greenberg, *Ezekiel 1–20*, 172–73.

Focus of Application

Many details concerning the idolatrous practices in Ezek 8 evade our understanding. Nevertheless, the heart of the vision is clearly signaled by *changes* between scenes (e.g., Ezek 8:6, 13, 15): first, the progressive closeness of idolatry in the direction of God's very presence (movement from outside the gateway to the porch of temple), and then the increasingly brazen attitude on the part of idolaters against God (hiding in secret to turning one's back on God's face). It is also helpful to bear in mind that Ezekiel is experiencing a *vision*, which like a dream-experience need not cohere to reality in every way. So, for example, attempting to make perfect sense of Ezekiel's tunneling into the gatehouse is irrelevant to the intention of the visionary experience and narrative portrayal.

It is often the case that severity of sin is measured by a hierarchy of behaviors, the exact order of which often varies from community to community. While not denying that there are degrees of severity to sin and its consequences (Ezek 8:17 is a reminder), the attitude of the individual toward God is equally important as we think about sin in our own life or in our faith community. God's tolerance measures the heart as much as the action (Pss 32:5; 51:17; compare Jesus' differing posture toward sinners and Pharisees).

The second scene portrays the complexity of practical atheism. Sins committed in secret or harbored in the fantasies of the heart are not hidden from God (cf. Pss 10:11; 94:7; Zeph 1:12; Prov 15:3), although even committed believers can fall prey to this illusion in practice. Positive correction for this attitude flows from Pss 19:12–14; 138:23–24.

More severe condemnation applies to brazen defiance. In contemporary terms, this would describe the person who confesses faith but at the same time insults God and tarnishes his reputation by publically flaunting their behavior. It is this sort of situation that elicits church discipline. The difference between those who struggle under sin's burden and those who flippantly ignore it is immense in God's eyes.

The concluding accusation in Ezek 8:17 reminds us that God does weigh different sins in their degree of severity. Unfortunately, communities of believers have too frequently devised their hierarchy of sins based on the types of behavior that permit easy evaluation. Those who do not measure up are censured. This obsession with "external" sin can result in a benign silence regarding "internal" sin. But the specific point in this vision (like the oracle of chapter 7) is that injustice, especially in forms that result in physical harm, tops the list. When one observes the moral issues that often play large on the agenda of churches, the hierarchy of popular Christian values often overlooks this.

MERCY FOR THE BROKEN OF HEART

Ezekiel 9:1–11

Ezekiel's Message

In the midst of complete judgment, God extends his mercy to those who grieve over sin.

Key Themes

- God shows mercy to those who grieve over sin.
- God's judgment is horrifying in its completeness.
- Judgment begins with the leadership of God's people.
- God's judgment is commensurate with the sin.

Context in Ezekiel

In Ezek 9, the focus of the vision changes from scenes of idolatry to a scene of the resulting judgment. The transition from the end of chapter 8 is marked by an ironic play on words in the the original text, which is captured by the ESV: "Though they cry in my ears with a loud voice, I will not hear them. Then he cried in my ears with a loud voice" (Ezek 8:18—9:1a). Those to be judged will cry out for help to the God who cries out for their judgment. But the passage sounds an important counter-note, that in the midst of judgment God shows mercy to those who grieve over sin.

Interpretive Highlights

9:1 *appointed to execute judgment*: This notion is similar to that in other texts in which God sends angelic agents to bring calamity in judgment (Ps 78:49 [the exodus plagues]; 2 Sam 24:15–16; 1 Kgs 22:19–22). In the historical outworking of this vision, it is the Babylonian army who destroys.

9:2 *a man clothed in linen . . . writing kit*: Six executioners plus the man in linen brings the total to seven, a complete number to thoroughly accomplish the task. Linen garments were worn by those who ministered in the presence of God (Exod 28:42; Lev 16:4; 1 Sam 2:18; 1 Chr 15:27), and so angels are portrayed in linen as well (Dan 10:5; 12:6). The writing kit most likely corresponds to the type known to be used by Egyptian scribes, containing a stylus and ink well.[1] The mention of this detail is striking, which raises curiosity and draws the reader's attention to the important task of this special angel among the seven (see below). The location where the executioners gather, the "bronze altar," is the original temple altar built by Solomon. It was later relocated by Ahab, who replaced it with his own altar styled after Assyrian worship practices. He then reassigned Solomon's altar for personal divination (2 Kgs 16:10–16). The executioners muster at the *legitimate* altar from which they will commence the destruction.

9:3 *the glory . . . went up*: Inside the temple building itself were two rooms—an outer room, where the incense altar, table of bread, and lampstand were located, and an inner room called the "the Most Holy Place," where two statues of heavenly creatures ("cherubim;" see discussion in chapter 10) stood guarding the ark of the covenant over which the cloud of God's glory appeared (1 Kgs 6:14–28; 7:48–50; 8:6–11; cf. Exod 40:34). The departure of God's presence from the temple begins as he moves from this inner room, the Most Holy Place, to the front door of the temple.

9:4 *put a mark*: The word translated "mark" is the name of the Hebrew letter, *taw*. In the ancient script, it took a form similar to the Latin letter "X." The letter served as a generic mark to indicate one's "signature"

---

1. For detailed description, see Block, *Ezekiel 1–24*, 305.

(Job 31:35). If this is the intention, it might suggest ownership.[2] But in this context, it may simply have been a mark to distinguish those to be preserved from judgment (Ezek 9:6), similar in function to the blood on the doorpost during the exodus (Exod 12:13).

9:5 *without showing pity:* The oracles of Ezekiel have already characterized God's impending judgment as pitiless (Ezek 5:11; 7:4, 9), but this verse draws out the implications in clear and shocking terms. The language is similar to the destructive judgment that God ordered against the Canaanite population during Joshua's conquest (Gen 15:16; Lev 18:24; Deut 7:1–2, 16; 20:16–17). Indeed, the point of such language in Ezek 9:6 is that the people of Jerusalem had become, practically speaking, no different than the Canaanites who were judged in an earlier generation. Consequently, the covenant sanctions now fall on Jerusalem (Lev 18:26–28; 20:22–23; Deut 28:49–50). Judgment is corporate and complete (see discussion below under Focus of Application).

9:6 *Begin at my sanctuary:* In Israelite society, the elder men were the leaders, hence the particularly reprehensible scene in Ezek 8:11. Presumably, the men worshipping the sun with backs turned against the LORD (Ezek 8:16) are elders as well, and as leaders they are relatively more culpable than the general community. Hence judgment begins with them. Normally, the altar is a place of mercy (Exod 21:14; 1 Kgs 2:28; 2 Kgs 11:15), but with God's holy presence leaving the temple, such sensitivities no longer matter.

9:8 *I fell face down:* It is a significant part of a prophet's vocation to intercede (Gen 20:7; Num 12:13; Deut 9:25; 1 Kgs 18:36–37; Amos 7:2, 5; Jer 14:11). Ezekiel's observation, that those preserved by the mark are few in number, is not surprising in view of Jeremiah's experience (Jer 5:1–5). Yet it is not just the numbers that matter to him; rather, by invoking the notion of the "remnant," Ezekiel shows his concern for the entire covenant plan of God. Without a remnant, the promise of God to bless the entire world though Abraham's descendants is jeopardized (Gen 12:3; Exod 19:5–6).[3] While concern for the nations is not a major theme in Ezekiel, it is nonetheless within the scope of his theology of hope (Ezek 47:22–23; see **Special Topic: The Remnant**).

One must be careful about interpreting prophetic language with undue precision. On the one hand, Jer 5:1–5 would lead one to think that

---

2. Taylor, *Ezekiel*, 102.
3. Wright, *Ezekiel*, 117–18.

there were none worthy of the protective mark. Indeed, Ezekiel himself uses language that would indicate the complete, unqualified destruction of Jerusalem's entire population (Ezek 5:1–4, 10; 7:11). At the same time, Ezekiel envisions a few survivors who escape (Ezek 6:8; 7:16). Such rhetoric makes the point that the number of those who "grieve and lament" must be a small minority.

Special Topic: The Remnant

Amos introduced the concept of a "remnant" in prophetic preaching to stress how complete judgment would be, such that only a few would survive (Amos 3:12; 5:3; 6:9–10; 9:1–4). Such use is ironic, rhetorically speaking, since "remnant" is hardly a positive image of hope in these texts. A similar use is found in Isaiah (Isa 1:9; 6:13), but Isaiah also introduces a reversal of this image to underscore the hope that God will ultimately restore blessing to his covenant people (Isa 7:3 ["Shear-Jashub" means a remnant shall return]; 10:20–23; 11:16; cf. Jer 31:7; 50:20; Mic 2:12; 4:6–7; 5:7; Zeph 2:7, 9). In these images of hope, there is an historical fulfillment in the restoration from Babylonian exile (Hag 1:12, 14; 2:2–3; Zech 8:6), but also an expectation for the permanence of Israel's blessing (Zeph 3:11–13). Since the nation's blessing did not endure in the postexilic period, the concept remains open to the future. The prophetic expectation is also for survivors from Gentile nations, who are blessed by Israel's surviving remnant (Amos 9:12; Zech 8:11–13) if they submit to Israel's saving God (Isa 45:20–22; cf. Mic 5:8, 15).

9:10 *down on their own heads:* As in previous verses (Ezek 7:23; 8:17), the language in this vision points to the most despicable element of Jerusalem's sin, violence and injustice (Ezek 9:9). This in turn determines the nature of judgment—violent desolation by warfare corresponding to their violent sin (cf. 1 Kgs 8:32).

Theological Bridge to Application

In tension with such a severe and complete description of judgment is the provision of protection for those who grieve over sin. God's heart of mercy is evident. Even if no one receives the protective mark (Ezek 9:6), it is not because God was unwilling. At the same time, God's mercy is conditioned on remorse ("those who grieve and lament" sin; Ezek 9:4).

Of greatest concern to God is the condition of the human heart (Ps 51:17; Isa 57:15). This expectation in Ezekiel finds a particularly relevant parallel in the prophet Zephaniah, where it is the humble who have hope to survive impending judgment (Zeph 2:1–3) and so are numbered among the remnant (Zeph 3:12).

Focus of Application

The completeness of judgment in this vision is horrifying. Particularly disturbing in Ezek 9:6 is the suffering of children, whom we characteristically hold innocent. One factor in weighing the ethics of such judgment is understanding the realities of total warfare. In the ancient Near East, practically speaking, warfare often meant targeting complete civilian populations. This happens in modern warfare as well. The horrors of World War II came at the hands of both sides, each of which judged that total warfare, including the killing of non-combatants, was a practical necessity. In the ancient Near East, when God used a nation as an instrument of judgment against another nation (as in the impending Babylonian destruction of Jerusalem), it brought with it the necessary tragedies of war. The mention of "children" in Ezekiel's language is the ancient way of referring to total warfare.

Another factor, no less important, is understanding that in some contexts guilt has corporate consequences (e.g., the Noahic flood, the plagues against Egypt, the conquest of Canaan, the destruction of Jerusalem, the subsequent destruction of Babylon, Jerusalem's conqueror [cf. Jer 51:56; Isa 13:16]). The judgment on Jerusalem stemmed from covenant curses, which by nature carried with them terrifying consequences for the entire population of God's people.[4]

We should not to confuse the historical outworking of temporal judgment on Jerusalem through the Babylonians with our theology of eternal salvation. Our doctrine of salvation is much more complicated in terms of the application of the atonement and questions of accountability in eternal perspective. There is no one-to-one correspondence between the physical death of individuals during the Babylonian destruction of Jerusalem and their eternal relationship with the LORD. The stress in this

---

4. For an overview of difficulties and possible solutions to the problem of divine warfare, see Copan and Flannagan, "The Ethics of 'Holy War,'" 201–39. With regard to the difficulties in Ezek 9, the commentary by Wright is particularly helpful (Wright, *Ezekiel*, 113–14).

passage is the totality of judgment apart from God's protection; and the condition for receiving God's mercy, as stated in this text, is a humble and contrite heart (see also the discussion at Ezek 18:9, 19 and Focus of Application there). How this balances in the scales of justice is beyond our perview, hidden in the yet unseen reckoning of all things.

Two other lessons on the nature of judgment also flow from Ezekiel's experience. First, God holds leadership especially culpable, as revealed in this passage by the "first priority" in executing judgment (Ezek 9:6; cf. Jas 3:1). Few things are more damaging to the reputation of God, his kingdom, and his own people than the failure of leaders. This bears out in the testimony of Christians who have been deeply wounded by sinful behavior on the part of those to whom they have submitted and depended. The media frenzies over public exposure of prominent Christian leaders are legendary. Second, the nature of God's judgment is commensurate with and often mirrors the specific sin in uncanny ways. Jacob deceived Isaac by means of an animal skin (Gen 27:16) and he himself was deceived through slaughter of an animal (Gen 37:31–33). David's greatest sin was orchestrating the violent death of Uriah (2 Sam 11:14–15) and so the sword did not depart from his house (2 Sam 12:9–10). Ezekiel's vision manifests the common biblical theme wherein people reap what they sow (Prov 22:8; Gal 6:7).

GOD'S PARTING JUDGMENT
Ezekiel 10:1–22

Ezekiel's Message

The withdrawal of God's presence results in reluctant yet destructive judgment.

Key Themes

- God's judgment springs from the purity of his glory.
- God's knowledge of human affairs is complete and penetrating.
- God's gracious attributes render him reluctant to leave and judge.

Context in Ezekiel

Ezekiel 9:3 reported the first stage in the departure of God's glory from the temple, as it moves from the cherubim over the ark in the Most Holy Place to the temple threshold. This first stage is repeated in Ezek 10:3 (the two scenes of Ezek 9 and 10 overlap), after a pause in Ezek 9:3b–11 to depict the anticipated judgment. The process of departure continues in Ezek 10:18–19 when the glory transfers to a cherub-born chariot, which carries God's glory to the eastern gate of the temple complex before final departure (Ezek 11:22–23). Within this context, God reveals to Ezekiel further aspects of judgment associated with the departure of his presence. The intention of Ezekiel's visionary experience is not to report a chronologically organized portrayal of the destruction of Jerusalem;

rather, these are "scenes of judgment" that convey what is actually "behind the scenes" of the impending Babylonian siege and destruction of the city.

Interpretive Highlights

10:1 *over the heads of the cherubim*: The flow of the narrative is not easy to follow, because Ezek 10:1 introduces into the vision a depiction of God's chariot-throne that is born by cherubim who differ from the cherubim over the ark of the covenant (Ezek 9:3; 10:4). That the cherubim spoken of in v. 1 are those of the chariot is clarified in v. 3, since they are stationed on the south side of the temple waiting for the glory of God to mount the chariot (Ezek 10:18). Details about these cherubim unfold as the vision focuses first on the judgment connected with their fiery presence (Ezek 10:2–8) and then on their transport of God's glory further away from the temple (Ezek 10:9–22).

10:2 *burning coals . . . scatter them over the city*: The phrase translated "burning coals" is identical to the words for coals from the altar (Lev 16:12) and also God's weapons as a divine warrior (Ps 18:12–13). The coals of the altar have the capacity to atone for sin (Isa 6:6–7), but in Ezekiel's vision they destroy. The image of fire over the city might compare Jerusalem's destruction with that of Sodom (Gen 19:24; cf. Ps 11:6), an association drawn upon by Ezekiel elsewhere (Ezek 16:46–49).

10:4–8 *radiance of the glory . . . take fire*: The vision of Ezek 1 climaxed in the description of God's glorious radiance (Ezek 1:28). From this radiance, God called Ezekiel and also signaled his presence with his people in exile. The vision of Ezek 10 employs the theology of God's glory to a different end, stressing that God's radiant presence departs with destructive judgment ("voice . . . the Lord commanded"; vv. 5–6). So dangerous is the fire associated with God's radiance that even the angelic "man of linen" dared not take it directly from such close proximity to the throne.[1]

10:12 *Their entire bodies . . . full of eyes*: For general discussion of the cherubim, see comments on Ezek 1; but here in chapter 10, there are three important distinctions to note.[2] First, Ezekiel now recognizes the identity of these same creatures from his initial vision as "cherubim"

---

1. Taylor, *Ezekiel*, 106.
2. See also Steinmann, "Cherubim," 112–13.

(Ezek 10:20–22). Overwhelmed at the outset of his first visionary experience, it was not until he recognized the God of glory (Ezek 1:28) that he could surmise the identity of the living creatures—Ezekiel reckoned that they must be comparable to the cherubim guarding the ark in the Most Holy Place.

Second, whereas in the vision of Ezek 1 only the rims of the creatures' wheels were covered with eyes (Ezek 1:18), here their entire bodies are covered. If the interpretation is correct that eyes connote awareness and knowledge (cf. 1 Kgs 8:29; Ps 11:4; Prov 15:3; 2 Chr 16:9), this change in detail underscores the importance of this attribute in Ezek 10. One might infer from the context of Ezek 8–11, which stresses the variety and depth of sin, that the Lord knows fully the sin of the city, contrary to the mistaken notions of sinners revealed in Ezek 8:12 and 9:9.

Third, compared to Ezek 10, the description in Ezek 1 concentrates on the *mobility* of God's chariot-throne in order to underscore his capacity to be present with his people in exile, away from Jerusalem. The vision in Ezek 10 magnifies the *awareness* of God on his throne concerning the culpability of his people in Jerusalem and stresses the capacity of his fiery radiance to destroy.

10:14 *four faces:* The faces of the living creatures in Ezek 1 included human, lion, ox, and eagle (Ezek 1:10). Even though the cherubim are described in Ezek 10:22 as having the same faces as the living creatures of the earlier vision, Ezek 10:14 indicates that instead of the face of an ox there is the face of a "cherub," which also receives first mention rather than the human face that was mentioned initially in chapter 1. Since cherubim in Mesopotamian temple architecture most often possessed the body of an ox, this change in detail might simply correspond to Ezekiel's recognition of the bovine component corresponding to chapter 1. In other words, in view of the cultural accommodation of these visions to the conventions of Ezekiel's Babylonian environment, the substitute of the "face" of a cherub for that of an ox is natural (see **Special Topic: Cherubim** in Ezek 1).

10:18–19 *Then the glory of the Lord departed . . . stopped:* These verses underscore judgment from the perspective of divine abandonment, which in the ancient culture preceded an enemy's destruction of a temple city (see **Special Topic: Divine Abandonment in Mesopotamian Religion**). The manner in which this is portrayed in these chapters might reveal something of God's attitude. The four texts that feature God's withdrawal present it in stages: Most Holy Place to temple threshold (Ezek

9:3/10:3–4), temple threshold to east gate (Ezek 10:18–19), east gate to an eastern mountain before departing further—presumably to the exiles in the east, where the Spirit carries Ezekiel at the end of the vision (Ezek 11:22–13). At each point God's glory pauses, as though reluctant to leave his temple abode.

Special Topic: Divine Abandonment in Mesopotamian Religion

In the culture of ancient Mesopotamia, people wrestled with the theological implications of defeat in warfare and the destruction of their cities. Assuming that defeat could not imply any inherent weakness with their patron god or goddess, societies drew the logical conclusion that defeat must be related to the anger of the deity; and the ensuing destruction of a city with its temple could not happen without the withdrawal of the deity's presence, a theme known as "divine abandonment." Many different kinds of literature exhibit this theme, including laments, hymns, prophecy, and royal inscriptions. For example, one of the best known city laments describes how deities leave their temples: "Enlil has abandoned the shrine (of) Nippur, his sheepfold (became) haunted"; and closes with the words, "May the hearts of its people that committed evil, be purified before you!"[3]

Block notes the irony in Ezekiel's treatment of divine abandonment, which contrasts Mesopotamian and Israelite understanding of the concept.[4] In Mesopotamia, the assumption is that the cause of abandonment is the sin of the people, but Ezekiel's vision reveals that the Jerusalemites have the causation backwards—the people seek other gods because they think the LORD has already left (Ezek 8:12; 9:9). In Ezekiel, the LORD leaves for his own reasons and on his timing, not because a council of other deities have determined the fate of his city for him, as is the case in some Mesopotamian hymns. In fact, Mesopotamian deities leave their temples because of the ruin of their images; but the LORD is not represented by any cult statue that could be defiled in such a manner.

---

3. Lament over the Destruction of Sumer and Ur (*COS* 1.166: 535, 538, lines 4 and 434).

4. See Block, "Divine Abandonment," esp. 93–95.

Theological Bridge to Application

Ezekiel 10 illustrates a balance within God's attributes that are associated with his glory. At Mt. Sinai, fire and cloud emanated from God's glorious presence and entailed either destructive judgment or forgiving grace (Exod 10–23; 24:9–11; 32:10; 33:5; 34:5–7). At Sinai, the balance of these attributes resulted in discipline, but ultimately the continuing presence of God's glory with his people. In Ezekiel's vision, the balance of these attributes results in the departure of God's presence with judgment in the wake, albeit a *reluctant* departure, revealing God's underlying compassion.

Focus of Application

One of the most striking images in this vision is that of the angel ("man in linen") being handed a coal from the center of God's radiant presence. As the ancient Jewish commentator, Kimchi, writes, the angel "did not obey the order . . . but acted as one who feared entering a place too holy and sublime for him. He halted beside the wheel to see what would happen; the cherub then took some fire from among the cherubs and filled his hands with it."[5] The degree of God's holiness relative to even his own angelic creatures is so startling; how much more should humans fear the danger into which their sin places them. The destructive capacity of God's glory must be taken seriously, whether a person stands outside the saving grace of God to face eternal judgment, or a redeemed believer presumes too much upon God's patience and faces the prospect of divine discipline. But this is a mere corollary to the central feature of this vision, the terrible consequences of separation from God's presence. For final judgment of unbelievers, Scripture often employs the image of God "sending away" from his presence (Matt 5:13; 7:23; 8:12; John 15:6).

There is no hiding our inner thoughts from God, let alone our actions and words. Ezekiel's vision of eyes covering the cherubim stresses the "situational awareness" of God's mobile throne. Inner thoughts might remain "inner," gossip might remain behind "closed doors," or computer technology might offer "privacy modes," but it is an illusion to imagine God's ignorance of our most secret lives. Practicing the presence of God is a helpful, positive corollary to the negative warning of Ezek 10.

---

5. Cited from Greenberg, *Ezekiel 1–20*, 181.

Yet in the face of God's overwhelming knowledge and purity, his glory consists of patient and tender feelings. In spite of all that his presence had endured in the temple, where idolatrous betrayal was flaunted in his face and where violent injustice filled the nearby streets, he withdrew his glory reluctantly. This theme resurfaces in Ezekiel when God reveals that he takes no pleasure in judgment (Ezek 18:23, 32; 33:11). This is an important truth to balance as we grimace under the realization of God's terrifying holiness; his attitude is like an aggrieved partner or a vexed parent.

HOPE AMIDST JUDGMENT
Ezekiel 11:1–25

Ezekiel's Message

God intervenes in the most desperate spiritual circumstances with necessary judgment but also decisive transformation, with the result that his people will follow his ways.

Key Themes

- The responsibility for spiritual failure by a community of God's people often resides with the leadership.
- The appearance of success must not be interpreted as a sign of God's favor over against others who appear less fortunate.
- God avails himself to his people in hard circumstances, even situations that are a result of divine discipline.
- God transforms people whose inclination is away from God into people who seek him and follow his ways.

Context in Ezekiel

The vision of judgment in Ezek 11:1–13 recalls similar portraits in chapter 8. However, this scene repeats Ezekiel's lament in Ezek 9:8 ("will you destroy all the remnant . . . ?"; cf. Ezek 11:13). The repetition of this question sets the context for an answer that was lacking at the end of chapter

9—a promise of national restoration (Ezek 11:14–25). For this reason, it is important to hold these two halves of the chapter together, as they cohere as a unit with "problem" and "solution." The chapter opens with an accusation against the city leaders (Ezek 11:1–6), followed by a sentence of judgment (Ezek 11:7–13). The logic of this passage is common to legal disputation speeches in which the words of the accused are quoted only to be refuted by the prosecution.[1] The answer to Ezekiel's concern for the remnant begins with a statement of the lamentable condition (Ezek 11:14–16a), followed by God's intervention to save (Ezek 11:16b–21). Accompanying the promise of Israel's return, Ezekiel's vision ends as the glory finally departs to be with the exiles in the east.

Interpretive Highlights

11:1 *twenty-five men . . . leaders:* This is not the same group envisioned in Ezek 8:16 ("twenty-five" is simply a round number), since they are located differently. Nor is "Jaazaniah" the same individual, since each has a different father. Although Ezekiel's visionary scenes do not necessarily take place in "real time," they do feature real leaders probably known to the prophet from his youth or through exchange of news between the city and the exiles. The word translated "leaders," (sometimes rendered "princes"; e.g., ESV, NKJV) denotes a wide range of political and spiritual officials (representatives of the king [1 Kgs 9:23]; military officers [2 Chr 21:9]; city rulers [1 Kgs 22:26]; temple officials [2 Chr 36:14]). The responsibility for wickedness in the people ultimately falls on them (Ezek 11:2).

11:3 *houses been recently rebuilt?* This phrase quotes the "wicked advice" of the city's leaders, but translations differ because the Hebrew in this verse is difficult. The NIV renders this quote as a rhetorical question by the leaders to the effect that their houses are in good order in spite of the threat of Babylon. In the context of Ezekiel's indictment of social injustice, this quote exposes the leaders' judicial malpractice, economic cruelty, and complacency at the expense of the less powerful (cf. Ezek 7:23; 9:9; esp. 11:6). Other translations offer: "The time is not near to build houses" (e.g., ESV, NASB). In this case, the "wicked advice" is that there is no *need* to build houses, presumably for similar reasons as just stated. As in Mic 2:2, the powerful are able to seize what they want

---

1. See Block, *Ezekiel 1–24*, 330.

(evidently land as well, cf. Ezek 11:15). The basic point is the same either way: the leaders have it good, so they have no worries ... or so they think.

The next line of the quotation is a metaphor taken from the domain of food vessels—a pot protects meat that is stored or, while cooking, protects meat from burning. In either case, the meat is the *choice portion* of food, to which these leaders liken themselves. Although the same word picture can be used in a reverse, negative way (cooked to destruction, as in Ezek 24:3–8), the connotation of the image here is a positive one, as clarified in the near context by Ezek 11:10–11. Probably, the leaders viewed themselves as especially favored in contrast to the leadership that had already been taken away to exile (Ezek 11:15). They were still preserved behind the protective walls of Jerusalem.

11:7–12 *The bodies you have thrown ... borders of Israel:* In a reversal, Ezekiel applies the metaphor of choice meat in a protective pot to the victims of violent injustice. It is the victims of injustice, not the city's leaders, who are in reality the choice citizens in God's estimation. Yet, Ezekiel categorically denies the wicked leadership any privilege or protection from the city walls. This announcement of judgment found partial fulfillment at the northern border town of Riblah (2 Kgs 25:18–21), where city leaders were slaughtered.[2] For the accusation against cultural conformity (Ezek 11:12), see comments on Ezek 5:5–7.

11:14 *The word of the Lord came to me:* This formula sometimes introduces new oracles (e.g., Ezek 6:1; 7:1; 12:1), but this does not necessarily disconnect the oracle from the preceding context (e.g., Ezek 12:26). Here it highlights a word of promise, the first hint of hope in the book of Ezekiel. The Lord directly answers the prophet's anguished question about God's ultimate plan for his people—will destruction be complete or will some be rescued (Ezek 9:8; 11:13)? There will be a "remnant," numbered among the exiles, to whom attention is next directed.

11:15 *They are far away ... the land ... our possession:* As in Ezek 11:3, the prophet again quotes the words of Jerusalem's leaders to set up a rebuttal. The leaders observed that those Judeans already in exile were cut off from the Lord's presence in the Jerusalem temple; so they concluded that the exiles also had forfeited possession of their ancestral lands that belonged to them by covenant. The exiles were disenfranchised of their status and their property.

---

2. Cooper, *Ezekiel*, 141.

11:16 *for a little while . . . a sanctuary*: Similar to the rebuttal in Ezek 11:1–13, the LORD reverses the wicked leaders' perception: God's glorious presence is departing Jerusalem; and instead, the LORD is with the exiles in the east, who without a temple nevertheless have access to God. This short expression reveals an important truth that Ezekiel conveys to his compatriots in exile, that regardless of outward appearances, God is with them (cf. comments on Ezek 1). The temporary nature of this circumstance ("for a little while") supports the promise that God will once again restore these captives to their homeland (Ezek 11:17). Even if the phrase, "for a little while," is translated "a diminished sanctuary" (NJPS, NKJV, NET) or "in small measure" (ESV margin), the point remains the same; God is with those in exile, *not* the condemned of Jerusalem.³ This anticipates the final vision of Ezekiel, when the LORD will again take up full and permanent residence in a new temple (Ezek 43:1–5; 48:35).

11:19–20 *an undivided heart . . . new spirit*: More important than physical restoration to the land is spiritual restoration that reverses the nation's idolatrous tendencies (Ezek 11:18, 21). The phrase, "undivided heart," also translated "one heart" (e.g., ESV, NASB), stresses integrity of purpose. In 1 Chr 12:38, the same expression occurs (translated "one mind," NIV) with the parallel phrase "whole heart" (cf. 2 Chr 12:33), referring to the devotion of David's men. Having "one heart" is the opposite of a "double heart" (Ps 12:2, ESV), which indicates hypocritical intent.

The problem of the leaders of Jerusalem is that they had wicked intentions ("what is going through your 'mind' [*ruah*]; Ezek 11:5). In contrast, here God promises Israel a new "spirit" (*ruah*; same word translated "mind" in v. 5).⁴ Ezekiel's metaphor "heart of stone," contrasted with a "heart of flesh," is unique to him (see Ezek 36:26) and recalls the problem of spiritual stubbornness, highlighted in Ezekiel's call (Ezek 2:3–4; 3:7). God promises that the mental determination of God's people will be redirected toward obedience.

Theological Bridge to Application

The corruption shown throughout Ezekiel's temple vision (Ezek 8–11) illustrates to the extreme what is the natural outworking of the human condition (cf. Ezek 2:3–5; 3:7). Only decisive intervention by God can

---

3. For discussion, see Block, *Ezekiel 1–24*, 349–50.
4. For thorough discussion see Block, "The Prophet of the Spirit," 27–50.

rectify the root of the problem, which is that the human mind lacks true, spiritual devotion (Ezek 11:19–21). In this Ezekiel shares the theology of his older contemporary, Jeremiah, who diagnosed a similar problem with the human heart (Jer 17:9; cf. Isa 1:5) and spoke of the work of God to transform a wayward mind into one that is singularly devoted to God (Jer 32:39). David speaks similarly of renewal of heart that results in willingness to follow the ways of God (Ps 51:10). Thus, Ezekiel's hope is built on nothing less than the transforming work of God himself.

Focus of Application

The influence of leaders on the spiritual and moral fabric of God's people receives yet another highlight from this passage, this time explicit in the note about their "counsel" (Ezek 11:2). The leaders alluded to in Ezek 11:1 are civic as well as spiritual. This might prompt the teacher to make quick application to political candidates today. Use of biblical values is one consideration in choosing civic leaders in our culture, but that is not the thrust of the passage here. Rather, Ezekiel's accusation is against leaders of the covenant community of God's people. If civic leaders in a post-Christian society act with deceit or malice, it comes as no surprise; however, accountability of leadership in the household of faith is God's immediate concern. This emphasis on accountability in Ezekiel's vision is striking (cf. Ezek 8:11; 9:6), particularly considering that he reports his visionary experience first to the *elders* gathered in his house (Ezek 8:1; 11:25). It is on church leadership that application should focus.

Although many Christians know better than to judge spirituality and measure God's favor by the material or social success of individuals and communities, the temptation to do so, if ever so subtly, remains. Leadership in churches and Christian organizations all too often betrays such values. In some Christian circles, the sort of spiritual hierarchy that places the "successful" on top is even explicit. The leadership left in Jerusalem after the first waves of deportation in 605 and 589 BC assumed a "winner take all" attitude toward positions of privilege and power. They disenfranchised those taken away to Babylon, concluding that God's favor was upon those left behind in Jerusalem who now prospered. Knowing the reality behind this prosperity, God judged the moral bankruptcy of the leadership. It is true that in Ezekiel's context, the exiles were at the time of the vision under covenant discipline. But desperate living conditions does not necessarily indicate divine disfavor, even under the more "contractual" system of blessing of the Mosaic Covenant (psalms of lament are ample testimony; see Theological Bridge to Application for Ezek 3:16–27 and comments on Ezek 3:18–19). The fact that God promised his presence with these exiles, *even* when they were under covenant discipline, underscores the certainty that God draws near to his people when they suffer in any circumstance.

The primary passage in Ezekiel that treats the promise of inward renewal is Ezek 36:24–28. If teaching through the whole of Ezekiel, one must decide where to place primary emphasis on this topic. Ezekiel 36 offers fuller attention. The placement of this promise here in Ezek 11, in a context of grim judgment, underscores the commitment of God to redeem hopeless circumstances by his own intervention to transform lives. Nothing in the stipulations of the Mosaic Covenant provided for inward transformation. Nevertheless, God committed himself to this work for ancient Israel, and it is part of the Spirit's ministry to effect spiritual formation in God's people today, a reality that offers hope to those frustrated by their brokenness and sin.

A WORD AGAINST FALSE HOPE
Ezekiel 12:1–28

Ezekiel's Message

God will vindicate his sure word against every contrary claim.

Key Themes

- Sometimes people simply refuse to accept God's truth and its realities set before them.
- Any apparent delay in God's judgment does not mean its realization is any less certain.
- Divine discipline has a redemptive purpose to spur repentance and restore relationship with God, resulting in the vindication of God's truth before others.
- False claims to divine knowledge will not prevail against God's sure word.

Context in Ezekiel

After the report of Ezekiel's temple vision (Ezek 8–11), Ezek 12 returns to the theme of chapter 7—the certainty of imminent judgment—forming a parenthesis around the temple vision. One could limit this unit to the dramatic enactment of packing for exile (Ezek 12:1–16) with anxious anticipation (Ezek 12:17–20). In this case, the second part of the chapter regarding the fulfillment of true prophecy (Ezek 12:21–28) would form a unit with the warnings against false prophets that follows (Ezek 13:1–23). However, the text division chosen in this commentary extends the unit to the entirety of chapter 12. In this configuration, the promise of the imminent fulfillment of prophecy supports Ezekiel's dramatic message that the people of Jerusalem might as well pack and wait anxiously, because their exile is surely imminent.

Interpretive Highlights

12:2 *eyes to see but do not see*: The chief characterization of Israel in Ezekiel is their stubborn, rebellious attitude (see commentary on Ezek 2:3). Here, the LORD compares this attitude to having sensory aptitude but lacking the will to use it. Jeremiah also utilizes this image to describe the people's conscious, if foolish, rebellion against the LORD (Jer 6:21–23). In Isaiah, the people (like their king, Ahaz) had already made up their minds not to trust in the LORD (Isa 7:10–13; cf. 2 Kgs 16:7–9). The people do not see or hear because they choose not to do so, being *unwilling* to respond to the message of the prophets.

12:3 *pack your belongings for exile*: Once again, Ezekiel adopts drama to reinforce his message (a "sign," Ezek 12:6; cf. Ezek 4 and **Special Topic: Prophetic Signs in the Ancient Near East**). Ancient Near Eastern artwork from Assyria depicts Israelite exiles of the northern kingdom being led into captivity. On their backs are knapsacks containing a few necessities.[1]

12:4–6 *in the evening . . . go out . . . dig through the wall*: Normally, one would expect an early start in the day for a long journey, such as to a foreign land of exile. However, Ezekiel's enactment takes place in stages, with packing in the day for a journey beginning at dusk. Probably, this alludes to an attempt at escape, which would take place under cover of darkness (cf. 2 Kgs 25:4; Jer 39:4). The action of digging through a wall (sun-dried mud bricks allow such) seems to support this idea, since such an attempt might take place in a discreet, unexpected location (such as the wall of a house along the city's perimeter) rather than through a gate. The significance of blocking the view of the land is a display of grief (cf. 2 Sam 15:20; 19:4) over the land left behind and the accompanying shame of exile (Jer 14:3; Mic 3:7). Commentators observe the ironic analogy

---

1. See Bodi, "Ezekiel," 429–30.

between the accusation of Ezek 12:2 (eyes that do not see) and the dramatic enactment of deportation without seeing the land.[2]

12:10 *the prince in Jerusalem:* The interpretation of the sign does not grant even the dignity of the title, "king," to Zedekiah (the uncle of the already deported king, Jehoiachin; 2 Kgs 24:15–17). Some commentators stumble over the lack of correspondence between Ezekiel's sign and the actual events of Zedekiah's deportation. Rather than escaping the city through a hole in a wall and fleeing with face covered, Zedekiah was smuggled through a city gate, captured, and blinded (2 Kgs 25:3–7). However, Ezekiel's prophecy applies to the "whole house of Israel," not just the specific fate of Zedekiah. So the ambiguity inherent in a symbolic act found essential fulfillment in the events that unfolded for all the residents who were trying to escape, it applied in an especially poignant way for Zedekiah. Ezekiel foretells the permanence of exile for that generation, exemplified in Zedekiah's death in Babylon (cf. Jer 52:11).

12:16 *so that . . . they may acknowledge:* This phrase reveals an important purpose for the horrifying covenant curses that God is bringing on the inhabitants of Jerusalem. The effect is ultimately redemptive for the remnant community, because it leads to repentance from idolatry and acknowledgement of Israel's covenant LORD (cf. Ezek 5:13; 6:7, 13–14; 7:27; 11:12). This acknowledgement not only signals reconciliation between Israel and her God; but also serves as a witness to the nations, among whom the exiles are dispersed, that Israel's LORD is God (Ezek 5:15).

12:17 *tremble . . . shudder:* A second sign-act in this episode stresses the imminence of exile by dramatizing the emotions that *ought* to be characterizing every day life in Jerusalem. While some are complacent (cf. Ezek 11:3), disaster is about to remove all sources of food and drink. These are an essential part of life, which represents loss of the whole land.

12:22 *every vision comes to nothing:* The word "vision" is a generic term for prophetic revelation. It describes the purely verbal message of prophets (1 Sam 3:1; Hos 12:10; Hab 2:2), a visually perceived experience (Gen 15:1), or a term covering both (Isa 1:1; cf. Isa 6:1). Ezekiel had other contemporaries, such as Jeremiah, announcing imminent doom for Jerusalem (Jer 6:1–2; 10:17; 34:1–3). Warnings also came from prophets a generation earlier, such as Zephaniah, who announced imminent judgment (Zeph 1:7, 14). But Jerusalemites had grown so skeptical that disregard for the warnings of doom-prophets became proverbial

---

2. Block, *Ezekiel 1–24*, 365.

(cf. Jer 7:4, where false belief in the inviolability of Jerusalem was also a proverb). The crucial point of this section is that Ezekiel's contemporaries will *experience* the word of judgment; it is no longer simply a warning of nearness as it had been for Zephaniah.

12:24 *false visions or flattering divinations*: Resistance to the warnings of God's prophets stemmed from other officials, who themselves claimed to have an opposing revelation (e.g., Hananiah in Jer 28; see Ezek 13:1–9); therefore, from God's vantage they are "false." In addition to verbal messages, alleged revelation also took the form of "divination." These practices utilized objects external to the practitioner to discern information from the supernatural realm; it is often linked with other, illicit revelatory techniques (Deut 18:10–11; 1 Sam 28:8; 2 Kgs 17:17). Such divination could be manipulated to satisfy the one seeking information, hence, "flattering" (see **Special Topic: Divination**).

12:28 **None of my words will be delayed**: This is the main point of the unit—the judgment that the prophets have announced as coming (even "near," Zeph 1:7, 14), is *now* upon them (cf. Ezek 7)—"in your days" (Ezek 12:25). The fulfillment of the prediction will be the final vindication of the truth of Ezekiel's prophecy (see **Special Topic: True and False Prophecy** under Ezek 13:1–23).

Special Topic: Divination

In the ancient Near East, the flow of information from the divine realm to humans was believed to come in two basic ways: (1) through an intuitive, subjective knowledge of the divine will, internal to the mind of the human, called "prophecy"; or (2) through more inductive, objective practices of observing or manipulating things external to the human functionary. This latter category includes such things as looking for signs in the movement of stars, casting lots, "reading" unusual patterns on the organs of sacrificed animals, interpreting the movement of oil in water or the behavior of birds. Although modern scholarship tends to group both types under the term "divination," in biblical terms "divination" refers to this second type of revelatory experience.[3]

The ancients were aware that such practices could be manipulated to serve the agenda of the practitioner. So, for example, the Assyrian King, Sennacherib, wished to ascertain why his father, Sargon II, had died

---

3. Hilber, "Prophecy, Divination, and Magic," 368–69.

unceremoniously on the battlefield. He had diviners inquire of the gods, and he confined them to separate rooms in order to assure that they did not collude with one another in their report.[4] In ancient Mesopotamia, inductive divination was regarded as more reliable than intuitive prophecy. But in Israel, the reverse was true—the regulations of Mosaic law prohibited divination (Deut 18:10–11), except for the Urim and Thummim of the high priest (Exod 28:30; Num 27:21; 1 Sam 23:9–12).[5]

Theological Bridge to Application

The primary thrust of Ezekiel's ministry in the first half of the book is trying to convince his contemporaries of the truth about their sin and the certainty of Jerusalem's judgment. But the people's stubbornness to respond (Ezek 12:2) is not due to any lack of clarity in communication—God speaks not only through the words of the prophet but also through Ezekiel's graphic visual aids. The manner in which God persists, in various ways, in confronting his wayward people reveals his longsuffering patience. In Isaiah's words, "I spread out my hands all day to a stubborn people" (Isa 65:2). At the same time, as the end of this chapter indicates (Ezek 12:25, 28), God's patience does have limits, his warnings are not idle threats, and he will surely follow up word with action. People may wish to believe other claims (Ezek 12:23, 27), but God's word is true and will be vindicated.

Focus of Application

The reasons people do not respond to God's word are many and complex. One aspect is that apart from the movement of God's Spirit, the human heart is naturally predisposed to rebellion against his will. Ezekiel's message about the Spirit's renewal of the heart (Ezek 11:19–21; 36:26–27) views the human problem from this perspective by addressing the *solution* to human need. But here, in Ezek 12:2, the Lord views the problem from the *dimension of human free choice*: people are simply *unwilling* to respond to God's appeals. They choose to believe alternative messages (Ezek 12:22, 27) rather than the harsher truth that God's word might be

---

4. The Sin of Sargon (Livingstone, *Court Poetry*, no. 33).

5. Further, see Van Dam, "Divination, Magic," 159–62; and Farber, "Witchcraft, Magic, and Divination," 1895–909.

speaking into their lives. In the context of Ezekiel's contemporaries, this was the false belief that judgment was either a distant time away or perhaps not coming at all.

A variety of alternative messages in our contemporary culture compete against God's call to respond to him with allegiance and obedience. Some of these messages reject the Bible altogether as a divine message of truth. But more subtle are alternative portraits about the nature and certainty of judgment—perhaps it is not imminent or not coming at all (cf. 2 Pet 3:4), or "there will be 'second chances' after death." Accounts of "near death" experiences report a peaceful encounter with the transcendent realm, regardless of one's religious disposition. Ezekiel warns against placing confidence in such alternative hopes, and he calls people to come to terms with God today (cf. Ps 95:6–8). This truth applies as well to believers who resist conviction. They must resist the temptation to justify their life-choices or to weave a false narrative about how God might look upon their behavior. For example, they might say "under these circumstances, this choice is understandable," or, "it's not that serious of a sin," or, "after all, God is graciously patient." Ezekiel would certainly affirm that God is patient, but God leaves no room for us to test how long his patience forebears.

For the Israelites who escaped destruction and experienced divine discipline in exile, God's design was redemptive. Indeed, it is important to recall that Ezekiel's immediate audience was a community in exile living under covenant sanctions (see comments under Ezek 1:1 and Theological Bridge to Application under Ezek 3:16–27). But these sanctions were not merely punitive. Rather, God designed the exile to move the community to forsake idolatry, declare allegiance to him only, and so testify to the nations among whom they live that their Lord is truly God (Ezek 12:15–16; cf. Ezek 5:15). By analogy, God might discipline his people today in order to move them to live by his will, giving them cause to testify before others that the Lord is God, who sovereignly works to vindicate his truth (cf. Pss 32:3–7; 51:12–13). When people humbly testify in this way, it dismantles the false hopes of a world that chooses more convenient narratives to live by.

SPEAKING PRESUMPTUOUSLY IN GOD'S NAME

Ezekiel 13:1–23

Ezekiel's Message

The LORD denounces those who presumptuously speak in his name and serve their own interests rather than bear the unwelcome task of challenging the community of believers.

Key Themes

- The LORD denounces those who presume to speak in his name but have not truly been moved by his Spirit.
- The LORD denounces leaders who speak whatever makes people comfortable and fail in the unwelcome task of challenging the community of believers.
- The LORD denounces those who use God's people for their own ends and offer false hope in times of trouble.

Context in Ezekiel

In the previous chapter, Ezekiel countered claims to visions and divinatory messages that judgment was not imminent. This flows naturally into accusations directed against the prophets themselves whose messages opposed the doom announced by Ezekiel. The passage follows the structure: (1) accusation and announcement of judgment against false prophets (Ezek 13:1–9); (2) against their message (Ezek 13:10–16); and (3) against false prophetesses (Ezek 13:17–23).

Interpretive Highlights

13:2–3 *out of their own imagination:* The translation "own imagination" (also rendered "own heart" [ESV] and "own inspiration" [NASB]), accurately stresses that the message originates from within the mind of the individual and not from the LORD. The next verse amplifies this using the phrase "who follow their own spirit" and "have seen nothing." In the book of Ezekiel, God's Spirit energizes Ezekiel to speak prophetically (Ezek 2:2; 2:24; esp. 11:5) and conveys Ezekiel to different visionary realms (Ezek 3:12; 8:1; 11:24). The prophets in Ezek 13:3–4 are not moved by the agency of God's Spirit (cf. Ezek 13:6–7, "the LORD has not sent them"). Since they have spoken presumptuously in God's name, they and their speech are "foolish," that is, morally corrupt (Pss 14:1; 74:18; esp. Isa 32:5–6).

13:4–5 *like jackals among ruins:* Ezekiel uses a metaphor about ruined walls and buildings to speak of the spiritual problems of his people. The image of "breaches" in the walls is particularly appropriate, since the city of Jerusalem faced an impending invasion. However, Ezekiel's interest is not in actual fortifications; rather, the target of his critique is the false message of hope announced by the prophets (Ezek 12:23–24, 27; "peace" in 13:10). Instead of challenging the people with the need for repentance before the "day of the LORD" (see comments on Ezek 7:7), these prophets speak words that reinforce their moral complacency; hence, they fail to repair the "breaches" (moral failures that lead to judgment; cf. Ezek 22:30). Psalm 106:23 refers to intercession in such an event as the proper course of action. When a city became uninhabited and went to ruins, it was taken over by wild animals (Isa 13:20–22; 34:11; Lam 5:18; Neh 4:3). Like jackals who make homes in the ruins and scavenge the dead (Ps 63:10), the false prophets take advantage of the ruined state of their society and effectively "eat" their own people. For "visions" and "divinations," see discussion on Ezek 12:24.

13:9 *council . . . records:* Ezekiel 13:1–8 contains the accusation against the false prophets, v. 9 is the announcement of judgment. These prophets enjoyed prestigious participation in the confidence of leadership

(Ezek 7:26; cf. analogous to God's "council"; Ps 89:7; Jer 23:18). To be listed in the "records" means to be recognized with full citizenship (Ps 87:6; Ezra 2:62). Failure to be listed entails loss of privileges (Neh 7:64). In addition to losing their social standing, none of these prophets would be part of the restoration to the land after exile (cf. Jer 29:29–32).

Special Topic: True and False Prophecy

Because prophecy entails an internal, subjective claim to having heard a word from God (see **Special Topic: Divination** under Ezek 12:1–28), it is easy to *claim* that one has received a revelation. In ancient Mesopotamia, because prophecy was subordinate to divination, such claims were sometimes put to an external test by divination to verify the credibility of a prophet. However, in ancient Israel, other tests for true prophecy were established in Mosaic law. The most important test was religious orthodoxy. Although performance of signs was one indication of prophetic authority (Exod 4:1–8; Isa 7:11; 38:7–8), even a miraculous sign could not authenticate a prophetic word if it contravened what had been revealed through Moses (Deut 13:1–5; Jer 23:13, 27). Moral integrity was also a crucial consideration (Jer 23:10–11, 14). Verification was especially necessary when two individuals offered contradictory prophetic messages, such as in the case of Jeremiah and Hananiah (Jer 28). In such cases, fulfillment of a short term prediction helped to adjudicate the true from the false (Deut 18:21–22; Jer 28:15–17; cf. Deut 18:20). Ezekiel's word would be vindicated against the false prophets when the Babylonians destroyed Jerusalem (Ezek 12:28; 33:33).[1]

13:10 *peace . . . flimsy wall:* Returning to the building metaphor, Ezekiel likens the "peace" message of the prophets to putting a cosmetic layer on a structurally unsound wall, the reality of which will be become evident with the storm. As in Ezek 13:4–5, the imagery is appropriate on two levels: first it describes the deceptive nature of the false prophecy, but at a second level, it is appropriate because it applies to the realities of the impending destruction of Jerusalem. The choice of imagery for the storm is similar to that found in Mesopotamian laments over the destruction of cities by attacking armies: "On that day, the storm was removed from the city, and that city was in ruins . . . In its walls breaches were made–the

---

1. For further discussion, see Hilber, "Diversity of OT Prophetic Phenomena," 250–54.

people groan."² The word translated "hailstones" (v. 11) is rare in the Old Testament (elsewhere only in Ezek 38:22) but is shared with the language of the Babylonians.³ This imagery, then, may have been familiar to the exiles living in Babylon and so it would have been particularly effective.

13:17–18 *daughters . . . who prophesy:* The denunciation of false prophets turns to prophetesses, although a technical change in the form of verb used for the word "prophesy" implies that these female counterparts might have differed somewhat in their form of divine mediation.⁴ This particular form of the verb often describes behavior that might be associated with prophecy (e.g., eccentric, prophet-like behavior [Num 11:25, 27; 1 Sam 10:5–6]) but not necessarily speaking forth the divine word. This broader sense of "prophesy" is appropriate in the context of Ezek 13:17–23, where the emphasis appears to be on divinatory practices involving external objects ("bands" and "veils").

The exact activities that these women engaged in is unclear. Most commentators have suggested that they were practicing some sort of magic, casting spells using the "bands" and "veils" mentioned in the text. Favoring this approach is the word translated "bands," which is related to an Akkadian word used in Babylonian magical spells for "binding" evil forces. Similarly, the term for "veils" might allude to a goddess of magic, or perhaps an amulet worn about the head, both ideas having support in Babylonian incantation texts.⁵ The intention of these women was "to ensnare the lives of my people." If the interpretation is correct that these women were employing magic to afflict or deliver people, then the practical effect had to do with health and physical life (cf. metaphorical use of "hunt for life" in Prov 6:26).

An alternate interpretation is that these women were engaged in necromancy, which is obtaining secret knowledge by conjuring the dead (1 Sam 28:3–19; Isa 8:19). The strength of this view is that it interprets the women's activities within the context of divination (accessing information from the divine realm), *not* magic (manipulating unseen forces through ritual and incantation). This accords with Ezek 13:23, which indicates that their practice corresponded to the purpose of the male prophets

2. The Lamentation over the Destruction of Sumer and Ur (*COS* 1.166: 536, lines 208, 212). See also Bodi, "Ezekiel," 432.

3. Bodi, "Ezekiel," 432.

4. Greenberg, *Ezekiel 1–20*, 239.

5. For examples of Akkadian texts using these terms, see Bodi, "Ezekiel," 433, together with helpful discussion in Block, *Ezekiel 1–24*, 414.

("visions" and "divinations"). In this view, the word translated "lives" has the sense of "ghost." This term most often denotes whole persons or their physical lives (see discussion on Ezek 3:18–19) but in related languages outside the Hebrew Bible, it can carry the sense of "inner life" or "disembodied spirit." The causing of death and life would refer to the alleged manipulation of the deceased, to conjure from and then send back to the realm of the dead. The metaphor of a bird taking flight, a common image in the ancient Near East for the deceased, supports this use here (Ezek 13:20).[6] Whatever the service, these women rendered it for pay (food to spare their own lives; Ezek 13:19), and the effect of their message was to contradict Ezekiel's sure word of doom (Ezek 13:22).

Theological Bridge to Application

Underlying Ezekiel's condemnation of false prophecy is the Third Commandment (Exod 20:7; Deut 5:11). One of the ways in which one can "misuse" the Lord's name is to speak presumptuously by it, claiming a word from the Lord when it is not really from him. When Moses preaches the law in Deuteronomy, the specific laws of Deut 12–26 illustrate and elaborate on the application of the Ten Commandments. Corresponding to the Third Commandment (misusing God's name) are laws governing prophetic speech in his name (Deut 13:1–5; esp. Deut 18:20). The conflict between Ezekiel and the false prophets was a duel over the honor of the Lord's name, which God himself would vindicate (Ezek 12:28; 13:9, 23).

Focus of Application

There exists a wide diversity of opinion and significant controversy about the place of prophecy in the contemporary church. Regardless of one's denominational tradition or viewpoint on this issue, Ezekiel denounces the ministry of anyone who *claims* to have received a word from God but has not. Criteria for testing such claims are found across the canon of Scripture, and this chapter stresses several points: First, the message of the false prophets failed to address the spiritual weaknesses of the people ("repairing the breaches"). Second, the ministry of these prophets was self-serving. The male prophets are likened to "jackals" (animals whose gain was in the ruin of humans) and the female prophets utilized their

---

6. For detailed presentation of this view, see Hamori, *Women's Divination*, 170–78.

special skills for financial advantage. Third, to the extent that some of these prophets utilized divinatory practices, they trafficked in illicit means of discovering the divine will. These tests are relevant for the church today. While popular forms of "divination" in contemporary culture (e.g., astrology, necromancy) are not common in church practices, Christians at times resort to such means of guidance. The popular idea of putting out "fleece" boarders on divination, since it is an attempt to force God's hand to reveal information. In this way, Gideon's action was a faithless act, and his practice ultimately led to outright divination with an illegitimate "ephod" (Judg 6:36–40; 8:22–27). In every case, the consequences of speaking falsely in God's name are severe.

Aside from outright claims to prophetic speech ("thus says the Lord"), there are more subtle claims of receiving a word from God to which the lessons of this passage might apply. Believers should weigh very carefully their wording about how God is "speaking" to them or "leading" them. This passage does not deny this common Christian experience; but by analogy to warnings against false prophetic speech, it serves to caution against speaking presumptuously in God's name, in particular, the manner in which that experience is reported to others.

By analogy to prophetic speech, this passage also addresses the duty of teaching and preaching more generally. God expects Christian leaders to discern the spiritual weaknesses of their communities and not turn away from such needs because the subject might make people uncomfortable. Much less should they encourage complacency where correction is needed. The temptation is greatest for leaders in cases where financial consequences might follow, for example, avoiding offense to the sentiments of wealthy supporters. The accusation against the prophets in Ezek 13 is relevant to the close social accord between these prophetic leaders and the privileged classes in Jerusalem (Ezek 7:26).

SIN AND HINDERED PRAYER
Ezekiel 14:1–11

Ezekiel's Message

The Lord rejects those who seek him when sin remains rooted in the heart, yet his severity works toward restoration.

Key Themes

- Idolatry is a matter of the heart as well as action.
- The Lord rejects those who seek him when sin remains rooted in the heart.
- People must turn from their idolatrous thoughts and practices.
- The severity of God works toward restoration.

Context in Ezekiel

Ezekiel 14 opens with a new scene (another visit from the elders); but because Ezek 14:1–11 continues on the theme of prophets, one could group this passage on a literary level with the previous unit, particularly since the prophets are enticed to speak when no message from God has truly been given (cf. Ezek 14:9–10 with Ezek 13:1–7). However, the topic of Ezek 14:1–11 (seeking God's word through an intermediary) stresses the character of those who seek God rather than the character and culpability of the prophets. Its emphasis on the internal nature of idolatry justifies separate treatment from the previous unit.

Interpretive Highlights

14:1–3 *the elders of Israel came . . . inquire:* Ezekiel's eccentric behavior and reclusion drew the leaders of the exilic community to him (see comments at Ezek 3:24–25; cf. Ezek 8:1; 20:1–3). As discussed at Ezek 3:26–27, it is part of a prophet's ministry to answer inquiries and to intercede on behalf of his or her people. The word "inquire," used in Ezek 14:3, often describes people seeking help from God for decision making in times of need (e.g., Exod 18:15; 1 Kgs 22:5 [both translated "seek," NIV]; 1 Sam 9:9; 2 Kgs 3:11; 8:8). In their distress in exile and with uncertainty about the fate of their homeland, the people were attempting to sort out the conflicting prophetic messages (cf. Ezek 12:21–28; 13:10).

14:4 *set up idols in their hearts:* This phrase could be translated "set [idols] over the heart", and so it has been suggested that it refers to wearing magical amulets around the neck; in effect, the idolatrous object lies on the chest over the heart.[1] This would be similar to magical practices mentioned in Ezek 13:18. However, elsewhere in Old Testament usage, this combination of words is an idiom for "setting one's mind" on something (e.g., 2 Kgs 12:4; Isa 65:17; Jer 3:16; 7:31; 19:5; 32:35; 44:21).[2] So the point is that the people had focused their thoughts and yearnings on their idols (see Ezek 14:7). For the words translated "idols" and "stumbling block," see comments at Ezek 6:4 and Ezek 3:20, respectively.

The elders hoped to hear a divine word *indirectly* through prophetic mediation; but rather than answer in *word*, the Lord would respond *directly* by his *actions* in judgment—"I, the Lord" is emphatic. The phrase translated "in keeping with" (NIV) expresses the idea that God's punishment is appropriate to the level of sin. The ESV and NASB render this verse "as he comes with the multitude of his idols," which is based on a slightly different Hebrew manuscript tradition; but the interpretation is not altered by this difference.

14:5–6 *recapture the hearts . . . repent:* If idolatry is rooted in the heart, the Lord's intervention aims at the same target. One might translate this clause "capture the house of Israel by their heart," which stresses

---

1. Bodi, "Ezekiel," 434.
2. Further, see Block, *Ezekiel 1–24*, 425.

the means by which the action occurs (cf. Gen 39:12, where the same Hebrew construction stresses how Potiphar's wife "caught" Joseph, but specifically by his cloak).

The words, "repent" and "turn," translate the same Hebrew word, so the command is repeated for emphasis. This word is frequently used for turning in direction of travel (e.g., "go back" [NIV], Gen 31:3; Exod 4:19; Ruth 1:8), and so it figuratively expresses a turn in spiritual direction. The purpose of judgment is restorative (cf. Ezek 14:11). For the meaning of "detestable practices," see comments on Ezek 7:3-4.

14:7 *Israelites . . . foreigners . . . separate themselves from me*: The Mosaic law placed some requirements on non-Israelites living in the land, particularly with respect to worship (e.g., Lev 17:8-16; 20:1-5; extended to idolatrous inquiries in Lev 20:6). Given that one of the purposes of the conquest was to rid the land of idolatrous worship (Exod 23:24; 34:13-14; Deut 7:5-6; 12:1-3), resident foreigners in Israel would be prohibited from idolatrous practices as well as Israelites. In the context of the exile, there may have been proselytes who were worshipping with Jews; or perhaps Ezekiel is merely using the legislation from Leviticus to underscore the gravity of the point.[3] From a rhetorical standpoint, if not even foreigners can worship idols in the land, how much less an Israelite whether in the land or in exile.

The word translated "separate themselves" describes consecration or dedication, usually to the LORD. It refers to the dedication of sacred offerings (Lev 22:2); and in the noun form of the word, it describes priests (Lev 21:12) and Nazirites (Num 6:1-21). For an Israelite to be consecrated to the LORD also means to be "separated away" from things that defile (Lev 15:31). However, it also refers to dedication to false gods (Hos 9:10). It is an ironic use of the word in Ezek 14:7 that, instead being dedicated *to* the LORD, the Israelites have separated themselves *from* him.

14:8 *an example and a byword*: The book of Deuteronomy warned that covenant sanctions against Israel would be so severe that their suffering in judgment would become proverbial among the nations (Deut 28:37; Jer 24:9; cf. Ps 44:14). The ultimate effect is to vindicate the character of Israel's God ("know that I am the LORD").

Since "my people" was a term for Israel as God's covenantal nation (cf. Lev 23:30; "my people," Exod 3:7; 5:1; 6:7; Hos 2:23), "removal" in this verse means expulsion from the covenant relationship. In the Mosaic

---

3. Block, *Ezekiel 1-24*, 429.

covenant, physical life and death were central to covenantal blessing or curse (Deut 30:15–20), so in effect, this warning is a threat of death. The combination of the expressions, "set my face against" and "remove," describes capital punishment in Lev 20:2–3.

14:9 *I, the Lord, have enticed:* This is similar to the scenario described in 1 Kgs 22:19–23, where the Lord sends a spirit to deceive the false prophets of King Ahab in order to "entice" him into battle (same Hebrew word for "entice"). Here, it is the false prophet himself who is enticed. The text expresses a world view in which various agents, both human and supernatural, engage in a course of events that are sovereignly directed by God himself. But presumably, the prophet in question here has brought divine deception on him or herself due to their own initial insincerity.[4] The point of this warning is to dissuade prophets from responding favorably to inquiries when people are only seeking God hypocritically.

14:11 *Then the people . . . will no longer stray:* God's refusal to tolerate such hypocrisy and to follow through in judgment has a redemptive purpose—to turn people from their sin to a sincere pursuit of God (Ezek 14:5). At the national level this would restore Israel to covenant blessing. The Hebrew word translated "then" (NIV) emphasizes purpose ("in order that," NASB). The stated goal uses language of intimate covenantal relationship ("my people" and "their God," see above comments on v. 8).

Theological Bridge to Application

Ezekiel's message reveals the complexities of divine and human interaction. In this passage, God rejects the approach of those who are seeking him; but he does so because he weighs the motives of people and judges them to be insincere. The message of Ezek 14:4, then, focuses on human responsibility by describing the willful devotion of people to idols. On the other hand, Ezek 11:19–21 stresses the divine initiative that is necessary to rid the human heart of devotion to idols and thereby effect restoration. Yet in Ezek 14:5 and 11, this restoration comes only after God allows judgment to run its course and have its intended effect on the human heart. Added to this complexity is the thought that other supernatural agents are also at work (2 Kgs 22:19–23), although that consideration is not introduced in this chapter of Ezekiel explicitly.

---

4. For more thorough discussion, see Block, *Ezekiel 1–24*, 432–35.

Focus of Application

It comes as no surprise that idolatry, indeed all sin, is a matter of the heart. The invisible, internal forms are varied and complex (see "Focus of Application" under Ezek 6 and 7). Often human sin creeps into our hearts slowly and subtly, perhaps by passively absorbing attitudes from our family of origin, friends, co-workers, or popular media. But the emphasis in Ezek 14:3-4 is how sin can be the result of intentional choice. The elders visiting Ezekiel "set up idols in their hearts." This addresses the conscious decisions we make daily as to what we watch, read, or listen to; it concerns decisions at work; it involves the people with whom we develop intimate relationships; it touches on the thoughts and fantasies nurtured in the heart.

It is also no surprise that the matters of the heart affect our relationship with God; but what often escapes our attention is how adversely sin affects our prayers and worship. In Ezekiel's context, the elders specifically approached him as a prophetic intermediary through whom they sought a word from God. But in general God does not respond to those who seek him with hypocritical lives or insincere motives. The Old Testament reveals the manner in which hidden sin hinders personal prayer (Ps 66:18; Prov 21:13; for not so "hidden" sin, see Isa 59:1-2). Similarly, both Jesus and Peter warn about the adverse affect of subtle sin (Matt 5:23-24; 1 Pet 3:7). And James's "double minded" prayer likely has to do with mixed motives (Jas 1:5-8).[5] Ezekiel warns us to turn from whatever might block our devotion to and relationship with God (Ezek 14:6). Whether one thinks on the individual or community level, God is reluctant to entertain petitions or accept worship from insincere hearts.

An important caveat is that prayer might remain unanswered for many reasons, none of which have to do with sin (e.g., John 9:1-3); so human opinion about the reasons for unanswered prayer should remain a matter of personal conviction on the part of the individual whose conscience might or might not be pricked regarding sin. Or in the case of a community, it is the responsibility of leadership to evaluate when corporate sin might be an issue.

God's firm refusal to answer prayer when unrepentant sin is involved reveals a severe side of his character. But this is balanced with the truth that God aims at restoration. The covenant sanctions specific to ancient

---

5. For characteristics of an effective petitioner, see Grenz, *Prayer*, 48-55.

Israel are not applicable today; but divine discipline in whatever form (it could be unanswered prayer), has the goal of turning hearts back to him.

NO RIGHTEOUSNESS BY ASSOCIATION

Ezekiel 14:12—15:8

Ezekiel's Message

Neither special relationships nor privileged status will avert God's just judgment.

Key Themes

- God ultimately judges each person on an individual basis regardless of their family or social network.
- Belonging to a spiritually privileged group does not avert individual judgment.
- The justice of God will be vindicated.

Context in Ezekiel

The formula, "The word of the LORD came to me," marks the beginning of a new oracular unit, but the announcement of judgment in Ezek 14:12—15:8 supplements the answer already given to the elders' inquiry in Ezek 14:1–11. Any hope for sympathetic mediation from the prophet Ezekiel was dashed by the announcement of judgment in Ezek 14:8, and the oracle of doom in Ezek 14:12-23 reinforces this message. The analogy of the vine in Ezek 15 is also a self-contained oracle, yet it complements the message of Ezek 14:12–23—both rebuke any false assumption that a special relationship (to the righteous) or status (belonging to a special group) will avert judgment.

Interpretive Highlights

14:13 *if a country sins:* The illustrations that follow (of Noah, Daniel, and Job) draw on people who lived in places outside Israel's homeland; hence, the statement is a principle that is generally applicable to any people or nation. Specific sins are not enumerated, because the main point is the irrelevance of any party's relationship with righteous individuals once judgment is decreed. But the Old Testament does offer some idea as to what moral standards are universally applicable to people outside Israel's covenant.

Although nations other than Israel were not governed by the Mosaic law, there are broad humanitarian and justice values to which God holds all people accountable. The Noahic Covenant, which was universal in scope (Gen 9:10), affirms the value of human life (Gen 9:6; cf. Isa 24:5). Consequently, when the prophet Amos announces judgment against nations outside of Israel, the accusations relate to the disregard for human life and dignity (Amos 1:3, 6, 11, 13; 2:1) as well as failure to respect covenantal relationships between people (Amos 1:9). Similarly, Joel accuses the nations of human trafficking (Joel 3:3, 6), Nahum castigates Nineveh for excess violence (Nah 3:1; cf. Jonah 3:8), and Ezekiel holds Philistia accountable for malicious vengeance (Ezek 25:15). God may also hold a country accountable for national arrogance (Isa 10:13; 16:6; Ezek 27:3; Hab 2:4). Ezek 14:13 presupposes an analogy between how God works with the nations in general and with Israel in particular. Since Jerusalem is even more guilty than the surrounding nations (Ezek 5:6–7), this general principle of judgment especially applies to it.

14:14 *these three men . . . by their righteousness:* In order to underscore the certainty of judgment for Jerusalem, the LORD alludes in a subtle way to the account of Abraham bargaining with God over the fate of Sodom and Gomorrah and the destiny of Abraham's nephew Lot (Gen 18–19). In that narrative, the assumption underlying Abraham's appeal is that God would be unjust if he destroyed a city with righteous individuals in it (Gen 18:19, 23–25). In this instance with Abraham, God agreed to spare the cities on account of the presence of Lot's family, since

Abraham assumed that surely Lot's family altogether would satisfy the minimal number, ten. As it turned out, this was not the case; and only Lot and three of his family, including two children escaped the city before destruction.

With this allusion in the background, the LORD draws on the example of three individuals from distant times and places who typify righteous men whose association might be expected to save their communities in the manner of Lot's family in Gen 18–19. If Ezekiel's audience hoped in such a scenario for Jerusalem, whereby a few righteous would save the city, they were mistaken. In the case of Jerusalem, not even an immediate family relationship to a righteous man, much less a civic relationship, can avert judgment (Ezek 14:16, 18, 20).

The examples of Noah and Job support the argument of Ezekiel at a literary level in two ways. First, both Noah and Job were "righteous" (Gen 6:9; or "blameless" and "upright," Job 1:1, 8; 2:3). Second, these men's children were involved in the story in various ways. Noah brought his children on the ark and Job offered sacrifice to atone for his children. Yet, in the case of Noah, he was unable to keep his son Ham's line from a curse; and Job's intercession did not prevent calamity on his children, even if it was not specifically in judgment. The children's fate is not determined by the will of their father.

The reference to "Daniel" is more difficult to assess because the identity of the individual is not as clear as most readers assume (see **Special Topic: Daniel of Judah or Dan'el of Ugarit?**). If the interpretation is correct that Ezekiel refers to king Dan'el of ancient Near Eastern fame, then this illustration parallels the others in this passage—righteous Gentile men (none of the three were "Israelites") from distant times and places who are ultimately unable to save their children from calamity. The rhetorical point is that there is even less hope that one righteous man could avert the judgment of an entire nation.

Special Topic: Daniel of Judah or Dan'el of Ugarit?

One of the more vexing, yet interesting, problems in the book of Ezekiel is the identity of "Daniel" named in Ezek 14:14 and 20 (also Ezek 28:3). The natural assumption is that this must be Ezekiel's contemporary, "Daniel" of the exiled Judeans who served in the Babylonian court (Dan 1:1–7). However, one difficulty with this identification is that the name is spelled differently in Hebrew in Ezekiel (*dani'el*) than in the book of Daniel (*daniyye'l*), the key difference being the letter "*y*." This could be two different forms of the same name, but it likely suggests two different individuals. Furthermore, as Ezekiel's contemporary, the biblical "Daniel" does not parallel the other two individuals in Ezek 14. Both Noah and Job are famous Gentile exemplars from the distant past and provide illustrations from non-Israelite contexts. Furthermore, because the biblical Daniel has no children (as far as the account indicates), he is not as suitable for literary effect as the other two figures whose children play a role in their stories.

There is another possibility, that "Daniel" refers to a famous king of ancient Near Eastern legend ("Dan'el"), whose story is known from extrabiblical texts found at Ugarit. The spelling of the name in the story better matches the Hebrew consonants used in Ezekiel. In addition, the story depicts him as a just king who cares for widows and orphans and earns the blessing of the gods; but such favor does not prevent the ultimate murder of his male heir.

One of the arguments against this identification is that a biblical text would not use a polytheist as a morally positive image. But the use of such a character as an example of a "righteous" individual is no more problematic than using an action hero from a modern story (e.g., Luke Skywalker of "Star Wars") to illustrate virtue. At a literary level in Ezek 14, Dan'el of west-Semitic fame functions in a parallel manner to Noah and Job much better than biblical Daniel.[1] The "Dan'el" of Ugaritic fame fits the context of Ezek 28:3 better as well (see comments there).

14:21 *four dreadful judgments:* These four calamities (corresponding to those mentioned in Ezek 14:13, 15, 17, 19) are stereo-typical instruments of judgment (see comments at Ezek 7:15; cf. Jer 15:2–3).

14:22 *some survivors—sons and daughters . . . consoled:* On the surface, this directly contradicts the claim of the previous context that a righteous man could not deliver his own children. But the rhetorical force of the illustrations can not be pressed beyond their intent. Ezekiel's contemporaries could find no hope that a few righteous in Jerusalem would avert judgment. The prophet has already mentioned that a remnant would survive the Babylonian siege. Here he employs the language of "sons and daughters" in an ironic fashion. Those who survive death

---

1. For further discussion, see Greenberg, *Ezekiel 1–20*, 257–58 and Bodi, "Ezekiel," 434. For defense of identification with biblical Daniel, see Block, *Ezekiel 1–24*, 447–50.

will serve only to vindicate the justice of God, since their character will expose the guilt of Jerusalem as a whole. Perhaps an extension of the analogy to Lot's family is implicit here. Those who survive illustrate the utter corruption that evoked judgment in the first place.

The word, "consoled," might give the impression that the exiles will be gratified to see some survivors and so their hearts would find comfort. However, the words translated "conduct" and "actions" are used by Ezekiel to describe the sinful behavior of the people (Ezek 20:43–44; 21:24; cf. Jer 7:3).[2] Therefore, Ezekiel's community will see the reason God judged Jerusalem and his justice will be vindicated.

15:1–2 *the wood of the vine:* In a new oracle (note the introduction formula "the word of the LORD came"), Ezekiel draws on another illustration to quell any hope that something "special" about Jerusalem will avert its judgment. When flourishing, the vine provides the all-important grape for winemaking. However, once a branch is cut, it offers no special value. The comparison of Jerusalem to a vine that ends up burned is ironic, because ordinarily a vine connotes a special status under God's care (Gen 49:22; Ps 80:8–11; Isa 5:1–7; Jer 2:21).

Theological Bridge to Application

In the face of God's judgment, a righteous person can sometimes move God to mercy (e.g., Gen 18:16–33; Exod 32:11–14; Num 12:13; 1 Kgs 17:1 with 18:1; 2 Chr 20:5–12; cf. Jas 5:16). However, there comes a point after which the decree of judgment is irreversible and the intercession or the protective presence of righteous people in society can no longer make a difference. This principle is relevant not only to communities as a whole (e.g., cities, nations; "a country," Ezek 14:13) but also to individuals, as noted by inclusion of "son" and "daughter" (Ezek 14:16, 20). At the heart of this issue is the justice of God, which Ezekiel defends on two points: First, God ultimately renders judgment on an individual basis, and second, when the cause of judgment is known, God's action is vindicated (Ezek 14:22–23; cf. Pss 51:4; 90:7–8; 96:13).

---

2. Greenberg, *Ezekiel 1–20*, 259.

Focus of Application

The most sensitive issue in applying this text is its relevance to *specific* nations or communities. It is true that God judges nations as a whole. However, the timing and causes of such judgment on specific cities or countries is not for us to discern; rather, knowledge of God's dealings in concrete cases is a matter of prophetic revelation only. When natural disasters strike communities, only God knows whether such calamity is the result of judgment for specific sins of the community. Unless it is prophetically revealed, announcing the cause of a catastrophe is purely human speculation. For example, when the World Trade Center was struck on September 11, 2001, some Christians were announcing that it was God's judgment for the spread of sexual immorality in the United States; but others were with equal passion pointing to the gross injustice of globalized corporations (symbolized by the World Trade Center). Both suggestions are dangerous proclamations, presuming to know the secret council of the LORD, which is disclosed only to genuine prophets of the stature of Ezekiel.

What we can say is that sin dwelling in any society has natural consequences that God allows to develop to the detriment of society as a whole. There may or may *not* be calamitous events that flow from the judgment of God, the nature and timing of which is not in human purview. What is certain is that judgment will eventually come to all human societies when God returns to judge the world (Pss 2:4–9; 46:8–10; 96:13; 98:9). In the meantime, God may honor the intercession and presence of righteous people in the society for a time; but once his judgment is irreversibly decreed, the presence of God's people is no assurance for the preservation of society.

These ideas are applicable as well at the level of the family. The intercession and presence of a righteous individual *may* contribute to the well-being of other family members and may even be instrumental in someone's path to eternal salvation (cf. 1 Cor 7:14). But the point to stress from Ezekiel's message is that the presence of righteous individuals in a family does not in itself avert the ultimate fate of family members when they meet God in judgment. This is similar to the point of Jesus in his discussion with Nicodemus (John 3:5–7). If someone ponders their relationship with God, they must realize that their dealings with him are one to one. Belonging to a Christian family, membership in the right church, holding special position in church leadership, association with a benevolent community group, or hanging out with the right friends avail nothing in the face of God's judgment.

Ezekiel's contemporaries perhaps hoped that the presence of a few righteous people in the city of Jerusalem would avert destruction. But as John Taylor observes, "This attitude is nothing less than using the saints as an insurance policy to cover the sinners . . . rather like the possession of a religious lucky charm."[3] Also, if they held any illusions that God's judgment might be unjust, Ezekiel warns that God's justice would be vindicated when the nature and depth of sin became manifest. The same is true in our lives and societies today.

---

3. Taylor, *Ezekiel*, 128.

GOD'S RELENTLESS LOVE
Ezekiel 16:1–63

Ezekiel's Message

God's covenant-love is relentlessly persistent even toward those who might scorn his mercy with hypocritical unfaithfulness.

Key Themes

- God's covenant-love is unmerited and persistent.
- Self-confident pride leads to lack of trust and unfaithful exploits.
- Seen for what it really is, spiritual unfaithfulness is abhorrent.
- Spiritual unfaithfulness has tragic consequences.

Context in Ezekiel

The previous unit ends with the accusation that Israel has been unfaithful (Ezek 15:8). This theme receives an elaborate and rhetorically poignant expansion in chapter 16. The surprising conclusion of the chapter, however, is that in spite of the inescapable judgment underscored in chapters 14 and 15, God promises to restore his covenant relationship with his wayward people. This long chapter divides into six units: (1) Israel's Inauspicious Beginning (Ezek 16: 1–5); (2) Israel's Rise though God's Love (Ezek 16:6–14); (3) Israel's Unfaithful Exploits (Ezek 16:15–22);

(4) Woeful Condemnation (Ezek 16:23–34); (5) Announcement of Judgment (Ezek 16:35–52); and (6) Promise of Restoration (Ezek 16:53–63).

Interpretive Highlights

16:2 *detestable practices:* Earlier in Ezekiel, the prophet used this phrase to focus on financial materialism and social injustice (see Ezek 7:3–4). As this chapter unfolds, the emphasis falls on idolatrous practices and the attendant, violent slaughter of children (Ezek 16:17–22).

16:3 *ancestry and birth:* God addresses the nation Israel in the person of its representative capital, Jerusalem. Since that city was originally a Canaanite city-state before being captured by the tribe of Judah (temporary conquest, Josh 1:8; recapture again by David, 2 Sam 5:6–7), it is rhetorically effective to compare Israel to Canaanites when the focus of accusation is on Israel's debauchery. Specifically, Jerusalem was inhabited by the Jebusites (Josh 15:8), who are distinguished from the Amorites and Hittites (Exod 3:8; Num 13:29; Deut 7:1; Josh 3:10); but Ezekiel furthers his derogatory description of Israel's origins by referring to such "parents" (cf. Ezek 16:44–45). The customary care of newborns evidently included rubbing of salt (Ezek 16:4), which was probably thought to have medical benefit, a practice reported to be in use today in some Middle Eastern places.[1]

16:8 *I spread the corner of my garment:* This action symbolized the protective relationship of a husband to a wife. It is illustrated in Ruth's proposal of marriage to Boaz (Ruth 3:9). In a text from the ancient Mesopotamian city of Mari, a queen exclaims, "Since my husband, Zimri-Lim, has spread the hem of his garment over me . . . , thereby indicating her special status.[2] The phrase "you became mine" alludes to the covenantal formula between the Lord and Israel (Exod 6:7; cf. Ezek 20:5; Hos 2:23).

16:15 *you trusted in your beauty and used your fame:* The important point to note is that self-confident pride leads to lack of trust, which is the spark for the unfaithful exploits that follow.

16:16 *he possessed your beauty:* The correct reading of the Hebrew text here is uncertain due to the extreme difficulty of the grammar, hence the different translations (compare with ESV, NASB, NET). In spite of

---

1. Bodi, "Ezekiel," 436.

2. Mari letter ARM 26 251, lines 16–18 (Durand, *Archives épistolaires de Mari*, 530–31). See Bodi, "Ezekiel," 438.

this ambiguity, the basic message of the verse is clear: Israel used its lavish resources to worship other gods. For "high places," see **Special Topic: High Places and Sacred Trees** at Ezek 6:1–14. In addition to covering divine images with gold as a sort of "skin," worshippers engaged in elaborate rituals to cloth idol statues and feed them on a daily basis (cf. Jer 10:9). Thus, the wealth of Israel (her "beauty") went to adorn idols in whom it trusted instead of the Lord (cf. Ps 115:8).

16:21 *slaughtered my children . . . sacrificed them as food:* The deep emotions of God flow in this text as he describes child sacrifice as destroying not just the people's children, but his own. The ESV and NASB translations specify what is implied by the Hebrew expression: child-offerings are roasted on altars (cf. Ezek 16:36; for condemnation, see Lev 18:21; 20:2–3; Deut 12:31; 18:10; 2 Kgs 16:3; 23:10; Jer 32:35).

Special Topic: Offensive Sexual Imagery

The language of this passage is offensive by virtue of its graphic and potentially misogynistic nature, even though softened to some degree in various translations (esp. Ezek 16:25–26 [cf. Ezek 23:20], 36–37).[3] It is important to bear in mind that Israel's idolatrous behavior was not innocuous, it involved the slaughter and burning of God's own children, arousing the passion expressed in this imagery. But rather than directed toward women or intended to deprecate feminine character, the message forces an ostensibly male audience to identify with a stereotype *they* themselves deplored. Ezekiel is not asserting something about women or the complex tragedy of prostitution; rather, he is using a reprehensible construct of his audience's own imagination against them. Such rhetoric "gets under the skin," so to speak, of the original male audience, even if not sensitive to a twenty-first century, western reader.

Some readers cannot dissociate the Lord's actions in this chapter from that of an abusive husband, calling into question the character of God. But a sympathetic reading allows God to play complex roles in the narrative, both embittered husband and just prosecutor of a covenant lawsuit, where he allows talionic justice to take its course (Ezek 16:43). One reads a multi-layered narrative in which the political realities of

---

3. For more graphic translation, see Block, *Ezekiel 1–24*, 467 and especially Greenberg, *Ezekiel 1–20*, 283, 285–86, who provides the details on word meaning. For expression of feminist concerns, see Galambush, *Jerusalem in the Book of Ezekiel*.

Israel's history interlace with the metaphor of prosecuting an adulteress. This imagery must not be read for more than it intends to affirm about theological reality—God is both jealous and justly hostile toward Israel's actions.[4]

16:26–29 *Egyptians . . . Assyrians . . . Babylonia:* At various times in Israel's and Judah's history, their kings made alliances with foreign powers (2 Kgs 16:7–10; Isa 31:1; 39:1–4; Ezek 17:15; Hos 7:11; 12:1). Ezekiel alludes metaphorically to the tribute paid to these powers for military protection when he speaks in terms of the prostitute paying her lovers rather than being paid by them (Ezek 16:33–34). Such subjugation to overlords came at the expense of Israel's "territory." The NASB has "rations," but the NIV rendering makes better sense in the context. This example gives concrete expression to the accusation of Ezek 16:15 that Israel has trusted in its own resources rather than the LORD.

16:30 *filled with fury against you:* The verb meaning in the first part of this verse is unclear (*'ml*: "be hot," NIV; or "be withered/dried out"). So based on the second option, other translations ascribe some sort of depravation to Israel's heart ("How sick is your heart," ESV; cf. NRSV and NJPS; or "languishing," NASB). Both the NIV and the alternatives are viable options and make good sense in context. Since nothing substantial in the message is affected, it is best to leave the choice undecided and make no point of exposition from it.

16:43 *because you did not remember:* Failure to "remember" is not merely a cognitive lapse but a failure to live in accord with the relational realities that once existed. Israel has fallen into the self-deception Moses warned against by taking pride in its own success (Deut 8:1–20).

16:49 *the sin of your sister Sodom:* Sodom is the classic example of a city that received just and devastating judgment (Gen 13:13; 18:20; 19:13; Deut 29:23; Isa 1:9; 13:19; Jer 49:19; 50:40; Amos 4:11). Some rightly observe that in Ezek 16:49, Sodom's specific sins concern arrogance and lack of concern for the needy, and not homosexual activity that traditional interpretation condemns. However, the choice of Sodom for illustrative purposes in a context dominated by sexual imagery, coupled with the mention of its "detestable" behavior (Ezek 16:50), implies that sexual deviancy is utilized for rhetorical effect. The word translated "detestable" is often related to sexual immorality (Lev 18:22–23, 29–30; Ezek 22:11). This sexual allusion impresses on Ezekiel's audience a level

---

4. For other considerations, see Block, *Ezekiel 1–24*, 467–70.

of self-disgust comparable to what they themselves would ascribe to the Sodomites (Ezek 16:56). The Jerusalemites were not guilty of sodomy in actual practice, but Ezekiel draws on elements of Sodom's sin that do condemn Jerusalem: self-confident arrogance and unjust social action (Ezek 16:52).

16:53 *will restore the fortunes of Sodom*: For Ezekiel's audience, this claim is as provocative as the accusation that Jerusalem is more vile than Sodom. Yet it sets the stage for the promise of restoration of Jerusalem itself. God's grace finds no higher illustration than here with the promise to redeem the "likes of Sodom."

16:60 *I will remember the covenant*: There are two covenants referred to in this verse. The covenant that God promises to "remember" looks back to the covenant brokered by Moses on Mt. Sinai in Israel's "youth" (Ezek 16:8). This verse also refers to the establishment of a future covenant. The word translated "establish" sometimes denotes the ongoing enactment of provisions of a covenant already inaugurated (e.g., Gen 17:7, 9; Lev 26:9, "keep"). There is a sense in which the establishment of a future covenant will bring to realization the blessings of the Mosaic Covenant. However, the word "establish" can also refer to the initial enactment of a covenant (e.g., Gen 9:9, 17; Exod 6:4). Since Ezekiel speaks of an "everlasting" covenant that will be newly inaugurated in the future (Ezek 34:25; 37:26), it is best to regard the "everlasting covenant" of Ezek 16:60 in this light. Hints of what this involves were introduced at Ezek 11:17–20. The unfolding of more detail awaits Ezek 34:25; 36:24–38; and 37:26.

Theological Bridge to Application

The potential for divine anger must be reckoned with—not by setting it aside as the construct of some ancient, barbaric culture, but by facing it directly with proper fear. Human love is deficient if its betrayal does not evoke anger.[5] So too, the Bible presents divine love and anger in analogous terms that humans are capable of understanding and appreciating (Exod 20:5; 34:14; cf. Num 5:14, 30). However, divine anger differs in that it is free of the malice and immaturity that often accompanies human jealousy (see comments at Ezek 5:13).

---

5. Taylor, *Ezekiel*, 140.

Focus of Application

Perhaps no other passage in the Bible juxtaposes divine jealousy and redemptive grace in such stark terms. Yet, due to the graphic nature of the imagery, the teacher must be sensitive even with adult audiences. Even though unrelated to Ezekiel's message, the language of this passage could stir painful memories of abuse. Also, both men and women may need to hear the qualifiers offered in **Special Topic: Offensive Sexual Imagery**. Ezekiel does not establish a stereotype of women or prostitutes. Rather, in a subversive manner, it uses prevailing assumptions in Ezekiel's audience to undercut self-righteous attitudes. While the text draws on imagery of sexual promiscuity, and alludes to sodomy, this passage is not a *direct* criticism of those sins and should not be used as such. That is not what Ezekiel is targeting in his oracle. Rather, Ezekiel insists that self-reliance, arrogance, spiritual unfaithfulness, violence, and social injustice provoke God's anger as much as *or more than* the sexual sins he uses as metaphors (Ezek 16:47-49). Self-confident pride leads people to improper reliance on human resources. This happened to Israelites when they turned to idols of their own creation or made treaties with ungodly nations around them. It is a temptation common even to believers. Confidence in one's own resources leads to lack of trust, and ultimately to failure (Ezek 16:15; cf. Prov 16:18).

It is too easy to establish a hierarchy of sins, ordered according to the severity we might consider more or less abhorrent. Not surprisingly, our own weaknesses end up near the bottom of the list and sins of others near the top. In this passage, Ezekiel draws on imagery from the kinds of sins his audience might judge most reprehensible, only to turn his audience's list upside down by naming arrogance and injustice alongside prostitution and sodomy. Granted, the slaughter and burning of innocent children should top anyone's list (Ezek 16:20-21), and North American society has done its share of sacrificing the unborn as an expedient remedy for social tragedy. But the mention of pride and lack of concern for the poor should convict everyone. Knowledge of who constitutes our "neighbor" (Luke 10:29) has reached global proportions. Wright notes how "affluence and complacency" have retarded sufficient outreach to the world's poorest countries.[6] This passage offers a stiff antidote for self-righteousness or any form of spiritual unfaithfulness.

---

6. Wright, *Ezekiel*, 148.

More staggering than the convicting imagery, when we see our unfaithfulness as God sees it, is the portrait of divine mercy and faithful love. God reaches out to the undeserving with compassion. His covenant love is unmerited at its beginning and unfailingly persistent in the end. Love triumphs, but only for those who respond humbly to the call of repentance implicit in the force of Ezekiel's message (Ezek 16:61).

THE SOVEREIGN LORD OF DESTINIES

Ezekiel 17:1–24

Ezekiel's Message

Human commitments are broken with dire consequences, yet the LORD controls the destinies of all.

Key Themes

- Even human covenants are binding in God's eyes.
- Breaking promises incurs God's displeasure and can have dire consequences.
- The LORD alone ultimately determines the success or failure of people and nations.

Context in Ezekiel

In this oracle, Ezekiel turns his focus from the inhabitants of Jerusalem to the actions of their king. But the logical force of his message is the same: considered from every angle, the city justly deserves judgment and so is doomed.

Interpretive Highlights

17:2 *an allegory... a parable*: The word, "allegory" (NIV), can be translated "riddle" (ESV; NASB; NJPS) because it emphasizes the enigmatic nature of the story (Judg 14:12–14; Ps 78:2 ["hidden things"]; 1 Kgs 10:1 ["hard questions"]; needing interpretation, Ezek 17:12). The word translated, "parable," captures the idea of a comparison. For example, in 1 Sam 10:2 (translated there as "saying" in NIV), Saul is *like* the prophets in some ways. In Ezek 18:2, this same word (translated "proverb" in NIV) describes a comparison between people and sour grapes. In Ezek 17, the comparison is extended into a longer story, hence an "allegory" in which people or events are symbolized in terms of descriptive images. The interpretation of the allegory (Ezek 17:11–15) clarifies who the referents are: the kings of Babylon and Egypt are like eagles and the kings of Jerusalem are like plucked branches and vines.

17:3–4 *A great eagle ... Lebanon*: In the ancient Near East, eagles were often used in royal imagery, which attributed to kings the dangerous swiftness of an eagle's attack (cf. Hab 1:8).[1] In the interpretation of the allegory, Jerusalem is the place to which this eagle comes (Ezek 17:12), and the place-name given to it, "Lebanon," is appropriate. Since Babylonian kings would use broader geographic descriptions for territories into which they campaigned, from a Babylonian perspective, "Lebanon" would include the region of Jerusalem. For another example, a Mesopotamian text called the Babylonian Chronicle narrates Nebuchadnezzar's military campaigns, and it mentions the exact events alluded to in this allegory. The account speaks of the territory as Hatti-land (northern Syrian, but also all of the Levant, including Jerusalem): "In the month of Kislev the king of Akkad mustered his army and marched to Hattu. He encamped against the city of Judah and on the second day of the month Adar he captured the city (and) seized (its) king."[2] The image of "Lebanon" is particularly useful because of its association with tall trees. These forests were regularly exploited by kings from Egypt to Mesopotamia, including Solomon (1 Kgs 5:7–9), whose palace included an architectural feature called the "House of the Forest of Lebanon" (1 Kgs 7:2).

17:3–4 *carried it away to a land of merchants*: The allegory begins with an historical allusion to Nebuchadnezzar's campaign against

---

1. Bodi, "Ezekiel," 441.

2. Chronicle 5, r. 11–12 (Early Reign of Nebuchadnezzar II; Grayson, *Assyrian and Babylonian Chronicles*, 102).

Jerusalem in 598 BC. At that time, he took king Jehoiachin back to Babylon as a political hostage, along with many from the nobility (Ezek 17:12; 2 Kgs 24:10-16). The description, "land of merchants" ("city of traders"), is a fitting description for Babylonia (Babylon), the economic hub of the emerging Neo-Babylonian empire.

Special Topic: Hostages in Exile

In order to appreciate the feelings of Ezekiel's audience (the elders gathered at his house; Ezek 8:1; 11:25), it is helpful to understand their status in exile. In the ancient Near East, nations took conquered peoples into exile for several reasons. Sometimes they served as slaves (Deut 28:68). In other cases, such as the Assyrian captivity, the intent was to dilute the populace of a conquered country so as to weaken cultural identity and thereby minimize the possibility of future revolt (2 Kgs 17:23-24). But sometimes, a conquering nation took captive select individuals from the upper echelons of society. They were political hostages to ensure the continued loyalty of their kin and social peers back home. This latter reason was the case with Ezekiel and his compatriots in Babylon (2 Kgs 24:12-16; Dan 1:1-5). As a political hostage, one's identity, status, and well-being was at the mercy of the host country.[3]

17:5 *one of the seedlings:* The term, "seedling," is a fitting image for an offspring of the Davidic dynastic, whom 2 Kgs 24:17 identifies as Zedekiah. The Babylonian Chronicle describes the action of Nebuchadnezzar: "A king of his own choice he appointed in the city . . ."[4] Likening Zedekiah to a "willow" suggests his *potential* to flourish under the rule of Nebuchadnezzar. Indeed, Jeremiah counseled Zedekiah to faithfully submit to Babylon so it would go well (Jer 27:11, 17). Willow trees are tenacious, capable of taking root from broken branches on the ground. Because of their extensive root system, they sometimes serve to stabilize stream banks. However, Zedekiah never realized this potential because he rebelled against Babylon. The shift in metaphor from "willow" to "low, spreading vine" suggests the relatively limited prosperity of Zedekiah's reign.

---

3. For further reading on the Jews in exile, see Fulton, "The Exile and the Exilic Communities," 230-35.

4. Chronicle 5, r. 13 (from the early reign of Nebuchadnezzar II; Grayson, *Assyrian and Babylonian Chronicles*, 102).

17:7 *another great eagle*: After Nebuchadnezzar placed Zedekiah on the throne in Jerusalem, the latter rebelled against his Babylonian overlord and turned his allegiance to the Egyptian Pharaoh, Psammetichus II, in whom he trusted as an ally against Babylon. Zedekiah's strategy succeeded in freeing him from Babylonian control for a while (Jer 37:5). But after some years, and with the succession of another Pharaoh, Hophra, Egypt was no longer a trustworthy ally.[5] As Jeremiah prophesied (Jer 37:6–8), the Babylonian army eventually returned to set siege. Ezekiel warns that this siege would be successful, with horrifying effects (Ezek 17:9–10). The effects of damaging east winds from the scorching desert appear several times in the Old Testament (Exod 10:13; 14:21; Ps 78:26; Jonah 4:8). Here, this wind is a metaphor for the Babylonian army that would come as an instrument of God's judgment (cf. Hos 13:15).

17:14 *so that . . . brought low*: On the surface, this verse might sound contradictory to Ezek 17:5, where Nebuchadnezzar establishes Zedekiah with the intent that his vassal would flourish. However, the final phrase, "surviving only by keeping his treaty" (NIV), expresses Nebuchadnezzar's motive. Nebuchadnezzar's subjugation of Jerusalem in 598 BC, when he placed Zedekiah on the throne, brought the city "low" in terms of independent status as a city-state. But this does not preclude the potential for economic success as a vassal of Nebuchadnezzar's vast empire.

17:16 *he shall die in Babylon*: As described in 2 Kgs 25:7 and Jer 37:4–7, after punitive punishment, Zedekiah was taken to Babylon.

17:18–19 *my oath . . . my covenant*: The word translated "covenant" in these two verses is identical in Hebrew to the word translated "treaty" in Ezek 17:14–15 (cf. ESV; NASB). Zedekiah had entered into a covenant (in political terms, "treaty") with Nebuchadnezzar, and according to custom, such covenants were inaugurated through the swearing of oaths before gods. The content of these oaths invited divine retribution on any party who violated the covenant. The gravity is underscored in 2 Chr 36:13, which notes that Zedekiah swore his oath to Nebuchadnezzar in God's name. This explains the subtle but significant change in wording between Ezek 17:18 and 19. Invoking God's name in an oath makes him a witness and guarantor to the covenant. Therefore, it was not simply a treaty between Zedekiah and Nebuchadnezzar but implicated the Lord as well.

---

5. For details of the political events, see Block, *Ezekiel 1–24*, 543–47.

17:22 *I myself will take a shoot:* The allegory of an eagle and tree refers now to the future work of restoration that the LORD himself will undertake. Whereas Nebuchadnezzar took a cedar sprig and intended to plant only a *willow* (Ezek 17:5), the LORD would raise up a *cedar*, a much grander tree. Human machinations failed, but God promises to cause greater flourishing than even the best of human intentions. Ezekiel offers a peek at the LORD's future plans for his people in Ezek 11:17-20; 16:60-63; Ezek 34:25; 36:24-38; and 37:26. But the promise of restoring a future king is specifically hinted at in Ezek 17:22, with amplification in Ezek 34:23 (see Isa 11:1; Jer 23:5; 33:15; Zech 3:8; 6:12 for other examples of horticultural metaphors for a messianic figure).[6]

17:24 *bring down . . . make tall:* Because Israel's God is the "Sovereign LORD" (see discussion at Ezek 2:4), the results are certain and will bring further vindication of his character ("all the trees will know"). These verses make use of the reversal-of-fortune theme, which receives discussion next in the Theological Bridge to Application.

Theological Bridge to Application

The notion that God sovereignly reverses the fortunes of people is an important Old Testament theme. Several passages are explicit on this count (1 Sam 2:6-8, Pss 107:41; 113:7-9; Dan 2:21). But narratives also illustrate it in a variety of ways. In the ancestral narratives, the reversal of birth order is significant, where the elder ends up submitting to the younger (Gen 25:23; 37:8 with 42:6; 48:19; 49:3-4 with 8-10). Hannah's prayer introduces this theological theme as backdrop for reading 1 & 2 Samuel: Hannah, Samuel, and David all rise above their opposition (Peninnah [1 Sam 1:6; 2:1]; Eli [1 Sam 3:2, 19; 4:17-18]; Saul [1 Sam 15:28]). Even David's fortunes ebb and flow relative to others (e.g., Absalom) after his failure with Bathsheba (2 Sam 15:6). The context of Ezek 17 is concerned largely with the fortunes of kings, which finds collaboration in 1 Sam 2:10 (David becoming king), and Dan 4, where Nebuchadnezzar is likened to a great tree. This demonstrates the sovereign wisdom and power of God, who often acts in ways that display his control of human lives and all of history (Prov 19:21; 21:30).

---

6. Block, *Ezekiel 1-24*, 550.

Focus of Application

Most often, believers in today's society do not enter into agreements by swearing an oath to God. However, marriage vows are usually taken with God as witness, and the custom in court of swearing an oath before testifying would be parallel to the ancient practice. Since the implied accusation of this chapter of Ezekiel is against Zedekiah for breaking his covenant oath, there is a message for today about the importance of such covenantal commitments. Even when formal oaths are not administered, God's reputation is at stake whenever a believer "shakes hands" in good faith or signs a legal contract. The world that Ezekiel projects is one in which God's character is appreciated because of the faithful dealings of his people.

When such agreements are broken, it is as though God considers himself one of the injured parties. A broken agreement means that God's reputation is tarnished because one of his covenant children has compromised their integrity, implicating God as well. The consequences cannot be predicted (we are not prophets), but they can be dire. Certainly, the unjustified breakup of a marriage has ripple effects not only in the immediate family, especially children, but extending beyond to the Christian's immediate faith community. The responsible parties cannot escape the practical effects and even risk divine discipline (see comments at Ezek 3:16–27; e.g., Prov 6:26–35). Broken covenants result in social chaos (Isa 33:8), even if the covenant is only implicit between people (Ps 55:20; Amos 1:9). This points to the idea that there must be an element of fundamental trust between people. Without this, society unravels. Understandably, God views this matter with utmost seriousness.

The good news is that regardless of human unfaithfulness to commitments, God has bound himself to restore what was lost when he exalts his king in the future kingdom (a "shoot" from the cedar; Ezek 17:22). The nature of God, who is sovereign over the rise and fall of any person or nation, underwrites this promise. Even in the here and now, believers can rest in God who ultimately works the "rise" or "fall" of all things, whether political, economic, social, or personal.

THE INDIVIDUAL RESPONSIBILITY TO REPENT

Ezekiel 18:1–32

Ezekiel's Message

It is not past deeds nor the actions of others that finally matter in judgment, rather the heart of the individual turned toward the ways of God.

Key Themes

- God judges individuals apart from corporate guilt or righteousness.
- God judges individuals based on the present disposition of the heart toward his ways, not past failure or merit.
- God does not delight in destroying the wicked, rather he calls for repentance in order to grant life.

Context in Ezekiel

After the standard introductory formula, "The word of the Lord came," the citation of a proverb from the lips of Ezekiel's compatriots frames a new topic of discourse: individual versus intergenerational accountability in judgment. The previous oracles addressed the causes of judgment due to unfaithfulness in the nation's history (Ezek 16) and leadership (Ezek 17). These chapters explored intergenerational and corporate dimensions, but this does not absolve the individual of responsibility to respond to the prophetic call.

Interpretive Highlights

18:2 *children's teeth are set on edge*: The implied backdrop for this proverb is the grumbling by those experiencing God's judgment either in Jerusalem or in exile. They complain they were suffering because of accumulated sins of previous generations of Israelites. This sentiment must have enjoyed some popularity, since it is disputed by the prophet Jeremiah as well (Jer 31:29–30). The concept of corporate guilt and punishment is indeed rooted in the warning of the Decalogue (Exod 20:5; Deut 5:9) and reinforced through prophetic teaching (2 Kgs 24:3–4) and lament (Lam 5:7). Even Ezekiel draws on the notion of corporate consequences in some oracles (see Focus of Application under Ezek 9:1–11). However, the complaint of the people that Ezekiel quotes here appears to express their belief in an "inevitable and uncontrollable determinism."[1] This misunderstanding of corporate guilt launches Ezekiel's rebuttal in the verses that follow.

18:4 *For everyone belongs to me*: The first rebuttal rests on the inference that since every human is the direct possession of God, he is capable of dealing directly with each individual and does not need to "get at" someone through another person, as though they are merely "the moral extension of another."[2] The illustrations to follow assert that individual responsibility is primary. For discussion of the word rendered "one" (who sins) in the NIV, but "soul" in the ESV and NASB, see Ezek 3:18–19.

18:6 *eat at the mountain shrines*: Worship places were often on high hills (see the **Special Topic: High Places and Sacred Trees** at Ezek 6:1–14); and frequently, worship involved communal feasting with the deity, whether it be orthodox worship of Yahweh (Exod 24:9–11; Deut 14:28–29) or illicit worship of other gods (Exod 32:6; Num 25:2).

Included in this list of immoral practices is having sex with a woman who is menstruating. While there is nothing inherently sinful about sexual relations between a husband and wife, nor with the natural reproductive cycle of women who menstruate, in the temple-oriented worship of ancient Israel, such activity or physical state rendered one "unclean,"

---

1. Block, *Ezekiel 1–24*, 560.
2. Greenberg, *Ezekiel 1–20*, 328.

that is, disqualified from entering the presence of God at the sanctuary (Lev 15:18–19). Even the process of childbirth rendered a woman "unclean" (Lev 12:1–8). This protected formal worship from syncretism with common human experiences of sex and reproduction that potentially could corrupt orthodox worship. In addition, Old Testament law prohibited a husband from *intentional* contact with the "impurities" related to menstruation (Lev 18:19); he should not knowingly "go out of his way" to render himself "unclean," which amounts to intentional disqualification for temple worship.

18:9 *That man is righteous; he will surely live:* The list of moral qualifications is similar to others found in the Old Testament (e.g., Pss 15:1–5; 24:3–4; Isa 33:14–16).[3] These possibly functioned as "entrance liturgies" for the temple, used to test the moral conscience of worshippers. Ezekiel repeatedly cites the list in the context of this oracle to define the characteristics of one who follows the ways of God ("righteous"), or fails to do so ("wicked," Ezek 18:20).

It is important to distinguish between the way the term "righteous" is used in the Old Testament, on the one hand, and the technical usage in Christian theological discourse on the subject of "righteousness by faith," on the other. In the Old Testament, the word "righteous" often denotes a class of individuals who are characterized by faithful commitment to the ways of God (Pss 1:2, 6; 37:30–31; Prov 2:20; 13:5; Hos 14:10) in contrast to the "wicked" who consistently violate God's laws and persecute the "righteous" (Pss 1:1, 5; 11:2–3; 37:12, 32; Hab 1:4). The description of the "righteous" in Ezekiel exemplifies this emphasis on one's course of life (esp. Ezek 3:20; 18:9, 24).

The sense of "live" and "die" in this chapter, like its use in Ezek 3:16–21, pertains first and foremost to surviving God's temporal judgment on Jerusalem and the generation in exile (see also comments at Ezek 33:15). Ezekiel does not have in mind questions about "eternal life." Nevertheless, Wright correctly notes that "there must be a deeper reality to 'life' and 'death' for Ezekiel's audience than simply its physical circumstances and timing,"[4] because some relatively innocent people likely died *physically* in the historical outworking of Jerusalem's destruction. For them, to "live" must include ongoing life with God after dying physically in the corporate judgment on the city.

---

3. For a similar example from an Egyptian temple, see Bodi, "Ezekiel," 447.
4. Wright, *Ezekiel*, 114.

18:17 *from mistreating the poor:* This is another case to be aware of alternate translations. For the Hebrew phrase translated "from the poor" (NIV; NASB), the ESV follows the ancient Greek translation of Ezekiel and reads "from iniquity" (cf. NET). However, there is not sufficient reason for the ESV and NET to follow the ancient Greek version here, which was likely attempting to harmonize this verse with Ezek 18:8.[5] The NIV's translation "mistreating" is a reasonable rendering of the Hebrew, literally, "keeps his hand from the poor," which makes good sense in the light of the following phrase regarding unfair interest.

18:19 *share the guilt of his father?* In the light of Exod 20:5 and Deut 5:9, this question is understandable—the Decalogue warns that the consequences of sin extend to four generations. Ezekiel does not expand his interpretive reasoning, he simply denies categorically that his audience is *applying* this principle correctly. He stresses the truth of Deut 24:16, that intergenerational punishment for a crime is unjust. In this, his theology corresponds with both Isaiah (Isa 3:10–11) and Jeremiah (Jer 31:29–30). In order to understand the interpretation of the Decalogue by these prophets, we note that the next verse in the Decalogue (Exod 20:6 and Deut 5:10) promises that consequences can be reversed for "thousands" based upon the choices the righteous make. So the principle of individualism has priority.[6] The difference between Ezekiel and his audience, then, comes down to proper application of the Decalogue to their situation.

18:30–31 *Repent . . . get a new heart and a new spirit:* The application of the entire discourse reaches conclusion in these verses where the prophet issues a direct call to repentance. For comments on the word "repent" (turning in spiritual direction), see Ezek 14:5–6. There is a strong link in this passage between someone's internal disposition (mind and will; see comments on "heart" and "spirit" at Ezek 11:19–20 and 36:26) and their external way of life. Jeremiah speaks of God identifying the "righteous" by probing the internal life (Jer 20:12). In a similar manner, throughout this chapter, Ezekiel defines the "righteous" by their way of life, which he couples with a proper, inward disposition.

The most difficult part of this verse is the command to "get" a new heart and spirit (note the parallel command "Rid *yourselves*"; cf. ESV).

---

5. See Block, *Ezekiel 1–24*, 577 n. 111. For support of the reading "from iniquity," see Greenberg, *Ezekiel 1–20*, 332.

6. Block, *Ezekiel 1–24*, 556 n. 9. The discussion by Wright, *Ezekiel*, 186–90, is particularly helpful.

Responsibility is placed on the individual human. But in Ezek 36:26–27, God promises this as a divine act. So the question naturally arises as to how humans can be co-actors in this with God. But to frame the question this way misses the force of the passage, which is not to explain anything about human/divine synergism, but to *convict* the individual of guilt and the *need* to change. It does not attempt to explain *how* this change happens. God's desire is to move people to change their ways so as to avoid destruction. The call to repentance invokes change and is one means by which God brings this about.

18:32 **Repent and live!** Frequently in a sequence of two commands, such as here, the second command carries the force of purpose or result (compare similar exhortations at Amos 5:4, 14–15 and Zeph 2:3). As noted above (Ezek 18:9), the expression "live" needs to be understood in the context of temporal judgment on the city of Jerusalem and the situation of Ezekiel's audience in exile. In order to escape impending judgment and destruction (i.e., "live"), the prophet calls on them to align their behavior with the ways of God. This would reveal inner attitudes of the heart valued by God ("new heart" and "new spirit"). As the concluding exhortation of the oracle, it expresses Ezekiel's primary application.

Theological Bridge to Application

Gaining "life" in Ezekiel's context meant escaping temporal judgment on Jerusalem. Therefore, Ezek 18 does not directly address our modern theological questions about eternal security. However, one careful inference of this passage is that God is concerned with the *present* state of an individual's heart and an *immediate* response to his word. This applies to a response to the gospel, or to conviction about our manner of life. So while aspects of our doctrine of salvation are not informed here, Ezek 18 challenges every individual to examine both their internal disposition toward God (heart and spirit) *and* their outward behavior as an indicator of this state. This serves the important theological emphasis of this passage, that God does not take pleasure in destroying anyone (Ezek 18:23, 32; cf. 2 Pet 3:9). It is consistent with the contrast in Exod 20:5–6 and Deut 5:9–10, which places a 250+ to 1 ratio ("thousands" of generations to four) between God's wish to bless and his willingness to curse. There is a climactic declaration in the oracle with God's final appeal for people to respond to his grace.

Focus of Application

As Ronald Clements writes, "We are neither prisoners of the past nor yet captive to the sins of others."[7] In this pithy statement he expresses two important truths of this passage. First, the manner of life that characterized one's past does not determine the status of one's relationship to God in the present. As Ezek 18 makes clear, this principle cuts two ways. There is no depth of debauchery that renders a person irredeemable if they turn away from their former manner of life and seek God. Similarly, a righteous lifestyle in the past does not earn "credit" toward God so that he must honor with blessing in the present. Each day requires a new commitment to seek God and his ways.

The second point in Clement's quote is this, while the principle of corporate guilt is valid, it is not a mechanically deterministic principle. People often suffer under the *consequences* of the sin of others, especially those living in the same household (theoretically, this could be four generations). But this is not the same as God directly transferring *guilt* from one person to another. Rather, Ezek 18 dispels this idea and offers hope to those who individually seek him. Conversely, there is no place for blame-shifting; each person is accountable to the divine Judge for choices made.[8] The emphasis on these two truths makes Ezek 18 superbly suited to the call to seek God regardless of past or present circumstances of life, whether there is need to respond to the gospel for the first time, to recommit to a life of discipleship, or to persevere in faith and obedience.

Another relevant application of Ezek 18 is the list of virtues and vices that the prophet uses to describe the "righteous" and the "wicked" person. Such conduct codes are common not only in the Old Testament (see above at Ezek 18:9), but they also feature in the New Testament (e.g., Rom 1:29–31; 1 Cor 5:9–11; Gal 5:19–23; Rev 22:14–15). In no case are they intended to be exhaustive lists; rather, they serve as examples of the types of attitudes and actions one might use for self-examination and correction. Ezekiel lists activities that frequently "top" the list of values of most Christians (e.g., adultery) as well as others that often do not receive as much emphasis (e.g., generosity toward the poor). However, the content of the list is not Ezekiel's main point; rather, it is the principle of individual responsibility to respond to God's invitation to repent and live.

---

7. Clements, *Ezekiel*, 81.
8. Wright, *Ezekiel*, 189.

A LAMENT OVER FALLEN LEADERS

Ezekiel 19:1–14

Ezekiel's Message

Believers should lament when brutally forceful or arrogant leadership leads to the the leader's downfall or devastates those being lead.

Key Themes

- God abhors leadership that is characterized by brute force and arrogance.
- Arrogance in leadership can bring the downfall of not only the leader, but also those being lead.
- Believers are called to lament when leadership and community fails.

Context in Ezekiel

The boundaries of this unit are bookmarked by the notation of its genre as a lament (Ezek 19:1, 14). The culpability of Jerusalem's leadership in the downfall of the nation was noted in Ezek 17. The following chapter, Ezek 18, focused on individual accountability in the context of judgment. This new unit returns to the culpability of leadership, however the accusation shifts from political guilt (covenant breaking) to moral failure (violence and arrogance).[1] The lament is composed of two parts marked by the phrase "your mother" (Ezek 19:1, 10): (1) lament for two lions (Ezek 19:1-9) and (2) lament for the vineyard (Ezek 19:10-14).

Interpretive Highlights

19:1 *a lament concerning the princes*: A "lament" is a genre designation for a song of grief. In Hebrew, a distinct rhythm marks the poetic form that reinforces the somber tone of a funeral dirge (cf. 2 Sam 1:17-27). Rhetorically, it can function as a celebratory taunt over an enemy's downfall (Isa 14:3-27; Ezek 27:1-36; 28:12-19; Amos 5:1-3). But given the concluding exhortation to use this song in liturgy concerning the tragic downfall of Jerusalem and the Davidic monarchy (Ezek 19:14), the mood of mourning, and not celebration, is intended. The song contains an allegory (see comments at Ezek 17:2) referring to several of Jerusalem's final kings, who here receive the title "prince" due to the intergenerational imagery of the allegory (queen mother and crown prince).

19:2 *your mother*: Common in laments, the second person ("you") addresses the one who has fallen (cf. 2 Sam 1:26; Ezek 27:3-4), so here it refers to the (royal) cubs born of a (queen) lioness. It is possible that "mother" refers to a specific queen, perhaps Hamutal (2 Kgs 23:31; 24:18). This fits if the two kings in the allegory of the lions are Jehoahaz and Zedekiah. However, "mother" could also simply be a generic image for purposes of the allegory.

19:3-4 *a strong lion*: In the ancient Near East, the lion frequently served as an image for kings due to their dominance in the animal kingdom and their fierce nature (see comments at Ezek 1:10; cf. Gen 49:8-10).[2] The identity of the first cub is Jehoahaz, who was the only king taken captive to Egypt (2 Kgs 23:30-34). The description of his behavior toward people constitutes an implicit accusation against his unjust and violent administration.

19:5 *another of her cubs*: Jehoahaz's immediate successor, Jehoiakim, ruled with the sort of bloodshed described by Ezekiel, and so the second "cub" may refer to him. He was deported to Babylon; but Ezek 19:9 implies that his deportation was permanent, which does not easily fit the doom prophesied by Jeremiah (for details, see **Special Topic: The**

---

1. Greenberg, *Ezekiel 1-20*, 359.
2. For illustrations in text and iconography, see Bodi, "Ezekiel," 446.

Last Kings of Judah).³ The next king, Jehoiachin, was also deported to Babylon (2 Kgs 24:15). He reigned only three months under siege conditions (2 Kgs 24:8–11), which is an unlikely circumstance to establish the reputation portrayed in this passage. The remaining possibility is Zedekiah, who would qualify as a second son of the same queen-mother as Jehoahaz. But all of this perhaps presses the queen-mother imagery farther than intended. An allegory does not necessitate perfect historical correspondence in all details. Greenberg may be correct to suggest that the entire lament is an amalgamation of these king's stories that is stereo-typical for the sort of violent brutality characterizing the royal administrations during Judah's final days (all Jerusalem's leaders were like ravenous lions; Zeph 3:3).⁴

Special Topic: The Last Kings of Judah

Josiah (640–609 BC) was killed in battle trying to intercept the Egyptian army that was marching to support a remnant of Assyrians being attacked by the Babylonians (2 Kgs 23:28–30; 2 Chr 35:20–24). He was thoroughly committed to orthodox worship of Yahweh, and his untimely death invoked heartfelt lament by the prophet Jeremiah (2 Chr 35:25–27).

Jehoahaz (609 BC), a son of Josiah, reigned only three months before he was deported by the Egyptians (2 Kgs 23:31–34; 2 Chr 36:1–3). Even in three months, he earned a reputation for idolatrous worship (2 Kgs 23:32).

Jehoiakim (609–598 BC), another son of Josiah (by a different queen-mother), was enthroned by the Egyptians (2 Kgs 23:34–37; 2 Chr 36:4). But Babylonian ascendency forced him to align with the Babylonians until the opportunity rose to rebel (2 Kgs 24:1). This brought swift retaliation from Babylon and its allies surrounding Judah (2 Kgs 24:2). Jehoiakim was either symbolically shackled for deportation and never actually taken to Babylon (only the temple vessels; 2 Chr 36:5–7; Dan 1:3), or he was deported and later released (like Manasseh; 2 Chr 33:10–13) at a date before the punitive Babylonian assault.⁵ One of these options is necessary to harmonize with Jeremiah's prophecy that seems to

---

3. For defense of this identification, see Block, *Ezekiel 1–24*, 604–6.
4. Greenberg, *Ezekiel 1–20*, 356–57.
5. Dillard, *2 Chronicles*, 299.

indicate he did not die in Babylon (Jer 22:19; 36:30). He ruled with the same violent injustice that characterized Manasseh's reign (2 Kgs 24:4–5; 2 Chr 36:8).

Jehoiachin (598–597 BC) replaced his father, Jehoiakim, for only three months before being deported by the Babylonians (2 Kgs 24:8–12; 2 Chr 36:9–10). He was later allowed freedom and privilege for the rest of his days in Babylon (2 Kgs 25:27–30).

Zedekiah (597–586 BC), a son of Josiah and uncle to Jehoiachin, was enthroned by the Babylonians (2 Kgs 24:17–18; Jer 37:1; 2 Chr 36:10; "brother" [ESV] here denotes a loose family relationship, cf. "kinsman" [NASB]). His unjust rule and rebellion against Babylon brought about the final destruction of Jerusalem (2 Kgs 24:19–20; 2 Chr 36:11–21).

19:7 *their strongholds:* There is ambiguity in the meaning of this Hebrew word, which explains the translation "widows" (ESV) over against "strongholds" (NIV; cf. NASB).[6] Either interpretation supports the portrait of brutal militarism.

19:9 *so his roar was heard no longer:* This is a crucial phrase for identifying the king to whom the second "cub" refers (see discussion at Ezek 19:5 and **Special Topic: The Last Kings of Judah**). If not a general composite description of several kings, Jehoiachin or Zedekiah might best suit the description.

19:10 *like a vine in your vineyard:* Ezekiel's change of imagery from lioness to vine suits the change in accusation. While "lion" connotes violence, which was the focus of the accusation in Ezek 19:1–9, the image of the vine and branches allows Ezekiel to convey how the king's arrogance ("height," see Ezek 19:11) lead to destruction not only of himself but also the kingdom, like a fire that spreads from branch to fruit (Ezek 19:14). For the positive associations of vineyard imagery, see comments at Ezek 15:1–2.

Where most modern translations offer "in your vineyard," the traditional Hebrew text has the phrase "in your blood" (see the NJPS translation and the marginal notes to NIV, ESV, and NASB). It is helpful for the teacher to be aware that a discrepancy exists here; but the word "blood" is too difficult to make sense, unless it is an oblique allusion to the lavish abundance of royal promise to Judah ("blood" [=wine] of grapes in Gen

---

6. For discussion, see Greenberg, *Ezekiel 1–20*, 351.

49:11; see below). Letter confusion during transmission of the text from "vineyard" to "blood" explains the difficult Hebrew reading.[7]

19:11–12 *ruler's scepter . . . high . . . throne to the ground:* The combination of the lion and vineyard imagery, together with the reference to a "scepter," triggers associations with the royal promise in Gen 49:9–11. This underscores the tragedy of this lament—what began as royal hope ended in a royal debacle (Ezek 19:14). Implicit in this description is an accusation. Often Scripture uses the language of a high or exalted status to describe those who have arrogantly elevated themselves. For example, 2 Chr 26:16; 32:25; Isa 3:16; Jer 13:15; Ezek 16:50; 28:2; Zeph 3:11; Ps 131:1; and Prov 18:12, all use the same Hebrew word translated "high" and "height" in Ezek 19:11. This loftiness is the cause for the vine being thrown down (cf. Isa 2:12; Prov 16:18; although a different Hebrew word appears in these two verses, it is conceptually parallel).

19:14 *to be used:* It is unusual to find liturgical instructions embedded within an oracle; so the application is explicit that this lament should teach future generations about the tragic consequences of violent and arrogant leadership that unraveled the Davidic monarchy. The final point of the allegory is that downfall of these last Judean kings ultimately brought about the destruction of those dependent on them ("fire spread . . . consumed its fruit").

Theological Bridge to Application

God graciously bestows upon chosen leaders privilege and endows them with great potential, as he did the Davidic dynasty (Gen 49:8–11). But he is not captive to human presumption and reverses the status of those who proudly flaunt their privilege and power in harmful ways. Even the great King David himself, who benefited from the reversal of fortune of his predecessor (anticipated in 1 Sam 2:3, 7–8, 10), did not escape this principle. He was brought to a state of humility after abusing power in the Bathsheba scandal (2 Sam 12:7–12). David's kingdom also suffered as a result of his pride (2 Sam 24). So the theology of Ezek 19 finds precedent even in the foundation of the Davidic dynasty. This is an important theological theme in Ezekiel, which finds even more graphic expression in the laments over Tyre and its king (Ezek 27–28).

---

7. See Block, *Ezekiel 1–24*, 607 n. 68.

Focus of Application

The genre of lament draws worshippers into a song of grief so they might experience the anguish of the original situation, learn from it, and know the ways of God better as a result. In Ezek 19, believers are urged to remember the tragic reversal of these Davidic kings, whose violence and arrogance brought their own downfall and that of their people. In contemporary churches, Ezek 19 does not lend itself, formally, to liturgical use in the same way as it might have for exilic or postexilic Jewish communities. However, the text can be used to remind leaders of their vulnerability; since it functioned this way in Ezekiel's context. In addition, Christian congregations can certainly offer corporate prayer to express sorrow over fallen leaders, even when it is the result of sin.

The most immediate application that comes to mind is political (Prov 29:2; Eccl 10:5–6; cf. Prov 11:10; 28:12). Politicians too often strive for the aggrandizement of their own power. Much of the suffering in the developing world stems from the inability of relief organizations to distribute aid due to war or corrupt government systems. In developed countries, men and women can serve their own interest in ways that ignore legal or ethical boundaries, because they have the resources to shield themselves from detection.

But perhaps closer at hand is the relevance of this passage to church leadership. Unfortunately, pastoral abuse of power manifests itself as sexual abuse, misappropriation of church funds, the distribution of opportunities to those "on the inside" relationally, or a "bullying" style of leadership. This style overpowers by wielding doctrine like a club or demanding submission of congregants for decision-making in life. More subtle is cajoling others to "go along with the program" or enticing support for leadership by the privilege of being closer to those in power. These are more "civilized" behaviors in which leaders act in a manner analogous to the violence and arrogance of the last kings of Judah. For more on "bullying" and "mobbing," see comments under application for Ezek 34:1–31.

God deals with such situations in his own ways and his own time. When such sins of leaders are exposed, anger is an apt response. However, it is also appropriate that believing communities grieve the manifestation of evil in their midst, and that individuals acknowledge any part they personally may have played in the organization or relational system that allowed the sin to manifest itself. That is the wholesome result of lamentation in these situations.

DIVINE PURSUIT OF A PURIFIED PEOPLE

Ezekiel 20:1–44

Ezekiel's Message

God will show himself true to his promises when he purifies his people through acts of judgment and restoration.

Key Themes

- God vindicates his integrity to keep his promises.
- The community of God's people fails when it behaves like the world.
- God will establish his rule over his people to bless them, if necessary through judgment.
- God's purposes to reach the nations through his people will prevail.

Context in Ezekiel

The report of a visit from the elders and the date formula signals the beginning of a new unit that ends at Ezek 20:44 (cf. Ezek 8:1). While the chapter continues to v. 49 in English, the Hebrew text begins a new chapter at v. 45. Ezekiel 20:1–44 coheres around three themes: (1) God's refusal to hear an inquiry from the elders, (2) the accusation of continual rebellion by Israel, and (3) the desire of God to vindicate his name by restoring a purified people. But the content of Ezek 20:45–49 introduces the parabolic nature of chapter 21 that follows.

As Block points out, chapter 20 addresses similar concerns about intergenerational sin and punishment as found in Ezek 14, 18 and 19. He traces the structure of the passage through seven phases: (1) Israel in Egypt (Ezek 20:5–9); (2) in the desert—first generation (Ezek 20:10–17); (3) in the desert—second generation (Ezek 20:18–26); (4) in the land (Ezek 20:27–29); (5) in exile (Ezek 20:30–31); (6) Israel transformed in the "desert" among the nations (Ezek 20:32–38); (7) Israel restored to God's holy mountain (Ezek 20:39–44). This long history of ancestral rebellion characterizes Ezek 16 as well, and the movements of this oracle find a close parallel in Ps 106.[1]

Interpretive Highlights

20:1 *In the seventh year . . . the elders of Israel came:* For reports about visitations from exilic leadership, see comments at Ezek 8:1 and 14:1–3. Nearly a year has passed since the last visit and two years have transpired since Ezekiel's call. The reason the elders approached Ezekiel at this time is unknown. Perhaps they inquired because the time constraint on Hananiah's prophesy regarding the end of exile was about to be tested (Jer 28:1–4); or perhaps there was renewed hope for Jerusalem stemming from the resurgence of Egypt against Babylon occurring about this time.[2]

20:4 *Will you judge them?* The refusal by God to respond as the elders hoped (Ezek 20:3; see comments at Ezek 14:1–4) is followed immediately by an accusation, so this is a rhetorical question urging Ezekiel to pronounce an oracle of judgment.

20:5 *I swore with uplifted hand . . . in Egypt:* Although God's covenant with Abraham promised a special election of his descendants as heirs of the land (Gen 12:1–3; 15:13–21; 17:7–8), it was in Egypt that God began to forge them as a chosen *nation* in keeping with this covenant (Exod 2:24; 3:6–10; 6:8 ["I swore with uplifted hand"]; 19:4–6; cf. Deut 7:6–8).

20:8 *rebelled . . . idols of Egypt:* According to Josh 24:14, some Israelites had adopted Egyptian gods during their sojourn in Egypt, and

---

1. Block, *Ezekiel 1–24*, 617.

2. For details, especially the chronological reckoning with Hananiah's prophecy, see Block, *Ezekiel 1–24*, 618–19.

some descendants had retained these idols even to the brink of entrance into the promised land. What form the outpouring of God's wrath took while Israel was still in Egypt is unknown. Ezekiel 20:7 implies that a prophetic voice called for exclusive worship of the LORD. From the beginning of Moses' announcement of deliverance until the crossing of the Sea of Reeds, the entire process of plagues may have been as long as nine months.[3] This window of time allows for such incidents of rebellion and punishment to occur.

20:9 *for the sake of my name:* See Theological Bridge to Application.

20:11 *people will live if they obey them:* The issue is not eternal life, rather enjoying the blessings of life under the covenant (see comments at Ezek 3:16–21; 18:9).

20:12 *my Sabbaths as a sign between us:* There are two important observations here that are crucial to understanding the Sabbath requirement for ancient Israel. First, the word "Sabbath" is plural. The Sabbath law (Exod 20:8; Deut 5:12; cf. Lev 19:3, 30; 26:2 [plural]) incorporates much more than special observance of the seventh day. The fourth commandment condenses into one simple command the requirements that were placed on Israel for their entire religious calendar of feasts, as well as some land and labor laws. The use of the plural in Exod 31:12–17 stresses the ongoing observance of seventh-day rests. But the plural ("sabbaths") is also consistent with the manner in which Moses explained the fourth commandment elsewhere to include other patterns of seven besides the Sabbath Day (Deut 15:1 [Exod 21:1]; 16:9–10, 13–15; cf. Lev 23:11, 15–16, 24; 25:4, 8 [Exod 23:10–13]; Num 28:9, 16 [two-sevens], 26; 29:1, 7).[4] So the Sabbaths were an integrated system that in practice cannot be reduced only to observance of every seventh day, even though it was the central feature of the system. Second, the Sabbath(s) served to distinguish the nation of Israel from other nations. The *nation* of Israel was a unique people who were bound to God in the Mosaic Covenant ("sign between us"; cf. rainbow as covenant sign of the Noahic Covenant, Gen 9:12). This is underscored by the phrase "to make them holy" (i.e., set apart). These two observations have important implications for application (see Focus of Application).

20:25 *statutes that were not good:* The contextual explanation to this puzzling, negative assessment is the next verse (Ezek 20:26). Ezekiel

---

3. Kitchen, *Reliability of the Old Testament*, 250–51.
4. For complexity of the Sabbath(s), see Barker, "Sabbath," 695–706.

frames the giving of God's laws purely in terms of the outcome, that is, what Israel ended up doing with the laws. Choosing the most outrageous example, sacrifice (see comments at Ezek 16:21), he describes how the people perverted the sacrificial system. First-born dedication (Exod 13:2; 34:19) became *mis*applied as child sacrifice, in spite of the explicit instructions to the contrary (Exod 13:11–13; 34:20; Jer 7:31; 19:5; 32:35). In this regard, the Israelites *did* become like the surrounding nations (see Exod 20:32; cf. Moabites, 2 Kgs 3:26–27).

20:26 *fill them with horror:* The translation of this Hebrew phrase in the NIV indicates that God's intention was to allow Israel to eventually see the barbarous outrage of its actions, thereby resulting in their turning back to him. However, the ESV and NASB render the verb "devastate them." If the ESV is correct then the idea is that, as a result of such deplorable acts, God declared them defiled (Ezek 20:30–31), and the consequence was judgment. The verb can be interpreted either way; however, the notion of appalling horror (NIV) is supported by Ezekiel's other uses of this verb form (Ezek 3:15; 32:10) and corresponds with Ezekiel's closing point in Ezek 20:43. In either case, the ultimate purpose was to bring Israel back to the knowledge of him (see comments at Ezek 5:13; 12:16).

20:29 *Bamah:* The name means "high place," for which, see **Special Topic: High Places and Sacred Trees** at Ezek 6.

20:33–38 *I will reign . . . gather . . . purge:* The commitment of God to be king over his people manifests itself in two ways. First, he promises to restore covenantal blessing of life in the land, which means return from exile. But, second, the process of restoration necessitates rooting out those who reject his rule. Ezekiel choses a shepherding metaphor to express this: "pass under my rod," which in Lev 27:32 describes the sorting of flocks for dedication to God. The return from exile is likened to the original entrance into the promised land by Israel's ancestors, during which rebels died in the wilderness on the way. How the return from exile worked out historically so that the rebellious failed to realize the blessing is unknown.

20:39 *Go and serve your idols . . . But afterward:* With sarcasm, Ezekiel releases idolaters to their ways (Amos 4:4; Jer 44:25); but there is warning and promise that idolatry will be reversed. The difficult Hebrew phrase, translated by the NIV as an oath formula ("you will surely listen";

cf. NASB), may be an incomplete conditional warning "if you will not listen to me . . ." (ESV).[5]

20:40 *For on my holy mountain:* The contrast with Ezek 20:29 (idolatry on high places) is important, setting up this description of final restoration (devoted worship of the LORD).

20:41 *I will be proved holy through you:* The founding purpose of the covenant (Exod 19:5–6) was to set Israel apart as a distinct people among the nations ("holy nation"; contrast Ezek 20:32) in order to show the way of submission to God's rule ("kingdom of priests"; contrast the need in Ezek 20:33). Restoration in the land would also restore this original purpose.

Theological Bridge to Application

Ezekiel highlights the vindication of God's prophetic threats in Ezek 12 and 13 and the vindication of God's justice in Ezek 14 (see Theological Bridge to Application in chapter 12; **Special Topic: True and False Prophecy** in chapter 13; and comments at Ezek 14:22). In this unit, the integrity of God's reputation regarding his promises to Israel is the focus (Ezek 20:9, 14, 22, 41, 44; cf. Num 14:13–16). The prominence of this theme is highlighted by its restatement in the final words of the oracle: "You will know that I am the LORD, when . . . for my name's sake." Crucial to knowing the LORD is understanding that he keeps his promises. When contrasted as it is here with the evil doings of his people, the fidelity of God's grace stands in stark relief.

Focus of Application

The worn out cliché still holds true: "It's not about me." Fundamental to the theme that Israel and the nations will know the character of God ("that I am the LORD") is his commitment to vindicate his word, his justice, and in this passage, his promises. In the big picture of human history, both of nations and of individuals, "it's about" God being known in all the earth (Ezek 20:41, 44). So the concern for the vindication of God's reputation should remain the central focus in expounding this passage.

Lest one accuse God of pure self-interest, Ezekiel reminds us that God's vindication of his character entails the realization of his blessing. In

---

5. For discussion, see Greenberg, *Ezekiel 1–20*, 374.

this chapter, that involves restoration of his covenant people. If one's view of the prophetic future includes restoration of a national entity, Israel, then the current condition of Israel illustrates how the nation continually fails to bear true witness to God and instead has created a stumbling block to the nations (see **Special Topic: Modern Israel in the Land** at Ezek 35:1—36:15). The relevance of this passage to God's faithful commitment to his church, both to bless and to reform, is illustrated by his dealings with his people in the Old Testament.

Unfortunately, as this passage also reveals, God's people often strive to be "like the nations." In the faith community, rather than following the ways of the LORD in our dealings with one another and our interaction with the world around us, there is a dangerous syncretism in adopting the manners of political machinery and corporate culture. We accomplish our ends through power or often cold-hearted treatment of those whose presence causes an inconvenient obstacle to our goals and objectives. At an individual level, our personal ethics can appear indistinguishable from the ethics of those who claim no submission to God at all. In this, God is not pleased. He refused to respond to the leaders of the exilic community for this very reason (Ezek 20:31–32).

Ironically, not only did Israel strive to be *like* the other nations (Ezek 20:32); they also disregarded the most evident sign of its covenantal distinctness *from* the other nations, that is, keeping Sabbaths. As discussed above, because Sabbaths were primarily a sign of national identity in the Mosaic Covenant, it would be a misuse of this passage to impose Sabbath-keeping on the church. This does not mean that the theology of Sabbath has no relevance to Christian practice and ethics. For example, Sabbath teaches the sovereignty of God over time and work (Exod 16:4–5, 23, 28–30), the necessity of worship (Lev 23:3) and rest for human well-being through recreation (Exod 23:12; Deut 14:26), and the need for humanitarian justice (Deut 5:12–15; 15:1). However, these lessons emerge from the message of other passages, not Ezek 20. To draw an analogy to the church, the predominant signs of the New Covenant are the LORD's Table and baptism. It is remembering the LORD at the Table that marks Christian worship as distinct from the worship of all other world religions. Unfortunately it suffers neglect in many churches. Similarly, baptism often is not taken seriously enough as an important sign of entrance into the new birth of the New Covenant.

Even as Israel included a mixed "rabble" (Num 11:4), the church is composed of "wheat and tares," and even those truly related to God have need of "pruning" (Matt 13:24–30; John 15:1–7; 17:14–17). God will intervene in his ways and in his time to purge the covenant community in order to shape it into the instrument he intends for reaching the world.

On the positive side, God desires faithful commitment to his kingship. In whatever forms our offering of service take, whether it be worship, ministry to one another, or outreach to the community, we must conform to his designs so that we are a "fragrant incense" to him and those around us (Ezek 20:41; cf. 2 Cor 2:14–16).

SOVEREIGN DETERMINATION OF JUDGMENT

Ezekiel 20:45—21:32

Ezekiel's Message

The LORD asserts the terrifying certainty of his judgment against the pretenses of any who would question his willingness or ability to follow through.

Key Themes

- Those who mock the divine word will be proven wrong.
- Realization of the horror and totality of judgment should prompt fear and grief.
- The LORD sovereignly controls all agents of destruction and any heavenly powers directing them.

Context in Ezekiel

Ezekiel 20:45 constitutes the first verse of chapter 21 in Hebrew. This division is shown to be correct by the continuity of geographical motifs throughout this section ("south to north"; Ezek 20:47; 21:4), the reference to "everyone" (Ezek 20:48) and "all people" (Ezek 21:5), which translate the same expression in Hebrew ("all flesh," ESV, NASB) thereby bridging the English Bible chapter division. Also there is an inclusio (literary bookends) formed by "fire" at the opening (Ezek 20:47–48) and closing (Ezek 21:31–32) of the unit. The motif of the sword also unifies the passage, in which four sub-units are recognizable: (1) the riddle of the sword (Ezek 20:45—21:7); (2) the song of the sword (Ezek 21:8–17); (3) the agent of the sword (Ezek 21:18–27); and (4) the taunt of the sword (Ezek 21:28–32).[1]

Interpretive Highlights

20:46 *the forest of the southland:* The hill country in the south of Israel was more forested in ancient days than today; nevertheless, we should not picture lush forests such as are found in the northern regions. Indeed, the word translated "forest" can also refer to arid scrub, hence Greenberg's rendering, "the scrub country" (cf. "thicket," NIV at Hos 2:14 and Isa 21:13).[2] This appropriately describes the geographical southlands in the region of Jerusalem, anticipating the point of Ezek 21:2 that this is an oracle directed against Jerusalem.

Questioning whether a wildfire image suits the botanical terrain well or not misses the point. The point is the all-consuming destruction of coming judgment. In fact, the metaphor changes from fire to sword in the next few verses of the oracle. Later in chapter 21, the imagery blends in "lightening" as well (Ezek 21:8, 15, 28). The interchange of these three divine weapons is common in the writings of ancient Near Eastern culture.[3]

20:49 *telling parables?* Ezekiel's poetic skill with metaphor evidently became the signature of his style (for "parable," see comments at Ezek 17:1–2). But there is little that is enigmatic about the meaning of this particular oracle. The reference to "south to north" clearly includes Judah and the city of Jerusalem. Therefore, it is likely that there was a growing opinion among Ezekiel's exilic audience to disregard his message as "flashy." Block offers the plausible explanation that in its *details*, the riddle is clarified in the next part of the oracle (Ezek 21:1–2), where the threefold reference to the "southlands" pertains to Jerusalem, its sanctuary, and the entire land of Israel.[4]

1. Block, *Ezekiel 1–24*, 659.
2. Greenberg, *Ezekiel 21–37*, 418.
3. Bodi, "Ezekiel," 450.
4. Block, *Ezekiel 1–24*, 668.

21:2 *preach against the sanctuary:* The ESV and NASB preserve the plural form of the Hebrew word, "sanctuaries." There is no significant difference in meaning here, since the plural form of a word in Hebrew sometimes refers to an object that is composed of parts, in this case the extensive temple compound. The same grammatical use of the plural in Hebrew for the temple appears at Pss 68:35 and 73:17.[5]

21:3 *both the righteous and the wicked:* On the surface, this declaration contradicts the statements in Ezek 18 that the righteous will live and the wicked will die. It is important to recognize the different rhetorical purposes of Ezek 18 and this oracle. In the former, Ezekiel challenges his audience's confusion between punitive judgment for individual sin and consequences for intergenerational sin (see discussion at Ezek 18:9, 19). In this oracle (Ezek 20:45—21:7), God reasserts the certainty of catastrophic judgment on the totality of Judah and Jerusalem. The emphasis is not on the *indiscriminate* nature of judgment; rather it is the *complete finality* that is stressed (see discussion at Ezek 9:5 and the Focus of Application there). The couplet, "the righteous and the wicked," is a poetic device to stress this totality. Bodi points to a similar expression in a Babylonian poem, the Erra Epic, in which a destructive deity kills both the righteous and the wicked: "O warrior Erra, you have put the just to death, You have put the unjust to death."[6] Yet at the end of the poem, a remnant survives the city's destruction.[7] The other hyperbolic language in this oracle, "all flesh" (ESV, NASB; Ezek 20:48; 21:5), reinforces this interpretation. The resolution of the potential contradiction with chapter 18 is in recognizing the situational nature of preaching. Ezekiel has the liberty to craft his rhetoric as appropriate to the context. Expectations for Ezekiel's preaching are different from expectations if he were writing a systematic theology.

21:7 *wet with urine:* See comments at Ezek 7:17.

21:10 *scepter of my royal son?* The Hebrew text of this verse is difficult, as a comparison of translations shows. In this context of the coming judgment, which will affect the royal house (Ezek 21:12, 25), understanding the "rod" (ESV, NASB) as a "scepter" (NIV; Gen 49:10; cf. Ezek 19:11, 14) makes good sense, as does the interpretive addition of the adjective "royal" before the word "son." Since the word, "despises,"

---

5. Greenberg, *Ezekiel 21–37*, 419.
6. *COS* 1.113: 414.
7. Bodi, "Ezekiel," 449.

is grammatically feminine, the logical subject of this verb is the "sword," which is also grammatically feminine and features as the weapon against the royal house in Ezek 21:12. The sense, then, is that the sword of judgment will strike the royal house, treating the scepter that symbolizes the royal house as though it were just another piece of wood. The royal house is nothing to rejoice about or find security in; rather it will be part of the tragedy (cf. Ezek 21:6). The NIV rendering of Ezek 21:13, which is also difficult, makes good sense in the light of these contextual considerations as well.

21:19 *mark out two roads:* This has the appearance of another dramatic act on the part of Ezekiel (cf. Ezek 4:1–13; 5:1–4), who perhaps traces a map on the ground. A hypothetical campaign route from Babylon would have passed through modern Syria and Jordan. At a point along the way, Nebuchadnezzar would need to choose between a road branching west across the Jordan River to Jerusalem, or a road continuing south to Rabbah, the Ammonite capital on the east side of the Jordan.

21:21 *to seek an omen:* Ancient Near Eastern kings regularly consulted their gods before going to war or before making important tactical decisions on a campaign.[8] Ezekiel portrays a plausible scenario in which Nebuchadnezzar consults his gods through three different forms of divination: The first, belomancy, involves drawing from a quiver arrows that have marks on their shafts to indicate the choice (like drawing straws).[9] The second employs a "teraphim" (ESV), which is a divine statue (cf. "gods," Judg 17:5; 1 Sam 19:13). The manner by which divine directives come from a teraphim is unknown. In the third method, a diviner examines the entrails (usually a liver) of a sacrificial animal, looking for patterns on the organ that would indicate a "yes" or "no" to a series of questions asked during the ritual.

21:23–24 *a false omen:* Ezekiel comments on the viewpoint of the Jerusalemite leadership who betrayed their oath of allegiance to Nebuchadnezzar when they rebelled (see comments at Ezek 17:18–19). They are incredulous that the arrival of Nebuchadnezzar's army at Jerusalem could have been directed by a truly divine word. Nevertheless, the outcome of events will prove their guilt and demonstrate the Lord's ultimate control, even over a foreign king.

---

8. For an interesting parallel example from an Old Babylonian text, see Block, *Ezekiel 1–24*, 685 n. 168.

9. An illustration from pre-Islamic Arabia is quoted at length in Greenberg, *Ezekiel 21–37*, 428.

21:27 *The crown . . . to whom it rightfully belongs shall come*: The NIV translation supplies words that fill in the ambiguity of a difficult Hebrew text: "The crown will not be restored . . ." The words "crown" and "restored" in this phrase are supplied by the NIV translation in order to clarify to whom the verse refers. More formally, the Hebrew can be translated "*this* shall not come" (cf. ESV). The word "this" is grammatically feminine, and so the word "crown," which is also grammatically feminine, could match this. However, the word "ruin" is also feminine and would provide a closer referent (ESV; cf. NASB). More crucial to the meaning of the verse is the Hebrew word translated "rightly" by the NIV (*mishpat*; as in Jer 32:7–8). The NIV interpretation is that the "legal right" to the crown belongs to another king who will one day be exalted after the time of destruction (perhaps alluding to the promise of Gen 49:10). The ESV renders this same word, *mishpat*, "judgment" (as in Ezek 23:24). In this interpretation, the "judgment" is the destruction of Jerusalem that has been granted to Nebuchadnezzar as the agent of God. Greenberg's comment is probably correct that "only a menacing sense [of the word] suits the context here," which is also consistent with Ezekiel's other uses of this Hebrew word (Ezek 5:8; 23:45; 39:21, where the NIV translates the word *mishpat* as "punishment").[10] Therefore, the verse anticipates judgment at the hands of the Babylonians, in keeping with the emphasis throughout the near context. Whereas Gen 49:10 is a positive word of promise, Ezekiel uses the wording from Genesis in ironic fashion to forecast the doom of Jerusalem and its wicked king, Zedekiah.[11]

21:28 *the Ammonites*: This oracle against this foreign nation is appropriate in this section because it might appear from Nebuchadnezzar's divination that the Ammonites escaped God's judgment (see the further oracle in Ezek 25:1–7).

Theological Bridge to Application

One remarkable lesson from this passage is the manner in which the one true God can use even illegitimate religious practices to serve his purpose. This is illustrated in the case of determining the draw of the lot, or the inspection of the liver during Nebuchadnezzar's omen consultation.

---

10. Greenberg, *Ezekiel 21–37*, 434–35. See the same assessment by Block, *Ezekiel 1–24*, 692–93.

11. Lyons, *Introduction to the Study of Ezekiel*, 102–03.

These inquiries would have invoked the names of Babylonian gods, yet the Lord exercises his sovereignty over all.

Focus of Application

These four oracles have been stitched together in the final literary form of the book of Ezekiel in response to the dismissal of Ezekiel's message as mere "parables" (Ezek 20:29). The oracles warn against setting aside the Bible as only a literary interest. The Bible is a literary masterpiece and merits close study as such, but it is not *just* an artful human composition. It calls people to face the God whose truthful word is bound together with these human words. The warnings in Ezek 20:45—21:32 had immediate relevance to the inhabitants of Jerusalem at the time of Ezekiel. But in the light of more general warnings in Scripture to all of humanity, the metaphor of the sword should paint an equally grim picture for any who think they need not give account to the God of all the earth. Two other features of these oracles support this universal application. There is the note that "everyone will see" (Ezek 20:48) and "all people will know" (Ezek 21:5) that it is the Lord who is judge. Furthermore, the inclusion of an oracle against a foreign nation (Ezek 21:28–32) reminds Judeans that foreigners are not exempt from judgment.

If the reality of God's *willingness* to judge should not be doubted, neither should his *ability* to judge. The destiny of the most powerful empire in the Near East, led by King Nebuchadnezzar, remained under the Lord's sovereignty and served his purposes. The Lord's control of the outcome of inquiries to other gods also testifies to his universal supremacy over forces in the heavens as well as on earth. In the pluralistic society in which American Christians now live, and in which most Christians have lived in the majority world throughout history, the importance of this truth cannot be understated. The practices of other religious communities and the machinations of government cannot thwart God's purposes. No agent of destruction on the planet operates outside the sphere of God's governance, nor is there any power that can offer hope of resistance to his final intention to rule his creation.

While the reality of God's ultimate justice brings courage to serve him, realization of the totality and horror of coming judgment should prompt grief on the part of believers (cf. Ezek 21:6). This is consistent with the teaching elsewhere in Ezekiel that God takes no pleasure in destroying his creatures (Ezek 18:23, 32).

EXPOSING SIN IN THE FURNACE OF GOD'S ANGER

Ezekiel 22:1–31

Ezekiel's Message

God notes the diversity of sin, and his judgment should never be doubted.

Key Themes

- The sins of people are varied and numerous, but what especially provokes God's anger is violent injustice against the vulnerable.
- God's severe judgment exposes the truth of sin.
- God's intention to intervene in judgment should never be doubted.
- Leadership is particularly culpable for moral failure.

Context in Ezekiel

Although the formula, "The word of the LORD came" (Ezek 22:1, 17, 23), punctuates this chapter, this set of oracles finds its unity in the lambast against leadership, which is largely accountable for the wide variety of Jerusalem's sins (Ezek 22:6, 25–28).

Interpretive Highlights

22:2 *will you judge*: The LORD calls Ezekiel to the task of a prosecutor who will enumerate the accusations he has against Jerusalem. More than any other passage in Ezekiel, the detailed list displays the variety of sins. Only Ezek 18:5–9 approaches this concentration of items (see comments at Ezek 18:6 and 9) where it serves to describe the moral failures that a righteous man *avoids*.

22:2 *city of bloodshed?* This is the same description used of Nineveh in Nah 3:1. The Assyrians were legendary for horrifying brutality in war; and if Ezekiel is alluding to Nahum or perhaps a commonly recognized title for Nineveh, then he is likening Jerusalem to its former hated enemy (cf. Ezek 7:23; 9:9).[1] The combination of violence with idolatry is expressed most supremely in child sacrifice (see comments at Ezek 16:21; 20:25; 23:36–39); but here Ezekiel unfolds a broader litany of moral failure.

22:4 *laughingstock to all countries*: The city that strove to be "cosmopolitan," like all the other nations (Ezek 5:7; 20:32), will instead receive the scorn of these nations (cf. Ezek 22:16).

22:6 *uses his power to shed blood*: The violence that Ezekiel has in mind is not ordinary street crime; rather it is the physical harm caused through the abuse of economic, judicial, or political power. For examples see comments at Ezek 7:23. The thrust of Ezekiel's accusation is against those in power.

22:7–12 *treated father and mother with contempt*: It may be inferring too much to draw from this text that family chaos lies at the root of a violent society. But Ezekiel does begin his list by alluding to the commandment that highlights the fundamental importance of respect for social authority, exemplified by the need to honor one's parents (Exod 20:12; Deut 5:16). Taylor and Alexander nicely summarize the cross references between the sins listed in Ezek 22:7–12 and the instructions from the Mosaic Covenant: exploiting the helpless (Ezek 22:7; Exod 22:21–24; 23:9; Lev 19:33; Deut 24:17); disregarding Sabbaths (Ezek 22:8; see comments at Ezek 20:12); false witness that leads to violent injustice (Ezek 22:9; Lev 19:16; 1 Kgs 21; Jer 6:28; 9:3); corrupt worship (Ezek 22:9; Deut 12:1–4; see comments at Ezek 6:3; 18:6); sexual sin (Ezek 22:9–11; Exod 20:14; Deut 5:18; Lev 18:6–23; 20:10–21; see comments at Ezek 18:6);

---

1. For a text in which the Assyrians boast of their own violence, see Bodi, "Ezekiel," 452–53.

illegal gain (Ezek 22:12; Exod 23:8; Deut 23:19–20; 24:6, 10–13; 27:25; cf. Isa 1:23; Amos 5:12; Mic 3:11).[2]

Rounding out the list of accusations, Ezekiel notes that all manifestations of sin are facets of failure to maintain covenant relationship with the Lord—"you have forgotten me" (Ezek 22:12; cf. Ezek 23:35). This alludes to the warning of Moses in the wilderness that complacency would result in failure to walk in the ways of the Lord (Deut 8:10–14; cf. Hos 4:1–6; 13:6; Jer 3:21).

22:13 *strike my hands together:* See comments at Ezek 6:11. After the accusation (Ezek 22:3–12) comes the announcement of judgment, "I will do it" (Ezek 22:13); specifically, the most extreme and final covenant curse will be invoked, which is exile from the land (Ezek 22:15; Deut 28:63–68; cf. Lev 18:24–28; 20:22).

22:18 *the people ... have become dross ... all of them:* Ezekiel employs a metaphor from metallurgy.[3] Ore is melted in a furnace in order to separate the desired metal from the matrix of rock that surrounds it. The "dross" is the waste material left over. This process can describe the purification of character that results from trial (Isa 1:25; Zech 13:8–9). But, as here, it can also denote people whose condition is proven worthless after being tested in the refining process (Isa 1:22; Jer 6:27–30). The metaphor shifts in Ezek 22:20–22 from the process of differentiating the metal from the dross to a picture of total destruction when ore is melted into liquid. The important point in Ezek 22:18–19 is that *all* the people are proven worthless, not just the leadership who are the primary targets of Ezekiel's accusations throughout this passage. As goes the leadership, so goes the people.

22:24 *not been cleansed or rained on:* Rainfall is associated with covenant blessing (Lev 26:4–5; Deut 28:12), but this is not the image here. Coupled with the phrase "in the day of wrath," the image is one of torrential downpour that can wash away dirt collected on stone surfaces. In this sense, it is similar to the metaphor of the smelting furnace to destroy impurities, as used in the previous verses. Judah's leadership needs purging.

22:25 *princes:* The word translated "princes" in the NIV (also NRSV and NET) follows an alternate reading of the original text that is preserved in the Old Greek translation (i.e., "leaders"). The ESV and NASB follow

---

2. Taylor, *Ezekiel*, 167; Alexander, "Ezekiel," 762.

3. For the technology involved, see King and Stager, *Life in Biblical Israel*, 172–74 and Block, *Ezekiel 1–24*, 717.

the traditional Hebrew text with "prophets." The difference between these two common words in Hebrew is only one letter, so confusion during transmission of the text would be easy. The prophets as a group are taken up in v. 28, so listing them here is redundant; and the image of lions coupled with "princes" fits Ezekiel's style (see Ezek 19:1, 3, 6; cf. Zeph 3:3).[4] Regardless of the translation decision, the point remains the same that multiple categories of Judah's leaders are responsible for leading the people as a whole to disregard the covenant stipulations (Ezek 22:29).

22:26 *profane my things:* An elaborate set of laws maintained a distinction between people, objects, and activity that belonged or did not belong in the sacred space of worship (see discussion at Ezek 44:17–31). The priests were the officials responsible for protecting the sanctity of worship (Lev 10:1–3; 13:3, 46; 15:31; 22:1–3; Mal 1:6–14) and to teach the people the lesson of God's law (Deut 33:10; Mal 2:6–7). Therefore, they bore responsibility for defiling God's holiness.

22:28 *false visions and lying divinations:* See comments at Ezek 12:24.

22:29 *mistreat the foreigner:* Along with orphans, widows, and the poor, the non-Israelite who sojourned in the land was an especially protected class, due to their vulnerability as non-citizens (Exod 22:21; 23:9, 12; Lev 19:33–34; 23:22; Deut 5:14; 10:18; 24:17–21; 27:19).

22:30 *stand before me in the gap:* At Ezek 13:5, the condemnation of false prophets included their failure to speak out in order to turn Israel from its errors. Ezekiel used the metaphor of standing in the "breaches" of the wall (same Hebrew word translated "gap"; see comments at Ezek 13:5). Here, the Lord broadens the accusation to include all classes of leadership.

Theological Bridge to Application

God does not bluff. At the head of the announcement to intervene in judgment is the Lord's declaration, "I will do it" (Ezek 22:14). The accompanying gesture of striking the hands together (Ezek 22:13) reinforces the decisiveness of his intention. One might infer from Ezekiel's repeated emphasis on the certainty of judgment (e.g., Ezek 7:1, 10; 12:25), as well as the repeated inquiry from the exilic elders (Ezek 8:1; 14:1; 20:1), that the prophet's constituency doubted whether God would

---

4. For defense of the NIV reading, see Block, *Ezekiel 1–24*, 720 n. 4.

truly follow through with destruction of his holy city. Such hope was ill founded then, and so today. God's rebuke of sin and his warnings of judgment should not be doubted.

Focus of Application

The ethical values embodied in Israel's laws reveal the heart of God for relationship with him and for relationships within the human community. As such, they are instructive for all people, even though only Israel was formally and directly regulated by the Mosaic Covenant. The extended list of accusations in Ezek 22:3–12 offers a broad sampling for self- and community evaluation.

Some of the accusations of Ezekiel pertain to right relationship with God, particularly unorthodox practices in worship (Ezek 22:3, 8–9). Idolatry is the pursuit of false substitutes for God. Making images, and the magical rituals associated with them at the mountain shrines, introduces into worship false ideas about God—believing that he can be manipulated or limited in some way. How often do Christians go through the motions of worship expecting to earn favor and glean a blessing from God? As Clements writes, "[one can] get things from the gods, without regard for a God-ordered way of life."[5] Also, disregard for the covenant sign in Israel (Sabbath) finds parallel in dishonoring or neglecting the LORD's Table or baptism in Christian worship (see discussion on Ezek 20:12). Despising God's holiness today might take the form of a cavalier or overly casual attitude (is it appropriate to sip our lattes while we offer up to God our sacrifice of praise?). Christian worship is not the same as going to a movie theater.

Many sins listed relate to inappropriate sexual boundaries, whether it be incest or adultery (Ezek 22:10–11). Economic greed leads to abuse of legal processes, making gain at the expense of those with less social capital, whether it be education, legal advocacy, or access to other support resources (Ezek 22:7, 12). In contemporary terms, most inner-city youth are "orphans" practically speaking, and women who have been abandoned by their husbands or boyfriends to care for children are as vulnerable as widows whose husbands have died. Businesses have shamelessly taken advantage of an immigrant workforce ("foreigners"). The number of men currently being released from death row attests to

5. Clements, *Ezekiel*, 100.

a dysfunctional legal system that seeks the satisfaction of a conviction over the just application of evidence and evaluation of witnesses. What attitude check is necessary in this light, whether it be judging another's culpability for their impoverished condition or choosing between social policies? Fortunately, as Ezekiel prophesied to his generation, God is not mocked; and he will bring to justice those who make gain by violence (directly or indirectly), which includes drug cartels, terrorists, and white-collar criminals.

As noted above, the head of the list concerns proper regard for parents. This highlights the more general importance of respect for social authority, but there is also a strong correlation between a society's regard for the aged and the measure of its capacity to choose mercy over greed (Eph 6:1–3; Mark 7:9–13).

Sins may remain hidden, either in the individual's mind or among a close cadre of conspirators, but the day will come when hypocrisy will be exposed as "dross."

There are parallels between Ezek 22 and Ezek 7 regarding the special culpability of leaders. But a broader responsibility is also evident. God calls everyone, not just leaders, to have the courage to challenge the faith community's departure from the ways of God. There might be secondary application for the church's voice in the public square, but Christians too often call out public sin without first applying the accusation to the church.

AN ALLEGORY OF POLITICAL PROSTITUTION

Ezekiel 23:1–49

Ezekiel's Message

Finding security through alliance with political power fundamentally undermines dependence on God and adulterizes loyalty to him.

Key Themes

- When God's people align themselves with political powers, it undermines dependence on the LORD.
- When God's people align themselves with political powers, it can result in behavior that is incompatible with the ways of God.
- Seen through God's eyes, turning allegiance away from God is as abhorrent as adultery.
- The consequences of disloyalty to God can be severe, but God's judgment has redemptive effects.

Context in Ezekiel

There are striking similarities between the allegory in Ezek 16 and the comparison of Israel's history to adulterous behavior in this chapter. Both chapters accuse Israel of forming political alliances to attain security, and both mention the abhorrent practice of child-sacrifice as part of Israel's idolatry. However, as Alexander points out, there is a relative difference in emphasis between the chapters. Ezekiel 16 stresses the origins of Israelite spiritual "adultery" in Canaanite religious practices; but Ezek 23 focuses on the description of the political powers with whom Israel formed alliances throughout its history, beginning with Egypt.[1] The passage consists of four units: (1) Identification of the accused (Ezek 23:1–4); (2) Accusation and announcement of judgment against the northern kingdom (Ezek 23:5–8/9–10); (3) Accusation and announcement of judgment against the southern kingdom (Ezek 23:11–21/22–34); (4) Repeated accusation and announcement of judgment against both the north and south (Ezek 23:35–45/46–48).

Interpretive Highlights

23:3 *prostitutes in Egypt*: Ezekiel traces the beginnings of Israelite idolatry to cultural influences while Israel was in Egypt (see comments at Ezek 20:8). There is a history of *political* alliances with Egypt as well, beginning with Solomon's alliance with Egypt through marriage to an Egyptian princess (1 Kgs 10:28—11:6; cf. Deut 17:16–17). Later kings would also align themselves with Egypt in order to hedge their security. Although not mentioned in the Bible, Assyrian annals record Hezekiah in league not only with other kings in the southern Levant but also with Egypt. Egypt became a hope for Judea against the Babylonia threat (see comments at Ezek 17:7).

23:3 *breasts were fondled*: The language of this chapter, like that of Ezek 16, is graphic and offensive. It is important that we not impose contemporary sensibilities and expectations on a culturally distant text from the sixth-century BC. The rhetorical purpose of this text was to shock the predominantly male audience by the comparison to which Ezekiel likens *them* (see **Special Topic: Offensive Sexual Imagery** at Ezek 16).

23:4 *Oholah . . . Oholibah*: These two names build on the common Hebrew word for "tent": the former name means "her tent" and the latter "my tent is in her." Ezekiel identifies the names as Samaria (the capital of the northern kingdom) and Jerusalem (the capital of the southern kingdom). The difference in the names contrasts the fact that Jerusalem was the place of God's rest (i.e., God's "tent," Ps 15:1; 2 Sam 6:17; then

---

1. Alexander, "Ezekiel," 766.

"temple," 1 Kgs 8:1–11; cf. Ps 132:13–14), whereas the northern kingdom developed its own illegitimate shrine (1 Kgs 12:26–30).

23:5 *Assyrians—warriors:* The Hebrew word translated "warriors" (NIV; ESV; NRSV) is related to another word that can mean "neighbor," hence the NASB rendering. However, the NIV translation is supported by the use of a similar word in Assyrian that means "bodyguard," which makes good sense in this context of terms for military officials. Ezekiel's mention of the colorful garments worn by Assyrian officers is confirmed by the wall reliefs discovered in Assyrian palaces.[2]

23:7 *[Oholah] defiled herself:* While not mentioned in the Bible, Assyrian records report that the northern kingdom began paying tribute to Assyria during the reign of Jehu (841 BC). The biblical record does indicate that Joash, Menahem, and Hoshea paid tribute to the Assyrians to gain support and strengthen their hold on the kingdom (2 Kgs 15:17–20; 17:3–4; cf. Hos 7:11; 8:9; 12:1).[3] One could argue that such tribute was forced and not voluntary; however, there was an alternative available to the northern kings. They could have turned whole heartedly to the LORD. But as it was, the outcome resulted in the total demise of the north (Ezek 23:10; 2 Kgs 17:18–23).

23:11 *Oholibah . . . was more depraved:* Although the northern kingdom pursued idolatrous ways (illicit shrines, images, and Baal worship; cf. 1 Kgs 12:25–32; 16:31–32; Hos 2:2–8; 4:12–13, 17; 8:5–6), the practices of the southern kingdom, Judah, reached more heinous proportions, particularly in child sacrifice (Ezek 16:2, 20–21). But Ezekiel's emphasis in this chapter is on political treason committed against the LORD. Like the north, Judah also paid tribute to Assyria for military protection.[4] One consequence was that the nation's leaders also mimicked their new overlord in some religious matters (2 Kgs 16:10–14). Yet Judah went beyond the north by also joining in allegiance to the Babylonians and the Egyptians (see comments at Ezek 16:26–29).

23:14 *figures of Chaldeans:* The dynasty that came to power in Babylon shortly before the time of Ezekiel was a Chaldean tribe from southern Babylonia. Their art portrayed mythological animal figures on the walls of buildings, as well as human, cultural heroes.[5]

2. For discussion and image, see Bodi, "Ezekiel," 454.

3. For Joash, see *COS* 2.114F: 276; for Menahem, *COS* 2.117B: 287; for Hoshea, *COS* 2.117C: 288. I thank K. C. Hanson for these references.

4. For Ahaz, see 2 Kgs 16:7–9; for Hezekiah, 2 Kgs 18:14–16; *COS* 2.119B: 302.

5. For descriptions, see Greenberg, *Ezekiel 21–37*, 475, 478.

23:22–23 *I will stir up your lovers:* Beginning in v. 22, Ezekiel turns from accusation to an announcement of God's intention to intervene in judgment, specifically, to bring against Judah the armies with whom they at one time or another had made alliances. The first of the three places, "Pekod," refers to a major Aramean tribe (modern Syria). The other two names, "Shoa and Koa," are of uncertain location; but texts from ancient Mesopotamia contain similar names that designate another Aramean tribe to the northwest of Babylon and a group from the mountains to the east.[6] The reference to Assyrians probably denotes mercenaries in the Babylonian invasion force.

23:25 *cut off your noses and your ears:* Assyrian laws prescribe this punishment in some cases of adultery, and Egyptian records describe the cutting off of the noses and ears of women in a harem who had illicit sex.[7] This verse anticipates the result of the Babylonian conquest of Jerusalem, where bodily mutilation and death by sword or fire overtake most inhabitants, while others are taken into exile. These cruel realities are graphically depicted on Assyrian palace reliefs and would have matched Babylonian treatment of the inhabitants of Jerusalem when it fell.

23:31 *her cup in your hands:* Drinking from a "cup" is often a metaphor for receiving the just desserts of punishment (Isa 51:22; Jer 25:15; Pss 11:6; 75:8). Israel and Judah sought alliances with political powers, but in the end these powers inflicted them with scorn and ruin.

23:35 *you have forgotten me:* The accusation of relational abandonment closed the summary of Judah's many failures at Ezek 22:12. Here Ezekiel stresses the same underlying relational failure, only as the opening summary of the detailed list that follows. The behavioral deviations and the relational betrayal are two sides of the same coin. For comment on child sacrifice, by which Judah desecrated worship on Sabbath, see the discussion at Ezek 16:21 and 20:25.

23:45 *punishment of women:* The default penalty for adultery was death (Lev 20:10; Deut 22:22). But the penalty of capital offenses, including adultery, could be satisfied under Old Testament law by payment of a ransom. Only murder could not be paid for in this way. Numbers 35:31–33 and Prov 6:32–35 make sense only if a ransom could be offered in lieu of the death penalty except in the case of murder. So when Ezekiel breaks from the metaphor of "adultery" twice in this verse to note the

---

6. See discussion in Bodi, "Ezekiel," 455.
7. Greenberg, *Ezekiel 21–37*, 482. See *ANET*, 181 and 215 respectively.

violent nature of the sins, he underscores the fact that only the extreme penalty is possible.

23:48 *So I will put an end to lewdness:* The horrifying consequences of Israel and Judah's treasonous behavior would ultimately have a redemptive effect. Jerusalem's destruction would teach the witnesses of judgment as well as future generations that the Lord is the supreme God, as claimed (see comments on the meaning of this divine name at Ezek 2:4).

Theological Bridge to Application

The Lord's covenant with Israel was technically a political treaty establishing him as the nation's king and Israel as his vassal. For this reason, making treaties with other nations was tantamount to political treason, because it encumbered God's people with commitments to foreign kings, and it necessitated some allegiance with their gods who were witness to political oaths (Exod 23:32; Deut 7:2). But the Lord tolerates no rivals, either religiously (other gods) or politically (other political powers). He alone is King of kings and Lord of lords (Exod 15:18; Pss 95:3; 99:1, 4; 145:1; Rev 19:16).

Focus of Application

Because Israel's covenant with God was political by nature, the implications were more restrictive than what would bind a believer today. In other words, the Mosaic Covenant restricted Israel's leaders from entering into political alliances; but one should not infer from this that any political involvement by a Christian today is prohibited. Some Christian traditions do not allow service in any public office or government enforcement agency, such as the police. However, such vocations do not necessarily threaten the fundamental commitment of a Christian to Christ's kingdom, which in this age is not political. The ethical sensitivity that a Christian brings to public service is no different than what is expected of working in the private sector. The message of this text is not against participation in secular, political power, *per se*; rather, it is against reliance on secular power and the risk that such participation presents.

This passage warns believers about the danger that political associations might pose to Christ's kingdom. This danger can function at the individual level or the corporate level of the church. Christians can unconsciously absorb values of political parties that are at odds with the vision of kingdom living. This is not just a matter of the *content* of its value system, but also the *mode of operation*. For example, it is easy to get caught in the sort of slander or misleading spin-games that often characterize politics. Also, real world politics operates on a *quid pro quo* basis, which can bind people to return political favors in compromising ways. Often, the ways of the secular, political world, have found their way from the public square into the corporate life of the church.

Whether in the culture wars of the public square, or in the manner how Christians operate within their churches and denominations, the church in North America has lost credibility and has been torn asunder. This is the result of spiritual adultery, when believers have abandoned their trust in the ways and providence of God in favor human power strategies. The imagery that Ezekiel uses in this passage is shocking. But the shock value is for nothing if it does not heighten our sensitivity to the danger of transferring our trust to the ways and means of political power.

A REAL CAUSE FOR MOURNING
Ezekiel 24:1–27

Ezekiel's Message

No institution is immune from the judgment of God who purges sin and demands recognition of his just ways.

Key Themes

- Divine discipline is sometimes necessary to purge people or communities of sin.
- No institution, political or religious, is too important or sacred to fail.
- Divine discipline evokes the recognition of real wrong.

Context in Ezekiel

Up to this point in the book, all oracles have served the purpose of convincing Ezekiel's compatriots that Jerusalem would indeed fall in judgment and that their hearts needed to turn in repentance rather than hope for deliverance. The time for such threats ends in Ezek 24, which marks the onset of judgment. Ezekiel's message is comprised in two parts: a prophetic metaphor (the destruction of residue in the cooking pot [Ezek 24:1–14]) and a sign-message revealed through the death of the prophet's wife (Ezek 24:15–27).

Interpretive Highlights

24:1 *In the ninth year*: This date formula converts to January 588 BC (cf. 2 Kgs 25:1; Jer 52:4), which is nearly two and a half years after Ezekiel's last notation (Ezek 20:1; August 591 BC).[1] Ezekiel's ministry spanned over five years at this point (Ezek 1:1–3; June 593 BC). His fellow-exiles had been listening to his warnings without fulfillment, so the need to mark the date (Ezek 24:2) supports the vindication of his messages (Deut 18:21–22).

24:3 *a parable . . . cooking pot*: Perhaps Ezekiel enacts another dramatic sign at this point to accompany his oracle, but the reference to "parable" (see comments at Ezek 17:2) suggests a rhetorical image. In Ezek 11, the prophet used the metaphor of a cooking pot as a protective image: a pot protects its contents from destruction by the cooking fire (see Ezek 11:3). Here, the metaphor depicts the opposite result: overcooking destroys the contents of the pot, and some residue can never be burned away (Ezek 24:10–12).

24:4–5 *choice pieces . . . pick of the flock*: Similar to the metaphor of Ezek 11:3, the cooking ingredients may be the leaders in Jerusalem, "choice" and "pick" describing their elite social status. If pressed, Ezekiel would include the entire population of Jerusalem in this image of judgment; but throughout his oracles, the leadership comes in for special attention. That this is the case here is supported by the accusation of bloodshed in the following verses, which Ezekiel attributes to Jerusalem's elite (Ezek 11:1–3; 19:1; 22:6, 25–29) as well as his announcement in Ezek 24:21 that his listeners' "sons and daughters" will be killed. It was the social elite who were taken into captivity (2 Kgs 24:15–16), so their socially privileged children would be the primary referent in Ezekiel's metaphor.

24:6 *the pot now encrusted*: What may have begun in Ezek 24:3–5 as an ordinary cooking song takes a macabre turn in this woe oracle. The Hebrew word translated "encrusted" (*helʾah*) is rare, and so its meaning is unclear. The ESV renders it "corrosion," and the NASB has "rust," which suggests that the metal of the *pot* ("copper," Ezek 24:11) has become tarnished in some way. However, throughout this context, it is the *contents* of the pot that are corrupt; therefore, the NIV probably captures the idea best. As Greenberg concludes, it is the "encrusted residue of cooked

---

[1]. For discussion of the change at this point from reckoning dates based on the year of exile to the year of Zedekiah's reign, see Block, *Ezekiel 1–24*, 772–74.

matter stuck to the inside of the pot."[2] The word translated "deposit" in the next line of the NIV is the same word (*hel'ah*). No amount of scrubbing can remove the filth from this pot, having been so cooked to the bottom. The phrase "in whatever order it comes" suggests that the cooked contents are all spoiled the same, so selection for eating matters not.

24:7 *on the bare rock:* According to Levitical law, when an animal is killed in the wild, the hunter must show the decency of covering its blood with dirt (Lev 17:13). This ritual acknowledges that even animal life has intrinsic value to God. Ezekiel's logic is that the violence of Jerusalem was so hideous that human life did not merit the respect that should be accorded even to animals. The bloody evidence of the city's murderous crimes was in plain sight. Now, God announces the slaughter of Jerusalem's population in similar terms, the punishment fitting the crime (Ezek 24:8).

24:11–12 *impurities may be melted . . . deposit burned away:* Even after removing what can be cleaned from inside the pot, there remains charred food encrusted to the bottom (cf. Ezek 24:6). The sins of the city (the worse of which are metaphorically portrayed as "deposits" encrusted in the pot) are so severe that not even the highest temperatures that threaten to melt the pot itself can burn away this deposit (same Hebrew word, [*hel'ah*], as in v. 6). This is similar to the metaphor from smelting metals to the point of destruction in Ezek 22:17–22 (cf. Jer 6:29).

24:13 *impurity is lewdness:* The word translated "impurity" (*tum'ah*) is the same Hebrew word as in Ezek 24:11. Ezekiel uses it to refer to the full range of Judah's sins, whether idolatry (Ezek 5:11; 20:18; 22:3–4, "defile"), child sacrifice (Ezek 20:31, "defile"), incest (Ezek 22:11, "defile"), or the totality of all their transgressions (Ezek 14:11; 20:43, "defile"). The word "lewdness" (*zimmah*) places Judah's sin in a category comparable to incest (Lev 18:19, "depravity"; Ezek 22:9), idolatry (Ezek 22:9), sexual perversion (Ezek 23:21), and the "abomination" of rape and mutilation (Judg 20:6). The futile efforts of "smelting" described in the previous verse find a more concrete expression here, probably referring to the succession of prophets whose proclamations failed to turn the nation away from sin (Jer 25:3–4; 26:5–6; 2 Chr 36:15–17). Leviticus 26 also speaks of covenant sanctions that increase in severity as warnings over time.[3]

---

2. Greenberg, *Ezekiel 21–37*, 499. See also Block, *Ezekiel 1–24*, 766, n. 14, 776–77.
3. Greenberg, *Ezekiel 21–37*, 503.

In later prophecies, Ezekiel speaks of God's promise to cleanse his people (e.g., Ezek 36:25, 29; 39:24-26). One of the pre-conditions for such cleansing is the purifying effect of God's exhaustive judgment ("until my wrath against you has subsided"). So even irrevocable judgment serves the divine plan to redeem.

24:14 *nor will I relent:* Often, prophecy carries the force of a warning of punishment that might be averted if people repent (e.g., Nineveh, Jonah 3:4-10, see the **Special Topic: Contingent Prophecy** at Ezek 29:19). In this case, the opportunity for repentance has passed, so the LORD expresses an irrevocable promise of judgment using a repetition of phrases that constitutes an oath to take action.

24:16 *do not lament:* Ezekiel's service as a living sign extends to his family (cf. Isa 8:18; see comments at Ezek 4:1 and **Special Topic: Prophetic Signs in the Ancient Near East**). The commands are not to prohibit Ezekiel from feeling any *emotion* at his terrible loss; rather the intention of God relates to his *outward behavior*. Both the command to "groan quietly" and the emphasis on customary mourning rituals (Ezek 24:17) support this inference. Ezekiel's behavior was a sign to provoke the inquiry of his fellow exiles (Ezek 24:19) and to illustrate for them the point of his message (Ezek 24:23-24).

24:21 *stronghold in which you take pride:* This phrase reveals an important theme underlying Ezekiel's agenda during the first 5 years of his ministry (Ezek 1-24)—to convince his fellow exiles that the importance of the Jerusalem temple offers no assurance of the city's invincibility (see comments at Ezek 7:22). Their trust was misplaced, and Jerusalem's destruction would overwhelm their refusal to listen and repent during these years of Ezekiel's ministry (Ezek 2:4; 3:7).

24:22 *you will do as I have done:* In spite of the temple's importance (see Theological Bridge to Application), the horrific loss is nonetheless just (see comments at Ezek 14:22). God demands that the people acknowledge this by their stoic response to the tragedy and mourning instead over their sin as the root cause of the catastrophe (v. 23).

24:27 *your mouth will be opened:* The terms of Ezekiel's initial call demanded silence in community contexts, except for messages inspired by God's Spirit (see comments at Ezek 3:26). But the vindication of Ezekiel's warnings over the previous five years allowed his restraint in speech to end. The sign that advanced his prophetic message was no longer necessary.

Theological Bridge to Application

The temple in Jerusalem was the symbol of God's presence on earth (Exod 15:17; 1 Kgs 8:29; Ps 132:13–14). It represented his rule and visually manifested his glory (Ps 24:7–10; 47:6–9; 96:4–9). From the temple, the LORD ruled invincibly against all armies (Ps 48). No institution on earth was more important. How significant that purging sin and purifying his people is far more important to God than preserving the temple that represented him. One can infer that the manifestation of the glory and just rule of God was vested more in his people than in any institution.

Focus of Application

Because of the emotional trauma, indeed the shock, associated with the death of Ezekiel's wife, this element of the passage can easily capture the focus of thought. Perhaps this is because the loss of a spouse is something most people can imagine, if they have not already experienced it. It can be tempting to consider Ezekiel's (and his wife's!) sacrifice as a lesson about the serious nature of God's call to ministry. While it remains true that God asks his people to suffer in various ways for kingdom purposes, this is not the intention of the sign or lesson from the text. Rather, the message comes from the demand that Ezekiel not observe *outward* mourning rights. His outward demeanor served as an object lesson as he redirected his fellow-exiles' attention to the real cause for morning. The exiles were not to mourn because they were mourning for the wrong reason; it is not the loss of the visible symbol (the city) that mattered but the internal sin that resulted in judgment.

Ezekiel warns against misplaced trust in institutions, particularly to the neglect of God's ways. No political or economic structure is invincible from failure or judgment. None are "too big to fail." No Christian organization is too important to the kingdom to be immune from divine discipline or destruction. Even the institution of the church, which Jesus himself promises will prevail against the forces of chaos (Matt 16:18), is not exempt from the purifying discipline of the LORD (Eph 5:26–27; Rev 2:5). Purifying his own people is more important to the LORD than maintaining the status of the religious organizations that purport to represent him. Believers are in spiritual danger whenever they depend on institutions to guarantee the fruit of kingdom life. This passage directs us to consider what matters most to God—it is the transformation of his people, including ourselves, and not the perpetuation of buildings or organizations.

JUDGMENT ON A VINDICTIVE SPIRIT

Ezekiel 25:1–17

Ezekiel's Message

The LORD judges those who delight in retaliatory violence, especially when it is directed against his covenant people.

Key Themes

- The LORD judges those who gloat over the suffering of enemies.
- The LORD will revenge the violence done to his covenant people.

Context in Ezekiel

Although Ezek 25 moves thematically from oracles of doom against Israel (Ezek 4:1—24:27) to judgment against foreign nations (Ezek 25:1—33:20), Alexander observes that at the literary level, chapter 25 is linked with Ezek 24 by the same date formula (the next dated unit begins with Ezek 26:1).[1] The significance is that while Jerusalem is being destroyed in judgment (Ezek 24), the foreign nations that gloat over its downfall will not escape either (Ezek 25). As such, these oracles against the foreign nations are actually oracles of salvation to Israel, serving to encourage

---

1. Alexander, "Ezekiel," 780.

Israel that the God of justice will act to keep his covenant promises (cf. Gen 12:3; cursing those who curse).

The structure of each of the four oracles follows a classic pattern recognized for judgment speeches: (1) Accusation ("because . . ."); (2) Announcement of Judgment ("therefore . . ."), which consists of (a) God's intention to intervene ("I am/will/have . . ."), and (b) results of his intervention ("so that . . ." or "[it] shall . . ." or "then . . ."). The judgment speeches are organized geographically, beginning with Ammon and moving clockwise, south to Moab and Edom, then west to Philistia.

Interpretive Highlights

25:2 *the Ammonites*: These descendants of Lot (Gen 19:38) settled the region east of the Jordan River directly across from Jericho and became early enemies of Israel during their settlement in the land (e.g., Judg 10:7, 9). More recent to Ezekiel's time, they were enlisted as allies with the Babylonians when they besieged Jerusalem in order to oust King Jehoiakim and his son (2 Kgs 24:1–2).

25:3 *Aha! over my sanctuary*: The first oracle against Ammon is comprised of two parts (Ezek 25:1–5 / 6–7), with parallel accusations and judgments in each part. The word translated "Aha" can be an expression of joy (as warming oneself by a fire, Isa 44:16). The LORD uses it to express satisfaction in just judgment (Ezek 21:15). Here, however, it denotes the malicious pleasure that the Ammonites took over the destruction of the LORD's temple and the exile of his people to Babylon (cf. malicious pleasure of the psalmist's enemies, Ps 35:25). The parallel accusation in v. 6 refers to clapping hands (see comments at Ezek 6:11; note the parallel between expressing "Aha" and clapping hands in Ezek 21:15, 17). For the profaning of the temple, see Ezek 6:5; 7:22; 22:26; and 24:21 with comments.

25:4 *people of the East*: The announcement of judgment ("therefore . . .") states God's intention to give over Ammonite territory and society to bedouin tribes from the Syro-Arabian desert to the east. These peoples constituted a continual threat to the kingdoms of the Jordan valley (Judg 6:3); and eventually their settlement of this region gave rise to the Nabatean Kingdom.[2] Ezekiel describes the "results" of judgment: a bedouin lifestyle (tents, milk, camels) will characterize the Ammonite

---

2. Greenberg, *Ezekiel 21–37*, 518; Taylor, *Ezekiel*, 186–87.

capital, Rabbah. Nebuchadnezzar may have chosen Jerusalem as his target over Rabbah (Ezek 21:18–23), but the Ammonite kingdom would be next.[3] The theological result of this judgment is the vindication of Yahweh's reputation ("I am the LORD").

25:6 *rejoicing . . . the malice of your heart:* This accusation begins the second cycle of judgment speeches against Ammon. The word translated "malice," along with its associated verb (Ezek 16:57; 28:26) is unique to Ezekiel (cf. Ezek 25:15; 36:5). It connotes extreme contempt with harmful intent, animosity in its most excess form. The advantage that Ammon took of Jerusalem's downfall continued beyond the Babylonian destruction (2 Kgs 24:1–2). In the aftermath, Ammon instigated the assassination of the Babylonian appointed governor of Judah (Gedaliah; Jer 40:14–15), and Ammonite hostility continued in the postexilic reconstruction (Neh 4:3–8).[4]

25:8 *Moab and Seir:* The second judgment speech focuses on Moab, although reference to "Seir" (i.e., the heartland of Edom; cf. Judg 5:4) in v. 8 and the "Ammonites" in v. 10 shows the entire region east of the Jordon river remains in view throughout these oracles and will suffer a common fate. The taunt by Moab and Seir, declaring Judah to have been reduced "like all the other nations," likely alludes to the fact that Jerusalem had survived the destruction of other peoples in the region at the hand of the Assyrians a century earlier but that Judah finally experienced downfall as well. The Moabites were enlisted to this end by fighting alongside Babylonian troops (2 Kgs 24:2). As Block notes, this taunt might be an outright repudiation by these people of Judah's self-perception that they were exempt from such calamity due to their special status with their God. In ironic fashion, Judah received her wish to be like all the rest (Ezek 20:32).[5]

25:9 *expose the flank:* The cities listed in this region were once possessed by the Israelites and are named as captured territory by the Moabite king in the famous Mesha Inscription (Moabite Stone).[6] It is rhetorically pointed that these former Israelite cities would be the first to fall to another conqueror, presumably the Babylonians. The word translated "flank" is a geographical description derived from the meaning of

---

3. Block, *Ezekiel 25–48*, 16.
4. Cooper, *Ezekiel*, 245–46.
5. Block, *Ezekiel 25–48*, 20.
6. Bodi, "Ezekiel," 458.

this word as "shoulder" (cf. Judg 16:3; Ezek 24:4). It is possible that the imagery of laying bare a shoulder alludes to the shameful exposure of a woman's body.[7] As far as the archaeological record attests, the lands of Ammon and Moab never recovered from the Babylonian destruction of their cities not many years after the destruction of Jerusalem.[8]

25:12 *Edom took revenge:* Edom's behavior and attitude in the plundering of Jerusalem was stereotypical of Judah's enemies, and so Edom warranted the focused attention of a separate prophetic book, Obadiah (Obad 10-14; cf. Ps 137:7). Perhaps because of the special family relationship between Israel and Edom their betrayal was so heinous (cf. Num 20:15; Deut 23:7-8).[9] While the term "malice" (*she'at*) describes the disposition of Ammon (Ezek 25:6) and Philistia (Ezek 25:15), the verdict differs for Edom: "very guilty"—a grammatical construction that combines two forms of the same verb for emphatic effect (*'asham*, to be guilty; Num 5:6; Hos 13:16; and Lev 6:7 for the noun "guilt").

25:13 *from Teman to Dedan:* While precise locations are uncertain, this geographical designation might name the southern and northern limits of Edom as a merism for the entire land (cf. Jer 49:7-8), similar to the way that "Dan to Beersheba" delimits the complete territorial homeland of Israel (Judg 20:1; 2 Sam 17:11).

25:14 *know my vengeance:* Whereas Ammon and Moab are punished with the purpose that they know the LORD, the outcome of Edom's judgment is uniquely described as experiential knowledge of God's vengence. This is consistent with the exceptional culpability of Edom, Israel's "brother" (see above).

25:15 *ancient hostility:* From the earliest days of Israel's settlement in the land, the Philistines were arch enemies and afflicted them with particularly harsh service during the days of the judges (cf. Josh 13:2-3; Judg 3:31; 1 Sam 13:19-20).

25:16 *Kerethites:* The Philistines settled the eastern seaboard of the Mediterranean from locations in the Aegean, and "**Kerethites**" designates the island of Crete in particular (cf. Zeph 2:5). This name sounds very similar to the Hebrew word "to cut off" (*krt*), and so the wordplay

---

7. Greenberg, *Ezekiel 21-37*, 520-21.
8. Greenberg, *Ezekiel 21-37*, 524.
9. Block, *Ezekiel 25-48*, 23.

provides a rhetorically pointed designation for the Philistines as the object of God's judgment.[10]

Theological Bridge to Application

This section of Ezekiel begins a series of oracles against foreign nations. Other than the instance of Jonah travelling to Nineveh to preach a message of judgment against it, there is no evidence in the Old Testament that prophets actually delivered messages to other places. Ezekiel was confined to a local district of Babylon and his words would never have been heard in such far off places. So, as noted above in the contextual introduction to this chapter, such oracles served more as assurances to Israel that God is universally just (e.g., Pss 9:19; 58:11; 96:10) and that he will fulfill his covenant obligations to Israel by defeating her enemies (cf. Gen 12:3). The judgment of God is a terrifying thing, but it is also a comforting realization that the God of all the earth will act justly to set things right.

Interestingly, Babylon is not mentioned among these nations, perhaps, as Block notes, because Ezekiel identified Babylon as God's chief instrument of judgment against Israel, so the absence is consistent with Ezekiel's emphasis. The nations mentioned, especially Tyre and Egypt, were enemies of Babylon and so stood in the way of Babylon's mission as God's unwitting agent (cf. Hab 1:6).[11]

The manner of God's judgment entails proportionate punishment. Ammon rejoiced in Judah's loss of land (Ezek 25:3), so Ammon will be dispossessed of their land (Ezek 25:4). The Philistines acted in vengeance (Ezek 25:15), so God will take vengeance on them (Ezek 25:17).

Focus of Application

As is often the case with prophetic oracles, since the announcement of judgment is specific to a certain people and situation, the most transferable lesson is found in the reasons for God's judgment (the accusation). The things that angered God in days of old continue to anger him today, regardless of the perpetrator. In this set of oracles, the common thread in the accusations is the excessively virulent attitude on the part of people

10. Bodi, "Ezekiel," 459.
11. Block, *Ezekiel 25–48*, 4.

who gloat over the demise of those they dislike. The same principle surfaces in wisdom literature (Prov 17:5). While the first half of this proverb applies the warning with respect to mocking the poor, the second line echoes this with a broader generalization. An insulting posture or desire for calamity on others is condemned here and in Ezekiel. This does not exclude the cry for kingdom justice (e.g., Pss 7:9; 12:3-4; 58:1-11; 59:13; 82:1-8; 94:1-7). Even in the New Testament one sees the call for retributive justice at the hand of God (e.g., 2 Thess 1:5-10; Rev 6:9-10). The key is that justice is left in the hand of God, who alone can judge with equity. The point of Ezekiel's message is that our attitudes must always be checked; excess animosity and malice is sin.

This passage speaks to Christians who fail to check the vehemence and malice with which they express their (sometimes legitimate) anger against those who threaten their values. The reputation of Christ has been damaged and the integrity of the church to proclaim the gospel has been diminished by the ill temperament and tongue of Christian voices in the public square. Ezekiel 25 is a call to civility.

Since God's vengeance pours out on Judah's enemies in this context, in accord with his special relationship with them (e.g., Deut 4:7, 33-34; 32:10; 2 Sam 7:23), the question arises whether it is appropriate to criticize modern day Israel. Genesis 12:3 is often used to teach that such criticism is never appropriate. On the one hand, the posture of the nations condemned in Ezek 25 is one of contempt and malice that is commensurate with the "cursing" referred to in Gen 12:3. But criticism is not the same as cursing, and neither Gen 12:3 nor Ezek 25 can be used as an excuse to muzzle legitimate criticism of a nation that should act according to the standards demanded by Moses and the prophets. Others can cite Israel's own Scriptures in regard to its failures and refuse to be complicit in them (see also **Special Topic: Modern Israel in the Land** at Ezek 35:1—36:15). But only God is entitled to gloat over Israel's catastrophes (e.g., Deut 28:63; Ezek 6:11).[12]

---

12. Greenberg, *Ezekiel 21-37*, 526.

THE SINKING OF TYRE'S WEALTH

Ezekiel 26:1—27:36

Ezekiel's Message

Material resources offer no security from calamity or the horror of judgment.

Key Themes

- The LORD will revenge the violence done to his covenant people.
- The judgment of God is a horrifying prospect.
- The most renowned human resources provide no insurance against calamity or judgment.

Context in Ezekiel

In Ezek 25, the LORD calls out nations who acted treacherously against Judah or gloated over its demise. This theme continues in chapter 26 (Ezek 26:2) with a declaration of judgment against the city of Tyre. However, the insertion of a date formula in Ezek 26:1 as well as the exceptional length of the prophet's treatment of Tyre (Ezek 26:1—28:19) underscores a special emphasis for this city. The same observation applies to Egypt (Ezek 29:1—32:32) which is characterized by its own date formula and similar length. Block notes that in the aftermath of Babylon's conquest of the Eastern Mediterranean, only Tyre and Egypt retained any degree of independence. He suggests, quite reasonably, that these two nations receive special emphasis because of Babylon's role as an instrument of the LORD's judgment in the region. Those standing against God's agent will in no way escape eventual judgment.[1]

Interpretive Highlights

26:1 *In the eleventh month of the twelfth year:* The ESV and NASB, following the Hebrew more closely, translate this phrase "In the eleventh year..." This is too early, since the oracle presupposes knowledge of Jerusalem's destruction (Ezek 26:2), but this news does not reach the prophet until the twelfth year (Ezek 33:21). The date formula is uncharacteristically short without a month designation, and the NIV translation fills out the calendar formula accordingly, assuming an accidental omission of these words some time during the transmission of the text.[2]

26:2 *I will prosper:* The material prosperity of Tyre is at the heart of Ezekiel's oracles against it. The downfall of Jerusalem meant the removal of its control over valuable trade routes ("gate to the nations") between the Mediterranean coast and the inland regions to the southeast. Since Tyre was the "entry point to the sea" (Ezek 27:3), the freer trade routes worked to its advantage. This combination of greed and gloating forms the foundation of God's accusation and judgment ("therefore," Ezek 26:3).

26:3 *many nations:* It is important to understand that the judgment of Tyre played out historically over a long period of time. Its demise came at the hands not only of Babylon, which destroyed the mainland settlements of this island fortress (Ezek 26:8), but Persia weakened its mercantile ambitions, and eventually the physical destruction of the island fortress itself was the work of Alexander the Great in 322 BC.[3] Comparing these successive attacks to sea waves lapping against the shore of the island is a fitting metaphor.

26:4–6 *a bare rock ... her settlements on the mainland:* The name of the city, "Tyre," means "rock." The primary center of the city was built on a bare island, providing stout defense for this maritime community with a robust navy. But across the narrow gap of sea on the mainland was an

---

1. Block, *Ezekiel 25–48*, 32.
2. For discussion of details, see Block, *Ezekiel 25–48*, 34–35 and n. 27.
3. Block, *Ezekiel 25–48*, 31–32.

urban extension of the city—literally, "daughters on the mainland" (e.g., ESV; NASB), referring to settlements that were secondary to the main urban hub. Complete destruction of the city entailed both parts. Reducing Tyre to a mere "rock" is a graphic way of saying that the aftermath of destruction would look as though there never had been settlement on the island at all.

26:7 **Nebuchadnezzar**: Of the "many nations," the most immediate onslaught was from Babylon, probably not long after the destruction of Jerusalem. The king never breached the city walls of the island fortress, but he laid waste to the city's expansion on the mainland (Ezek 26:8). The island fortress submitted to Nebuchadnezzar's siege and its king was deposed.[4] The shift in pronouns from third singular ("his," i.e., Nebuchadnezzar's) used throughout Ezek 26:7–11 to the first singular ("I," i.e., God), resumed in v. 13 might be significant. The *complete* destruction of Tyre, including the island fortress, would eventually be carried out by later instruments of God's judgment ("many nations," v. 3; "they," v. 12; i.e., Alexander the Great).[5] Ezekiel never predicted that the complete destruction would come at Nebuchadnezzar's hand alone. God would bring other nations, like waves, against Tyre's shores.

26:15 **the coastlands tremble**: Prophetic oracles often begin with an accusation of wrong doing (Ezek 26:2), followed by an announcement of judgment ("therefore . . . ," Ezek 26:3; see Context in Ezekiel for Ezek 25:1–17). This announcement consists of God's intention to intervene (marked by "I will") as well as descriptions of the scene of judgment (e.g., Nebuchadnezzar's attack in Ezek 26:7–12). Beginning in Ezek 26:15 is a further description of the result—the former trading partners of Tyre will become aghast at what they hear and witness ("coastlands" refers to ports of trade, Ezek 27:3, 6, 15, 35). Fear and mourning is displayed by laying aside royal attire (Jonah 3:6), as well as sitting on the ground (Job 2:12–13). The leaders of these regions utter lament at the desolation, which not only diminishes their own prosperity in partnership with Tyre's trade, but it also signals the potential for their own demise. If the greater is vulnerable, then how much more the lesser.

26:17 **a lament**: This word describes funeral songs (2 Sam 1:17; Amos 8:10), and is a frequent theme in Ezekiel's grim prophecies of judgment (Ezek 2:10; 19:1, 14; 27:2, 32; 28:12; 32:2, 16). The reversal of fame

---

4. Bodi, "Ezekiel," 461.
5. Cooper, *Ezekiel*, 253–54.

and power marks the central theme of this lament. While it flourished, Tyre put fear into the hearts of people. Tyre continued to generate terror in the hearts of others at its collapse, but its glory days were over.

26:19 *I bring the ocean depths over you:* If the focus of Ezek 26:15–18 was on the results of judgment, Ezek 26:19–21 revisits the personal intervention by the LORD himself. As a fortress island that earned its wealth by mastering ocean trade, Tyre represented the highest accomplishment of humanity against the forces of the sea. Yet, in ironic fashion, Ezekiel describes Tyre's death in terms of the sea's destructive potential on the city (cf. Jonah 2:3, 5; Job 38:8–11).

26:20 *the pit . . . people of long ago:* The word translated "pit" can refer to any hole dug in the ground, usually a cistern (Gen 37:20; Exod 21:33). But often in Old Testament usage it designates the manner of burial, and as such, it also denotes the underworld realm of the dead (Pss 30:4; 55:23; 88:6; Ezek 32:22–23). The permanency of death, and so Tyre's destruction, is emphasized by the expression, "people of long ago" (cf. Ps 143:3; Lam 3:6).[6]

26:20 *you will not return or take your place:* The Hebrew text is difficult and possibly corrupted in transmission (compare the ESV, "you will not be inhabited, but I will set beauty . . ." [with NASB]). The NIV (with NET; NRSV) follows the ancient Greek translation here as the best witness to the original text. But either reading leads to the same interpretation, namely, that Tyre will be permanently destroyed, in contrast to the vitality enjoyed in the land of the living.

27:2 *take up a lament:* Tyre's renowned sea power, noted briefly in the lament by Tyre's trading partners (Ezek 26:17), receives expanded elaboration in chapter 27. The lament adopts the metaphor of a ship, whose eventual sinking graphically illustrates the demise of the city and its maritime prowess. The flow of this long unit can be summarized in three parts: (1) the matchless beauty of the ship's construction and its elite crew (Ezek 27:3–11); (2) the extensive reach of the ship's trading network and the riches of its cargo (Ezek 27:12–24); (3) the cataclysmic sinking of the ship (Ezek 27:25–36).

27:3 *I am perfect in beauty:* The first part of the lament is framed by the theme of perfect beauty (Ezek 27:3 and 11). The ship's construction exhibits the finest craftsmanship and materials (Ezek 27:4–7).

27:10 *soldiers in your army:* At first impression, the language of Ezek 27:10–11 sounds like a mercenary force employed as land infantry. While

---

6. Block, *Ezekiel 25–48*, 48–49.

one normally thinks of soldiers as infantry on the ground, warships in ancient days utilized marines for combat ("all the men of war who are in it," Ezek 27:27). The modern distinction between freighters and warships was not strictly maintained. Artwork dating from before Ezekiel's time portrays shields hung on the deck rails of such ships.[7] However, the mention of "walls" and "towers" in v. 11 shows that the difference between city and ship are blurred in this poetic rendition.[8]

27:12 *Tarshish:* Tyre's trade network extended to the coasts of modern Spain and Morocco. The details of locations and products listed in Ezek 27:12–24 are unclear due to a heavy concentration of rare words. But the main point is clear. As Block notes, while Tyre was dependent on its trading partners, the controlling power in this extensive network was clearly Tyre ("entry point to the sea," Ezek 27:3).[9]

27:26 *east wind will break you:* In spite of the wealth in the ship's cargo (Ezek 27:25), all will be lost when it suffers shipwreck (Ezek 27:27, 34). The danger that east winds posed for maritime travel is showcased in Ps 48:7.[10] The catastrophic loss elicits two responses from partnering nations. First, implicit in the lament is the awareness on the part of the nations of their own lost opportunity for gain (Ezek 27:33). Second, the lament gives way to horror (cf. Ezek 26:16, 18) and taunt (Ezek 27:36). But it is the "horrible end" of Tyre that carries the final note, both of this chapter and the last (Ezek 26:21).

Theological Bridge to Application

As noted in the commentary above, the exceptional treatment of Tyre (Ezek 26–28, and Pharaoh in Ezek 29–32) makes clear that, in spite of temporary appearances, God's judgment is inescapable. In the case of Tyre, judgment was ongoing over two hundred years, beginning with Nebuchadnezzar (586 BC) and ending with Alexander the Great (332 BC). God is patient in the execution of his judgment; its timing is under his control. It may be imminent and without delay (e.g., Ezek 7 and Hab 2:3 for Jerusalem's judgment). At times his patience allows for repentance

---

7. Greenberg, *Ezekiel 21–37*, 552. For an illustration of an ancient Phoenician warship from the period (probably of Tyre), see Bodi, "Ezekiel," 463.

8. Block, *Ezekiel 25–48*, 63.

9. Block, *Ezekiel 25–48*, 54, 71.

10. Greenberg, *Ezekiel 21–37*, 561.

(Jonah 3:4, 10). But it is foolish to imagine that any measure of human resources, in this case Tyre's wealth, can hold his judgment forever at bay.

Focus of Application

The accusation underlying this oracle (Ezek 26:2) is the same as the previous chapter of Ezekiel—God will not tolerate gloating attitudes or vindictive actions against his people (cf. Prov 17:5 for gloating over disaster of any kind). But what makes the oracle against Tyre different is the lengthy description of judgment, especially the unusual lament that eulogizes the power and renown of the city. It is the unique strength of the city that highlights the gravity of its fall and the power of God to bring it to pass.

Bodi notes that over time, Tyre shifted the goals of its trade from satisfying basic domestic needs to commercialization. Using its monopoly on sea transport, it exploited its neighbors for the maximization of profit. A line from Homer's *Odyssey* recounts the reputation earned by Phoenician sea trade (of which Tyre was at the center): "Phoenicians, men famed for their ships, greedy knaves, bringing countless trinkets in their black ship."[11] Ancient historians report that it was not just trinkets, but kidnapped youth as well, whom they sold as slaves. Ezekiel 27:13 notes their purchase of slaves from others. The admirable qualities of Tyre's prowess bore a dark side, expressed in commercial exploitation and human trafficking. It is not surprising that John's vision in Revelation alludes to Tyre's attributes to describe the downfall of "Babylon" (Rev 18:9–22). Human greed today aspires to maximize wealth, driving inexorably toward international proportions, witnessed today in the dark side of globalization. And human trafficking respects no international boundaries.

But no amount of wealth, commercial power, or human resources can offer insurance against calamity, let alone God's judgment. Nor does human flourishing equate with the accumulation of more "stuff." It is not difficult to recall the many famous and powerful nations, institutions, or people who have met shocking ends. Like Tyre's partners, we also respond with dismay and horror when we witness a tragic downfall (Ezek 26:16–18; 27:30–32, 35). In such moments, we catch a glimpse of our own inherent vulnerability.

---

11. See Bodi, "Ezekiel," 460–61 for discussion of Tyre's commercial empire. For quote from Homer, see *Odyssey* 15.415–416.

THE CORRUPTION OF TYRE'S PRIDE

Ezekiel 28:1–26

Ezekiel's Message

The Lord brings down the proud and greedy for the rescue of those who trust in him.

Key Themes

- Stockpiling wealth can lead to self-sufficiency and self-aggrandizement.
- Arrogance and greed lead to destruction.
- The Sovereign Lord commits himself to the rescue of those who trust in him.

Context in Ezekiel

The proclamation of judgment against Tyre continues from chapters 26–27 into chapter 28 with a second oracle, but the emphasis shifts from addressing material wealth to the pride that it engenders. This second oracle follows the same structure: (1) Judgment speech against Tyre (Ezek 28:1–10 [Ezek 26:1–21]); (2) followed by a highly metaphorical Lament (Ezek 28:11–19 [Ezek 27:1–36]).

Concluding Ezek 28 is an oracle against Sidon and an announcement of salvation for Israel (Ezek 28:20–26), which technically speaking comprises its own literary unit. However, it is included in this commentary with the second oracle against Tyre for several reasons. First, for practical reasons it may not justify its own treatment as a homiletical or teaching unit. But the connection with what precedes is not forced. The city of Sidon is part of the Phoenician culture that shared maritime success; and Sidon was second only to Tyre in power, succeeding Tyre in preeminence after its demise. In addition, the oracle against Sidon brings closure to the group of judgment oracles against the nations that participated in and gloated over Judah's destruction (Ammon [Ezek 25:3, 6]; Moab [Ezek 25:8]; Edom [Ezek 25:12]; Philistia [Ezek 25:15]; Tyre [Ezek 26:2]; Sidon [included in Ezek 28:24]). This broader literary unit from Ezek 25:1—28:24 is capped by a brief promise of restoration for Israel (Ezek 28:25–26). As noted in the contextual introduction to Ezek 25, oracles of judgment against foreign nations are conversely oracles of salvation to Israel. They serve to encourage Israel that the Lord will act to keep his covenant promises (cf. Gen 12:3). The end cap to this section makes this theological point explicit.

Interpretive Highlights

28:2 *ruler of Tyre:* The word translated "ruler" ("prince," in most translations) is a generic term for any high ranking leader (priest, Jer 20:1; military officer, 2 Chr 32:21). Its use in parallel with the word "king" in Ps 78:12 cautions against finding any significant difference when Ezekiel addresses the "king of Tyre" in Ezek 28:12. The prophet interchanges different words for the same individual elsewhere ("princes/kings" of coastlands in Ezek 26:16; 27:35).[1]

28:2 *pride in your heart:* The prophetic accusation shifts from Tyre's self-reliance on its wealth to the arrogance of its representative ruler (the word, "because," is explicit in the Hebrew text; cf. ESV, NASB). The heart is the center of both emotional and mental activity—a term that can refer to feelings (Ps 25:17), wishes (Ps 21:2), intellect (Ps 90:12), and will (2 Sam 7:3; literally, "in your heart"). As such, it denotes the controlling disposition of an individual, which in this case is self-exaltation to the highest grandeur.

---

1. Greenberg, *Ezekiel 21–37*, 580.

28:2 *I am a god:* In the ancient Near East, divine kingship was not a political-religious belief anywhere except in Egypt. There is evidence that Tyrian kings participated in a ritual that celebrated the revitalization of the patron god of Tyre in which the human king played the role of the deity.[2] And the name of their god was "Melqart" (*mlk qrt*) which means "king of the city." Whether the king of Tyre actually claimed divine status is not crucial to the point. Ezekiel's accusation stands, if only because the king's arrogance was so excessive that it amounted to a claim to divinity ("you are a man, not a god, even though you set your heart like a heart of a god"; cf. ESV; NASB).

28:3 *Daniel:* This could either be the "Daniel" of the Bible, a contemporary of Ezekiel, or the Ugaritic "Dan'el," who ruled as a legendary king in the same geographical region as Tyre. It is true that wisdom plays no special role in the one surviving story about Ugarit's Dan'el; however, such a reputation for a legendary king is not surprising. The close geographical and cultural association between Ugarit and Tyre is a strong argument in favor of comparison between these two in Ezekiel's rhetoric. Also, the Ugaritic Dan'el better fits the rhetorical argument in Ezek 14, where the name appears as well (see **Special Topic: Daniel of Judah or Dan'el of Ugarit?** at Ezek 14:14).

28:5 *because of your wealth:* This verse is the key to understanding Ezekiel's accusation. Accumulation of wealth is a dangerous thing, not only because it can lead to a sense of security in one's independence (Ezek 26–27) but also because it can lead to prideful celebration of one's own skill.

28:7 *beauty . . . shining splendor:* The wealth of Tyre was admired by surrounding nations and taken to heart by the Tyrians in an unwholesome way (Ezek 27:3, 11). In ancient Near Eastern texts, kings are frequently described in glowing terms ("awe-inspiring luminosity") that befits divinity.[3] Such language even appears in the Old Testament for Israel's king (compare Ps 45:3 with Ps 29:2). But the ruler of Tyre took such accolades to a prideful level.

28:10 *death of the uncircumcised:* If the ancient historian Herodotus is correct, the Phoenicians practiced circumcision (unlike the Philistines).[4] Hence, they would abhor this fate. The connotation would

---

2. Bodi, "Ezekiel," 465; Greenberg, *Ezekiel 21–37*, 577.

3. Bodi, "Ezekiel," 465.

4. Herodotus, *The History* 2.104. See also Greenberg, *Ezekiel 21–37*, 575–76; and Bodi, "Ezekiel," 466.

be comparable to our modern Western term, "heathen"; and the disgrace associated with it can be seen in Israelite attitudes (Gen 34:14; Judg 14:3; 1 Sam 17:26).

28:12 *king of Tyre . . . seal of perfection:* Like the movement from Ezek 26:1–21 to 27:1–36, after an announcement of judgment in Ezek 28:1–10, the second part of this judgment cycle also shifts to a poem of lament (Ezek 28:11–19). For the question whether the king of Tyre is Satan, see **Special Topic: Is the "King of Tyre" Satan?** The most likely identification is the human king of Tyre, whom Ezekiel casts as a prototypical ruler, whose rebellion is described in terms reminiscent of Adam in the garden of Eden. The "first man" motif is employed in Job 15:7–8 as well.[5]

The translation, "seal of perfection" might allude to the stamp of the divine image on Adam, who was God's ideal representative. This interpretation necessitates a change of one vowel in the Hebrew word (*hotem* to *hotam*) to carry the meaning "seal" (Jer 22:24 and Hag 2:23).[6] This was the understanding of the Old Greek translation and is reflected in most modern English translations. Alternatively, as the vowels stand in the Hebrew text, the NET Bible translates the phrase, "sealer of perfection." If this is the correct reading, then this Edenic character is one who sets the seal on perfection.[7] Both alternatives attribute perfection to this individual.

Special Topic: Is the "King of Tyre" Satan?

One can find both ancient and modern interpreters who identify the "king of Tyre" with Satan. While this view still finds some scholarly defense,[8] most modern commentators, both conservative and mainstream, consider a figurative interpretation for the human king to be more persuasive, being rooted in the contextual flow of these chapters.[9] In both cycles of judgment-lament (Ezek 26:1—27:35 and 28:1–19), the lament poem is a highly figurative recast of the preceding judgment speech. In addition, the language of Ezek 28:11–19 does not require more than a human figure. Lest a human identification of the king of Tyre be dismissed as just

---

5. Allen, *Ezekiel 20–48*, 94.
6. Greenberg, *Ezekiel 21–37*, 580–81; Block, *Ezekiel 25–48*, 104 and n. 86.
7. For defense, see Greenberg, *Ezekiel 21–37*, 580.
8. Cooper, *Ezekiel*, 266–68.
9. See, for example, the comments of Alexander, "Ezekiel," 800.

another example of modernist avoidance of supernatural themes, it is instructive to note the view of John Calvin. His Ezekiel commentary never reached these chapters; however, his comments on Isa 14:3-27, which employs similar language for the king of Babylon, reveal his thoughts about this issue—only a human referent does justice to the context of the passage, and Calvin dismisses a Satanic identification as "arising from ignorance" and based on "useless fables."[10]

28:13 *every precious stone adorned you:* The list of stones matches nine of the twelve named in the High Priest's breastplate (Exod 28:17-20), which leads some to suggest a priestly character for this perfect, primeval man in God's garden temple. Or, if not the priest's breastplate specifically, then the stones simply describe the splendor of the king's royal attire.[11] Others view the stones as ornaments in the garden surrounding this king, similar to the listing of mineral wealth that surrounded Adam (Gen 2:11-12). The Gilgamesh Epic describes an orchard of jeweled trees in the habitat of the immortal Mesopotamian flood hero.[12]

28:14 *You were anointed as a guardian cherub:* This sentence is the primary reason interpreters have identified the figure with Satan. But as Block observes, every word in this sentence is problematic in meaning and grammatical function[13]—a questionable foundation for constructing a doctrine of Satan's fall. Following the ancient Greek translation, some modern versions render the Hebrew text: "I placed you *with* the cherub" (Old Greek; cf. NET; NRSV). This affirms an Edenic location but places the first man in company *with* cherubs rather than identifying him *as* a cherub. Consistent with this, these translations describe the cherub in Ezek 28:16 as the agent driving the man away (cf. Gen 3:24). However, in Ezek 28:16, the Hebrew can be read naturally as an identification of the king ("O guardian cherub"). So the translation found in most modern English versions may be correct. But even so, this does not necessarily identify the king of Tyre as a cherub literally. Rather, the description could be a metaphor, since kings were the ultimate sponsors and protectors of temples in the ancient world. Across the ancient Near East, composite creatures (usually winged bulls or lions) were presented in iconography or in statuary form to depict guardians of divine or royal space (cf. Isa 6;

---

10. Calvin, *Isaiah*, 1:442. See also Block, *Ezekiel 25-48*, 119 n. 139.
11. Taylor, *Ezekiel*, 196; Block, *Ezekiel 25-48*, 112.
12. Bodi, "Ezekiel," 466-67.
13. Block, *Ezekiel 25-48*, 112-13.

Ezek 1). Hence, the king had a cherub-like function, even as Adam was placed in the garden to protect (Gen 2:15). The dragon-like identity of Pharaoh in Ezek 29:3 nicely illustrates the figurative use of such imagery (see comments there).

28:14 *holy mount of God . . . fiery stones:* The "holy mountain" can refer to the location of God's temple (Ezek 20:40; Pss 48:1; 99:9; Isa 56:7), or more broadly, his presence anywhere in all of creation (Isa 11:9; 65:25). It would appropriately describe either the garden of Eden or his throne in heaven, wherever there is access to his divine presence.[14] The "fiery stones" is more difficult to interpret. Some have suggested it pertains to a ritual of fire through which Tyre's patron deity, Melqart, was revitalized; and the human king of Tyre participated in these rituals in a representative way.[15] But a simpler explanation is that they are related to the brilliant gemstones mentioned in the previous verse.[16]

28:15–16 *You were blameless . . . you sinned:* This echo of Adam's fall and expulsion from the garden continues the depiction of the king of Tyre as the first, primeval man. The return to the theme of his ruthless control of maritime commerce reinforces the interpretation that the referent here is the human king.

At the time of Ezekiel's oracle, the king of Tyre was still proudly enthroned. This is not incompatible with the narrative's past-tense viewpoint. Rather than a retrospect of Satan's fall, Ezek 28:11–19 is a lament such as would be performed at a funeral (cf. 2 Sam 1:17–27). The lament anticipates the downfall and death of the king that is still future (Ezek 28:9–10) at the time of the oracle. The rhetorical viewpoint is similar to the use of another funeral term, "woe" (1 Kgs 13:30, translated "Alas"), to reinforce the certainty of doom in prophetic oracles (cf. Amos 5:1–2 with 5:18).

28:18 *you have desecrated your sanctuaries:* Part of the profit from the king's commercial success would have been offered in the sanctuaries of the various deities worshipped by the Phoenicians. However, due to the violent and dishonest means by which they were attained, these offerings actually polluted their temples. Israel's God judged sacrifices as worthless if offered in the context of injustice (cf. Isa 1:10–17; Amos 5:21–24).

---

14. Block, *Ezekiel 25–48*, 114.
15. Alexander, "Ezekiel," 802–03; Bodi, "Ezekiel," 467.
16. Block, *Ezekiel 25–48*, 114.

28:18 *I made fire come out from you:* The internally oriented sin of the king (arrogance, vanity) is the very source of his destruction. Taylor observes that "Ezekiel's imagination wandered freely" in the use of a wide variety of symbolic imagery; so here, "the temptation to sin comes to the city not from without [as in Eden's garden] but from greed and pride within."[17]

28:21 *against Sidon:* The introduction to this chapter noted that the oracle against Sidon is an independent unit on the one hand, but as another Phoenician city, it also belongs with Tyre (see above).

28:24-26 *No longer ... malicious neighbors:* Taken together, the political entities addressed in Ezek 25-28 represent the nations antagonistically set against God's people. Oracles of judgment against them function as an announcement of salvation to Israel. God's sovereignty over the nations, demonstrated through his judgments, encourages Israel that they are still destined for life in the land promised to their ancestors (Ezek 28:25-26; see comments at Ezek 35:15—36:13). The mention of "houses" and "vineyards" alludes to the reversal of covenant curses (Deut 28:30).

Theological Bridge to Application

The demonstration of the sovereignty of God is a crucial theological foundation throughout these oracles against the nations. This theme finds expression in Ezek 28:24, where the result of all his judgments leads to the recognition of his identity as "Sovereign LORD." It is striking that the king of Tyre should not attribute his success to his own capabilities; rather, it must be recognized that it is Israel's LORD who is the real king-maker and king-breaker ("I set you" [on the mountain], Ezek 28:14; "I set you" [to the earth], Ezek 28:17). As Block notes, the use of the Hebrew word "to create" in two places in this account (Ezek 28:13, 15) points to the identity of Israel's God as Creator, the LORD of all history.[18]

Focus of Application

A primary theme in this passage is the indictment of arrogance and pride, as well as the closely related sin of vanity (Tyre boasts in "beauty"). This corresponds to Ezekiel's attention to wisdom (Ezek 28:3-5), which

17. Taylor, *Ezekiel*, 197.
18. Block, *Ezekiel 25-48*, 118, 120.

ironically should have led the king away from these vices (Prov 8:13; 16:5; 18:12; 31:30). In the case of Tyre's king, the accumulation of wealth contributed to a sense of self-sufficiency and self-aggrandizement (Ezek 28:5, 17). Israel's own experience taught the same lesson (Deut 8:10, 14, 17; cf. Ezek 16:15; Hos 12:8).

Observing the harsh realities of a fallen world, one often finds that greed and violence accompany one another. Even if economic and social injustices are not directly violent, they invariably have physical consequences to the detriment of the those who suffer; and this contributed to the guilt of the king of Tyre (Ezek 28:15–16). When greed leads to ill-gotten gain, it is especially repulsive to God (cf. desecrated sanctuaries at Ezek 28:18).

The above commentary argued strongly against the traditional interpretation that Ezek 28 narrates the fall of Satan. At the same time, in the world view of Israel, there was no clean separation between evil human rulers and the cosmic powers behind them. Psalm 82 (and probably Ps 58; cf. Ps 58:1 in ESV; NASB) attributes injustice to both cosmic and human powers (cf. John 10:34–35). Daniel 10:20–21 also affirms the reality of supernatural players at work on the world scene. So while not an account of Satan's fall specifically, Ezek 28 depicts the sin of Tyre's king in language appropriate to other-worldly beings (cherubs), perhaps implicating the unseen forces at work in history more generally.[19]

There are passages more central in Ezekiel on the spiritual and physical restoration of his people than the brief section found in Ezek 28:24–26, but of note here is the relationship between God's judgment and his promises. His announcement to bring down those who have acted with malice is not because he merely delights in their destruction (cf. Ezek 18:23; 33:11) but because it is a necessary step in the fulfillment of his commitment to right what is wrong and secure the peace of those who trust in him. See also the contextual introduction to chapters 31–32.

---

19. Further, see Heiser, *Unseen Realm*.

LEANING ON UNRELIABLE ALLIES

Ezekiel 29:1—30:26

Ezekiel's Message

Relying on human resources is ultimately a doomed strategy.

Key Themes

- The LORD will bring down those whose strength is in themselves.
- Dependence on human allies rather than the LORD is a doomed strategy.

Context in Ezekiel

Ezekiel's oracles against the nations began in Ezek 25:1 and culminates with Egypt, the seventh nation to receive an announcement of judgment (Ammon, Moab, Edom, Philistia, Tyre, Sidon, and now Egypt). As the climax of this section, Egypt itself is the object of seven oracles (29:1–16; 29:17–21; 30:1–19; 30:20–26; 31:1–18; 32:1–16; 32:17–21).[1] In addition, comprising four chapters, Egypt receives noticeably more attention than any of the other nations. This is likely due to the strategic role Egypt was playing in the events surrounding the final downfall of Jerusalem and the misplaced hope that Egypt might deliver the city from Babylonian siege.

1. Block, *Ezekiel 25–48*, 128.

More than once had Israel and Judah looked to Egypt for help against Mesopotamian adversaries. First was Hosea's revolt against Assyria (2 Kgs 17:4), then Hezekiah allied with Egypt against Assyria (Isa 30:1–7; 31:1; 36:9), and Egyptian interference in Judah's affairs resulted in the placement of anti-Babylonian Jehoiakim on the throne (2 Kgs 23:31—24:7). Finally, during the days of Zedekiah, Egypt failed in an attempt to relieve the city from Babylonian siege (Jer 37:1–8).[2] This track record of political alliances is important, because it explains why these extensive oracles against Egypt are a warning to God's covenant people (see below, Ezek 29:16). For practical reasons, it is difficult to treat each of the seven oracles individually in exposition. So, they will be treated in two parts (Ezek 29–30 and Ezek 31–32)—an attempt to organize them into workable units. Chapters 29 and 30 are unified by the extensive consideration of Nebuchadnezzar's role in Egypt's demise as well as the theme of temptation that Egypt offered to Israel as an alternative source of trust. Chapters 31 and 32 are united by the conclusion to each of these two chapters, depicting Pharaoh's entry into the netherworld.

Interpretive Highlights

29:3 *you great monster:* The word translated "monster" (*tannin*) is used in several ways in the Old Testament. It can mean "serpent" (Exod 7:9–12; cf. Exod 4:2–5 where a more precise word for "snake" [*nahash*] appears). But in Ezekiel, the creature has feet (Ezek 32:2) and scales (Ezek 29:4). Therefore most interpreters equate it with the crocodile, especially here in the context of the Nile River. Furthermore, Egyptian texts depict Pharaoh as a crocodile (see comments at Ezek 32:2).[3] But a crocodilian image does not erase the mythological overtones. Elsewhere in the Old Testament this word refers to the aquatic monster associated with evil forces of disorder (Ps 74:13; Job 7:12; Isa 27:1; 51:9), hence "dragon" in some translations (ESV, NRSV, KJV, Old Greek). This connection with the sea-monster, who is the arch-enemy of God's rule, fits the accusation against Pharaoh, since Egypt routinely interfered with God's movement of nations to judge his people Israel and Judah (see Context above). The judgment of this monster is portrayed as pulling it from its aquatic habitat

---

2. Greenberg, *Ezekiel 21–37*, 608–09. See Greenberg for extra-biblical evidence as well.

3. For texts, see Bodi, "Ezekiel," 467.

and leaving it as food for the desert creatures (Ezek 29:4–5). This is similar to God's treatment of the sea-monster, Leviathan, when the Lord asserts his sovereign kingship over forces opposing his rule (Ps 74:12–14).

29:3 *the Nile belongs to me; I made it:* Ezekiel bases the accusation against Pharaoh in terms of the Egyptian king's arrogant, self-reliance. The pretentious boasting that *he* made the Nile, and that for himself (restated a few verses later in Ezek 29:9), is in direct opposition to the rightful claim of Israel's God to be the sole Creator, who made both the waters of the earth as well as the "sea-monsters" who inhabit them (Gen 1:9–10, 21 [*tannînîm*]; Pss 95:5; 104:25–26; Jonah 1:9, 17).

29:6 *a staff of reed for the people of Israel:* The NIV leaves untranslated a word in the Hebrew text ("because," cf. ESV, NASB) that marks an accusation (i.e., the reason for judgment). The strength of Egypt, whether real or imagined, offered continuous temptation to Israel and Judah when they felt the need for military allies (see "Context" above). But rather than providing help against invading armies, on each occasion, alliance with Egypt resulted in more disastrous consequences. So Ezekiel compares this to self-inflicted injuries resulting from dependence on an unreliable crutch, a metaphor used even by one of Israel's invaders (cf. 2 Kgs 18:21).

29:10 *Migdol to Aswan:* These locations can be identified with the border fortresses on the north in Egypt (Exod 14:2, "Migdol" can refer to a fortress tower, 2 Kgs 18:8) and the southern most cataract of the Nile ("Aswan"). The entire extent of Egypt will suffer.

29:11 *forty years:* Forty years is a measures for the length of a generation in the Old Testament (Num 14:33; 32:13). And it is used schematically to mark periods of approximately one-generation lifespan (Judg 3:11; 5:31; 8:28; 13:1). In an extra-biblical inscription left by Moab's King Mesha, he approximated the span of time over which Israel occupied his land as 40 years.[4] This is the length of time Egypt will endure oppression, with some inhabitants in exiled captivity. This period presumably ended about the same time as Israel's exile, when the Persians overthrew the Babylonian empire and allowed return of exiles to their native lands.

29:13 *I will gather the Egyptians:* This is a striking statement about the reversal of God's judgment, not expressed for any other peoples in this series of oracles against the nations. Block offers the plausible suggestion that the reason lies in the differences between the accusations

---

4. The Inscription of King Mesha (Hallo, and Younger, Jr., *The Context of Scripture*, 2.23: 137).

against the other nations and that which is stated against Egypt. While the six nations treated before Egypt were accused of gloating over Israel's destruction and taking its land (Ezek 28:24), Egypt, whatever their motives, tried to prevent Judah from losing its land.[5] But the consequences remain that Egypt's international status would never recover. The phrase translated "a lowly kingdom" (Ezek 29:14) suggests a vassal status; the same phrase in Hebrew describes Zedekiah's vassal status in Ezek 17:14.[6]

29:16 *no longer be a source of confidence:* There are two accusations against Egypt in this oracle. First, the LORD rebukes the self-sufficient arrogance of Pharaoh, who stylized himself as creator and possessor of the Nile, the backbone of Egypt's strength. The second accusation drives at the manner in which Egypt lured God's people to misplace their trust. The fact that the oracle ends on this note highlights its importance for Ezekiel's message to his own people.

29:17 *In the twenty-seventh year:* This date formula indicates that this is the last of Ezekiel's oracles from a chronological perspective, trailing the other oracles in this section of the book by five to seven years. So why is it placed so far out of chronological sequence? In terms of subject matter, it concerns the city of Tyre (Ezek 26–28); yet it is also relevant to the downfall of Egypt. Therefore, its placement here in the book of Ezekiel is as close as it can be to the oracles against Tyre, and at the same time it makes sense contextually among the oracles against Egyptian. What is known about the fate of Tyre from extra-biblical historical sources indicates that after a thirteen-year siege of Tyre, Babylon's Nebuchadnezzar was able to bargain with Tyre only for the deportation of its king, without the benefit of plundering the island fortress.[7] The mainland settlements had been sacked, but not the island fortress itself. Evidently, the spoils of the mainland were insufficient to reward Nebuchadnezzar's army for thirteen years of siege labor (heads and shoulders rubbed raw; Ezek 29:18).

Special Topic: Failed Prophecy?

It is not uncommon to read in contemporary interpretations of Ezek 29:17–21 that this passage is the prophet's attempt to recover credibility

---

5. Block, *Ezekiel 25–48*, 144–45.
6. Block, *Ezekiel 25–48*, 143 n. 77.
7. Bodi, "Ezekiel," 469.

in the face of a failed prophecy.⁸ Ezekiel prophesied the downfall of Tyre by the Babylonians (Ezek 26); now it is Egypt. However, it was noted above (see comments at Ezek 26:3, 7, 12) that Tyre's destruction would unfold in successive attacks by different nations. In addition, a more nuanced understanding of the nature of prophecy and fulfillment is needed. Many assume that, by its nature, biblical prophecy provides absolute, detailed predictions of what will come to pass in the future. But such an assumption needs correction. Because prophecy is a speech-act, it does more than simply predict the future (i.e., assert information committing God to action). Prophecy also declares a new state of affairs (Hos 2:2), directs the actions of others (Isa 1:16–17), expresses attitudes (Amos 5:21), comforts (Isa 40:1 with 43:1), and warns (Jonah 3:4). It is in the latter capacity that it is easiest to see how prophecy is often contingent on human response. *By "contingency," this does not mean that God does not know the future; rather, it merely recognizes that on the horizon of human experience, the manner and timing of God's actions are appropriate to human choices.* Sometimes, this conditionality is explicit (Isa 1:19–20; Jer 22:4–5). Sometimes, God does commit himself to action without qualification, and the promise of irrevocability can be expressed explicitly (Isa 45:23; Amos 1:3). But, rather than assume absolute unconditionality and simplicity as the default posture of prophetic speech-acts, contingency and complexity are normal (Jer 18:7–10).⁹ On the human horizon, the manner and timing are rarely specified, and "fulfillment" is a more complex affair than usually expected. So, regarding the prophecy against Tyre, it is helpful to recognize that a complex outworking of history is expected, and indeed, this was already anticipated in the initial oracle (i.e., "many nations," Ezek 26:3, 7, "they," Ezek 26:12).

29:21 *a horn will grow*: One suggestion is that the "horn" refers to hope for a revitalized Davidic kingdom (1 Sam 2:10; Ps 132:17; with Ezekiel's stated expectations in Ezek 34:23–24; 37:24–25).¹⁰ But this may be a premature introduction of this theme in the book as a whole. The image of a horn denotes "strength" (1 Sam 2:10; Pss 18:2; 75:10; 92:10; Jer 48:25), and the need to mention Israel's restoration in the context of

---

8. For example, see Greenberg, *Ezekiel 21–37*, 616–18.

9. The contingency of prophecy is discussed at length in Pratt, "Historical Contingencies," 180–203 and Chisholm, "When Prophecy Appears to Fail," 561–77. To deny God's freedom to amend his own prophecy is to "deny to God a proper freedom and sovereignty" (Clements, *Ezekiel*, 134).

10. Cooper, *Ezekiel*, 275.

Tyre is linked with the nature of the prophecy against Tyre. If God would reward his servant Nebuchadnezzar, surely he would do the same for his people. Block argues that both notions could be in view.[11]

30:3 *the day of the Lord is near*: The phrase, "day of the Lord," denotes any event when God intervenes into human history in judgment or deliverance (see also discussion at Ezek 7:7). The complexity of its historical outworking is illustrated well by Zephaniah's use of the phrase: judgment of Assyria in 612 BC [Zeph 2:13—context of the day of the Lord, cf. 2:1]; judgment of Judah in 586 BC [Zeph 1:14-18]; return from exile in 539 BC [Zeph 3:16]; future restoration of the Gentiles [Zeph 3:8-9]). God's interventions have been manifest numerous times over the course of history, and from the standpoint of this oracle, Egypt's destruction at the hand of Nebuchadnezzar (Ezek 30:10) is on the horizon (possibly 568 B.C).[12]

30:5 *people of the covenant land*: Ezekiel names numerous, non-native elements in Egypt, perhaps mercenaries (cf. Jer 46:9).[13] The ESV and NASB render this phrase, "people of the land that is in league" (cf. NKJV), stressing an alliance of these people with Egypt, but leaving their identity ambiguous. But the more formal NIV translation (cf. NET) places proper emphasis on the fact that the word "covenant" functions adjectivally to specify the identity of the "land." The Old Greek translation has "people of my covenant." The peculiar expression "covenant land" is most likely an oblique way of naming Judeans, who have, in Block's words, "prostituted themselves by serving in Egypt's armies."[14] Another possibility is that these are not Judean mercenaries but Judeans in general who have sought refuge in Egypt (2 Kgs 25:23-26).[15] Whether Judean mercenaries or general citizenry, the message here reinforces the message in Ezek 29:16—a rebuke for choosing alliance with Egypt over protection from their covenant Lord (cf. Ezek 30:6).

30:13 *images in Memphis*: The Lord's day with Egypt will attend to its gods as well (cf. Isa 19:1). Memphis was one of Egypt's most ancient and venerated political-religious centers.[16] The focus on Egypt's deities

11. Block, *Ezekiel 25-48*, 152.
12. Block, *Ezekiel 25-48*, 151.
13. Bodi, "Ezekiel," 470.
14. Block, *Ezekiel 25-48*, 160.
15. Cooper, *Ezekiel*, 278-79.
16. For survey of the geographical references throughout this oracle, see Bodi, "Ezekiel," 471-72 and Block, *Ezekiel 25-48*, 166-70.

recalls the exodus tradition, where through plagues the Lord executed judgment on Egypt's gods (Exod 12:12; Num 33:4). In Ezekiel, as in the exodus, the goal was that Egypt would know that Israel's Lord is the true God (Ezek 30:19; Exod 7:5; 11:9; 14:18). If Egypt's gods are impotent in the face of the Lord, then reliance on the resources of their land is surely a greater folly.

30:21 *broken the arm of Pharaoh:* The peculiarity of this oracle is the two-stage manner by which it describes the crippling of Pharaoh; first one arm described as a past event and then the other arm described as future. This invites comparison to the historical outworking of the oracle. A title of Pharaoh was "possessor of a strong arm," used specifically by Hophra, the Pharaoh at Ezekiel's time.[17] We cannot be certain of the precise identity of the two stages. The first breaking could be that of Necho, who was defeated by Babylon at the Battle of Carchemish (Jer 46:2). More relevant to Ezekiel's interest, however, is Hophra's aborted effort to relieve Jerusalem during Nebuchadnezzar's siege (Jer 37:1–8; 2 Kgs 24:7).[18] The future breaking of the other arm would be at the hand of Nebuchadnezzar (Ezek 30:24–25). But fulfillment of biblical prophecy unfolds progressively; on the heals of Babylon was Persia, followed by Alexander the Great, and then Rome. Egypt never recovered. Never again could it offer a source of refuge to God's people.

Theological Bridge to Application

The Lord tolerates no rivals. This idea underlies Ezekiel's proclamation in these chapters. First, he does not allow any of his creatures to presume the status of God, which is his prerogative alone. Pharaoh's pretentions about being Creator and self-reliant are directly and soundly rebuked. Second, when the Lord's servants turn their trust to others, it is an affront to the exclusive claim that the Redeemer-Savior has on them (cf. Exod 20:2–6).

Focus of Application

Two themes dominate these two chapters. Primarily, these are oracles against Egypt's Pharaoh because he asserted himself with divine

---

17. Block, *Ezekiel 25–48*, 175–76; Bodi, "Ezekiel," 472.
18. Greenberg, *Ezekiel 21–37*, 633–34.

pretenses—creative power and self-service (Ezek 29:3, 9, 15). The breaking of Pharaoh's arms is a direct rebuke of Egyptian royal ideology (Ezek 30:22). Even the Egyptian gods, with whom Pharaoh finds company, will be destroyed by the Lord's sovereign power (Ezek 30:13). This warning today extends to any who feel they are invincible in their own strength. Regardless of physical prowess, social standing, economic resources, or intellect, the Lord will bring down those whose confidence is in themselves.

A second theme follows from the first. Dependence on human allies rather than the Lord is a doomed strategy. When Ezekiel denounces Pharaoh for offering false hope to Israel (Ezek 29:6–7, 16), it is an implicit rebuke to Ezekiel's audience for the habitual reliance on Egypt that characterized their past. Recent decades have witnessed the growing tendency among Christians to align themselves with political power in order to strengthen their voice in the public square and advance their agenda in the culture wars. The results have been disastrous for the church and the integrity of its witness (see Focus of Application at Ezek 23:1–49).

A GREAT FALL
Ezekiel 31:1—32:32

Ezekiel's Message

The LORD brings low the proud and renders terror to those who spread terror.

Key Themes

- The LORD brings down the mighty who revel in their pride.
- Those who terrorize others will themselves face greater terror in judgment.

Context in Ezekiel

These chapters continue Ezekiel's oracles against Egypt. For the context of this section and the rationale for grouping these two chapters together as a unit, see the above discussion on the context for Ezek 29:1—30:26. If the oracles against Egypt (Ezek 29–32) must be divided for practical reasons, it is possible to work with a difference in emphasis between chapters 29–30 and chapters 31–32. In the first instance (Ezek 29–30), the prophet challenges Egypt's arrogant usurping of the place of Israel's God (Ezek 29:3, 9, 15–16; 30:6, 9, 22). Pharaoh is neither self-reliant nor someone who can be relied on. The latter two chapters (Ezek 31–32) might be united by imagery of the proud falling: a great tree or a mighty monster brought down to earth, and ultimately to judgment, in the underworld of the dead. This underworld destiny concludes and unites both of these chapters.

Interpretive Highlights

31:2 *Who can be compared*: An important theme throughout these oracles against the king of Egypt is arrogance. The language of "incomparability" is a rhetorical device that is used to show supremacy. For example, Isaiah uses it to extol the unique attributes of the one, true Creator-God (e.g., Isa 40:18, 25; 44:7; 46:5; cf. Exod 15:11). Ezekiel uses this rhetoric in mocking fashion to describe Pharaoh, who would fashion himself as one of the most elite of kings in the history and culture of the ancient Near East.

31:3 *Assyria*: Arguably the most supreme nation up to that time in the history of the ancient Near East was Assyria—perhaps the first "empire" by definition. While previous nations extracted tribute from other nations and had commercial influence over them, no kingdom before Assyria incorporated other nations into its permanent, governing control. Therefore, when Ezekiel chose Assyria for his case-study of what befalls powerful nations, he chose the most supreme example.

31:3 *cedar*: The cedars of Lebanon were the most magnificent trees in the Middle East, and kings from Babylon to Egypt sought timbers from Lebanon for their great building projects. The cedar's qualities are extolled in a campaign inscription of king Nebuchadnezzar in terms similar to Ezekiel: "mighty cedars, high and strong, of precious beauty."[1]

31:4 *deep springs*: The word translated "deep springs" (*tehom*; NIV), or simply "the deep" (ESV; NASB), refers to the subterranean waters that were thought to be the source of ground water (Gen 8:2; 49:25; Ps 136:6; Prov 3:20; cf. Ezek 31:7). In Egyptian and Mesopotamian thought, there existed the image of the cosmic tree, whose branches reached to heaven and whose roots sank into the deepest parts of underworld waters. The Babylonian Erra Epic describes it in these terms: "Whose roots reach down into the vast ocean through a hundred miles of water, to the base of Arallu, Whose topknot above rests on the heaven of Anu."[2] Of course,

---

1. Nebuchadnezzar's Expedition to Syria (*ANET*, 307). See also Bodi, "Ezekiel," 472.

2. Erra and Ishum (*COS* 1.113: 407–8). See also Bodi, "Ezekiel," 472.

Ezekiel and the exiles were living in the heart of Babylonia, so this was well known imagery in their cultural environment.

31:6 *All the birds:* Also associated with great trees was their capacity to house wildlife, both birds and beasts. This is a common motif in ancient Near Eastern texts and can be seen in the description of Nebuchadnezzar's dream of himself as a great tree (Dan 4:10–12). The point of the imagery throughout is to highlight the grandeur of the tree and its life-giving qualities.

31:8–9 *garden of God . . . trees of Eden:* Ezekiel employed associations with the Garden of Eden in his taunt against Tyre (Ezek 28). Here he writes in hyperbolic language, as though Assyria (and so Pharaoh) was so magnificent as to surpass the splendor of Eden. Like the king of Tyre, this rhetoric sets the stage to underscore the greatness of Pharaoh's fall into judgment.

31:10–14 *because it was proud:* The description of the great tree carries an implicit accusation of arrogance that becomes explicit in these verses. Assyria was indeed great, but pride in such grandeur resulted in its destruction at the hand of the next kingdom, Babylon. Its ruler is called "most ruthless" and is identified with Nebuchadnezzar in Ezek 32:11–12, who will summarily cut the tree down. The lesson from the cosmic tree is that Israel's God will tolerate no rivals to his supremacy over the cosmos (Ezek 31:14). Pharaoh will be judged and consigned to the realm of the dead just like every other mortal.

31:15–16 *mourning . . . nations tremble:* The tree whose roots descended to the "deep" now resides there in withered form. It is important to keep in mind throughout this passage that it is similar to a parable; not all details should be examined for correspondence to the real, historical world (let alone the underworld). The point is that Assyria, with a "crash" like that of a great fallen tree in Lebanon, struck fear in the hearts of other national leaders. If this could happen to Assyria, then no nation was exempt from a similar fate. For leaders and nations already fallen, there was consolation. As the saying goes, "misery loves company" (Ezek 31:17; see **Special Topic: Sheol**). Perhaps Ezekiel borrows here from similar imagery in Isa 10:33–34 and 14:8–10.[3]

---

3. Greenberg, *Ezekiel 21–37*, 646.

Special Topic: Sheol

The NIV translates the Hebrew word *sheol* in Ezek 31:15 as the "realm of the dead" (cf. "Sheol" in ESV; NASB; NET). This word denotes the dwelling place of the deceased, graphically illustrated in Num 16:31–34 where the rebellious Korahites descend "alive" to this underworld realm. Hence, Sheol was located in the lowermost region of the earth, below the subterranean waters (Job 26:5, hence "depths" in Ps 139:8) and at the root of the mountains (Deut 32:22; Jonah 2:2–6). The Old Testament presents a gloomy and unclear portrait of human existence after death.[4] People became only a shadowy image of the former, living self—the word *repa'im* is translated "shades" in the ESV and "spirits" in the NIV (Isa 14:9; 26:14). The same word is translated simply as the "dead" by the ESV and NIV in Job 26:5 and Ps 88:10. Death contrasts with the "land of the living" (Pss 27:13; 116:8–9). Because burial was associated with decomposition in an earthen grave, one finds metaphors such as "pit" (Hebrew word *bor*, Pss 30:3; 88:4, 6), "decay" (Hebrew word *shahat*, Ps 16:10; 49:9) or "Destruction" (Hebrew word *'abaddon*, Ps 88:11). In moments of most extreme distress, even the righteous despaired in fear, viewing death as a hopeless end (Job 17:10–16; Ps 88:3–5). But in moments of inspired faith, the Old Testament offers a better, if still unclear, hope (Ps 49:15 contrasted with vv. 7–14; see also Pss 73:23–26; 139:8; Isa 26:19; Dan 12:2).[5] However, for those outside of covenant relationship with Israel's God, Yahweh, there was no hope but for a miserable existence in the company of other "miserables," as depicted in Ezek 31:16 and 32:21, 31. One must not press the details in Ezekiel's description. As Block states, Ezekiel's portrait of Sheol is more a "literary cartoon" than a "literary photograph."[6]

31:18 lie among the uncircumcised: As discussed in connection with Tyre's fate in Ezek 28:10, to be "uncircumcized" was regarded as a shameful condition, with connotations similar to what we might associate with the word "heathen." Therefore, an afterlife with the uncircumcised was an ignominious death. The imagery of this fate is expanded in Ezek 32:17–32.

---

4. For a comprehensive discussion of the topic, see Johnston, *Shades of Sheol*.

5. Further, see the sidebar "Death and the Underworld" in Hilber, "Psalms," 348–49.

6. Block, *Ezekiel 25–48*, 234.

32:2 ***lion . . . monster:*** For discussion of the water monster ("dragon," ESV), stylized here as a crocodile stirring mud in the Nile River, see Ezek 29:3. This same terrifying pair of beasts, from land and water, is utilized in a portrait of Pharaoh Thutmosis III: "I cause them to see Your Majesty as a crocodile, lord of fear amidst the waters, unapproachable . . . I cause them to see Your Majesty as a ferocious lion."[7]

32:4 ***gorge themselves on you:*** The psalmist describes a similar fate for the aquatic chaos monster (Ps 74:13-14).

32:7-8 ***darken their stars . . . sun . . . moon:*** When God intervenes in the most extreme forms of judgment, the prophets use cosmic imagery to highlight its scope and severity (cf. Isa 13:10; Joel 2:30-31). These astral objects were associated with the chief gods of ancient Near Eastern religions, and the sun in particular was the supreme deity in Egypt. The LORD's control over the sun announces the cutting off of all hope for Egypt's Pharaoh (cf. Exod 10:21-23).

32:14 ***I will let her waters settle:*** While the lament of this chapter opened with the Pharaonic crocodile muddying the waters (Ezek 32:1-2), after God has finished his judgment, he will be the one to restore what chaos has disturbed; and on that note the lament closes (Ezek 32:16).

32:19 ***Are you more favored:*** This question restates implicitly the accusation against Pharaoh that underlies these chapters, his excess arrogance (Ezek 31:2, 10, 14; 32:12). Egypt will suffer the same fate as all other nations who have spread terror by the sword (the recurring motif in this death poem).

32:22 ***Assyria:*** As discussed above, the Assyrian Empire offered the prime comparison to Egypt, and so it heads the list of nations here.

32:24 ***Elam . . . shame:*** Elam was located to the east of Babylon and was a constant threat to whatever nation dominated the Mesopotamian flood plain (Babylon or Assyria). Noteworthy in this funeral epithet is Ezekiel's comment about bearing shame.[8] This reinforces the connotation of the term "uncircumcised," referring to an ignominious death (see Ezek 31:18).

32:26 ***Meshek and Tubal:*** These peoples populated the center of modern day Turkey, and their importance emerges in Ezek 39:1 in connection with Gog.

---

7. Triumph Hymn for Thutmosis III (Kitchen, *Poetry of Ancient Egypt*, 172-73, lines 17 and 19; or *ANET*, 374). See also Bodi, "Ezekiel," 474.

8. For the importance of honor and shame in ancient Near Eastern culture, see Hilber, "Psalms," 343.

32:27 *warriors of old*: Before discussion of this verse, it is necessary to explain a translation difficulty. The NIV, with the NET and NRSV, reads "from of old." This follows the text of the Old Greek translation, which witnesses to the Hebrew consonants *m ʿwlm*. The ESV, NASB, and NJPS retain the traditional Hebrew text, "from the uncircumcised," which has the consonants *m ʿrlym*. As one can see, the two are very similar, and the crucial letters *w* and *r* can easily be confused in Hebrew. Considering all the times the phrase "uncircumcised" appears in this passage, most likely a scribe inadvertently misread "from of old" as "from the uncircumcised."[9]

Who then are these warriors "from of old"? Two suggestions have good merit: First, they could be legendary heroes of the ancient Near Eastern tradition, such as Gilgamesh. These merit a more noble memory than the fate of Meshek and Tubal, who are contrasted. Second, the passage might allude to the antediluvians (i.e., mighty warriors of pre-flood days; Gen 6:4). So the rhetorical thrust is that the warriors of Ezekiel's dirge are worse than the notorious antediluvians.[10]

32:29 *Edom*: Perhaps this close neighbor of Judah is chosen to represent the peoples of the Levant; however, at the beginning of Ezekiel's oracles against the nations, Edom was singled out as "very guilty" (see discussion at Ezek 25:12).

32:30 *All ... disgrace ... shame*: The geographical scope of Ezekiel's death poem is complete, and once again he stresses the ignominious nature of their fate. If Pharaoh proudly thought of himself as the best in the present life, his afterlife existence would certainly be as miserable as anyone's.

32:32 *Although I had him spread terror*: All these nations operated under the sovereign hand of God, which utilizes human powers as secondary instruments to accomplish his work of judgment. But those powers in their turn also become objects of his justice (cf. Isa 7:18; 10:5 with 10:12).

Theological Bridge to Application

The LORD tolerates no rivals, or anyone who pretends to possess incomparable greatness. He uses the powerful for his own purposes, but also

---

9. See Allen, *Ezekiel 20-48*, 135; Greenberg, *Ezekiel 21-37*, 665; Block, *Ezekiel 25-48*, 220 n. 54 and 228.

10. For discussion, see Block, *Ezekiel 25-48*, 228.

sovereignly holds them accountable without privilege over others. There are no cosmic powers that are not under his control, whether it be the deified celestial objects (sun, moon, stars) or chaos itself (embodied in Egypt's Pharaoh). The realization of God's incomparable greatness forces the conclusion that there is only one God—"then they will know that I am the LORD" (Ezek 32:15).

Focus of Application

Like the previous two chapters (Ezek 29-30), these two chapters focus on the arrogant pride of the king of Egypt (Ezek 31:10, 12, 14; 32:12). God will not allow the powerful to remain so, lest others begin to depend on them (cf. Ezek 29:15-16). By making an example of the powerful, God instills reverence in those who witness the demise of the "rich and famous." All nations are put on notice that God's justice plays no favorites (Ezek 31:16; 32:9). As Block notes, this serves to warn any who might rely on secular power.[11] Even at the level of the average person, these chapters warn against arrogance, illustrating the lesson of Prov 16:8. Finally, the closing death poem of Ezek 32:17-32 offers a sober view of God's judgment. Clements notes that the repeated condemnation of killing "by the sword" is a "damning indictment of human militarism and military showmanship."[12] Power is a somber trust and not an excuse for exuberance or exploitation of others.

---

11. Block, *Ezekiel 25-48*, 197.
12. Clements, *Ezekiel*, 142.

NO PRIVILEGED STATUS
Ezekiel 33:1–33

Ezekiel's Message

There is no privileged status before God, rather, the demand that we walk in his ways.

Key Themes

- God vindicates his word and the ministry of his servants.
- God judges on the basis of current disposition toward him and his ways.
- There is no resting on past laurels nor taking refuge in community identity, rather the expectation is that we walk in his ways.

Context in Ezekiel

Ezekiel was commissioned as a watchman at the outset of his ministry (Ezek 3:17); and Ezek 33 opens with a return to this theme, which serves as a closing "bookend" to this phase of Ezekiel's ministry. The end of the chapter highlights the vindication of the prophet's ministry (Ezek 33:33), demonstrated when the news arrives of Jerusalem's destruction (Ezek 33:21–22). This phase of Ezekiel's ministry was dominated by a message of doom; he had indeed been a faithful watchman, warning of the destruction to come. Beginning in chapter 34, the book of Ezekiel pivots toward oracles of salvation, dominated by a message of hope. As in the message of prophet's commission (chapter 3), the first half of Ezek 33 (Ezek 33:1-20) warns against leaning on one's laurels of righteousness. At the same time, it offers continuing hope for the penitent. The second half of the chapter (Ezek 33:23-32) undermines anyone's confidence in ancestry (Ezek 33:23-29) or the mere show of religiosity (Ezek 33:30-32). As already noted, embedded within this chapter is the vindication of God's spokesman, Ezekiel (Ezek 33:21-22, 33).

Interpretive Highlights

33:2 *watchman:* The commissioning recorded at the time of Ezekiel's call (Ezek 3:17) was a private, personal message to the prophet. This time, the call of the watchman is delivered in the form of a parable directed for the benefit of Ezekiel's compatriots. The change in form and audience vindicates Ezekiel's call to public ministry. As the chapter draws to a close, it is evident that he has been faithful to his call and is free from guilt for the death of any who fall in God's judgment. For the role of a watchman, see the comments at Ezek 3:17.

33:9 *they will die . . . you yourself will be saved:* It is important to differentiate the notion of life and death in Ezekiel's context from that usually associated with our Christian proclamation of the gospel. Ezekiel's message pertained to the covenant curses, where life and death were physical and not "eternal." The English translations can create a problem when they translate the Hebrew word *nepesh* as "soul." For example, the ESV and NKJV translate this word "life" in v. 5 but inconsistently as "soul" here. In contrast, other translations more accurately use the English word "life" in both places (see also NASB; NIV; NET; NRSV). For full discussion, see the commentary at Ezek 3:18-19.

33:10 *weigh us down . . . wasting away:* As Taylor notes, this is the first indication in the book of Ezekiel that the people express any self-awareness of sin.[1] The phrase "wasting away" echoes the words predicting judgment in Ezek 4:17 and 24:23, marking the realization of covenant curses in exile (Lev 26:39).[2] This suggests a public recognition that Ezekiel's warnings are coming true in the present experience of the people. In the light of this, how might they survive? But in view of the people's

---

1. Taylor, *Ezekiel*, 215.
2. Block, *Ezekiel 25-48*, 246; Greenberg, *Ezekiel 21-37*, 673.

accusation against God (Ezek 33:17) and their yearning for entertainment (Ezek 33:31–32), commentators rightly express doubt about the depth of contrition. The saying of the people in v. 10 is more likely a cry for relief than a repentant confession. Nevertheless, it presents a "teachable moment," and Ezekiel seizes the opportunity.[3]

33:11 *I take no pleasure*: In an apologetic manner, the LORD expresses his heart regarding the nature of judgment. Even for him, judgment is unpleasant business and designed to lead people to repentance (cf. Ezek 18:23 and comments at Ezek 18:30–32).

33:12 *righteousness will count for nothing*: The parallel to Ezek 3:18–21 continues in small measure in Ezek 33:12–20; but the language of chapter 33 follows more closely the oracle in Ezek 18:21–30. In both Ezek 18 and 33, the message is that God judges according to the general orientation of each person's heart *in the present*. However, the purpose to which this principle is applied in each chapter differs. In chapter 18, the issue was the moral autonomy of each succeeding generation, but here the problem is despair at ever recovering from a wicked past.[4] With such a dark history of sin, is there any hope? The answer is a resounding "yes"! And to those who have walked in God's ways, the message is to persevere. On the reconciliation with Exod 20:5 (Deut 5:9), see comments at Ezek 18:19.

Greenberg notes that the watchman's duty in Ezek 33:1–6 is to the people collectively, meaning that the individual is not in view. Rather, Ezekiel's charge is to minister to the house of Israel as a whole. Therefore, he concludes that the individual language in Ezek 33:12–16 is simply legal in style, using quasi-legal language for the individual as an illustration for the collective.[5] However, the corporate principle is predicated on the assumption that individualism is valid, whether in socio-legal contexts or in the disposition of individuals toward the LORD and his ways (cf. Ezek 18:5–20, especially comments on Ezek 18:9). The corporate is composed of many individuals; and Ezekiel later appeals to individuals to respond in spite of what the majority are doing (Ezek 33:17).

33:15 *decrees that give life*: The word translated "decrees" refers to legal customs (translated "statutes" in ESV; NASB). The relationship between obedience and life is set forth clearly in Moses' sermons recorded in

---

3. Block, *Ezekiel 25–48*, 246–47.
4. Greenberg, *Ezekiel 21–37*, 679.
5. Greenberg, *Ezekiel 21–37*, 679–80.

Deuteronomy. As long as Israel follows the statutes of the covenant, they will flourish in the land of promise (Deut 6:2; 30:9–10, 15–16). Failure to keep covenant results in sanctions of the curse (Deut 28:15, 45). Ezekiel, being a priest, was especially attuned to the language of Leviticus, and his words echo the words of Lev 18:4–5: "Keep my statutes and judgments, for whoever does them will live by them." In Lev 18–20, these statutes are elaborated in terms of the Decalogue (e.g., Lev 19:11–13; 20:9–10). It is by following these statutes that Israel maintains its identity as the priestly nation to which they were called (Lev 20:7). So, abundance of life in the Mosaic Covenant was predicated on faithfulness to the stipulations of the covenant. As noted in comments at Ezek 18:9, this oracle applies to questions of eternal life only in a limited and indirect way. In both the Old Covenant and the New Covenant, loyalty to the LORD and walking in his ways are characteristic of someone in relationship to him (see **Special Topic: Transformation of Heart in the Old Covenant** at Ezek 36:26). Obedience does not *create* the relationship; rather, it is a *byproduct* of loving God.

33:17 *the LORD is not just:* In spite of the hint in Ezek 33:10 that the people (some at least?) acknowledged the imposition of covenant curses for their sin, this verse shows that, characteristically, they remained hardened (cf. Ezek 2:4–8; 3:7). Ezekiel's response is to continue the message that regardless of the community response, individuals are responsible for their disposition toward the LORD.

33:21 *In the twelfth year . . . tenth month:* Nebuchadnezzar's siege of Jerusalem began in the winter of 589/588 (= Zedekiah's ninth year and tenth month; 2 Kgs 25:1; Ezek 24:1).[6] By the date system used in Ezek 33:21, two years later Ezekiel receives the promised word (Ezek 25:25–26) that the city had fallen. The breach of city walls was actually in the eleventh year and fourth month (2 Kgs 25:2–8), and the trip from Jerusalem to the region of Babylon normally took about five months (cf. Ezra 7:9). This prompts the question why the fugitive would take around eighteen months to arrive. The date notations in Ezekiel generally follow the year of his *exile* ("our exile"; cf. Ezek 1:2), not the customary system that follows the year of reign of the king (as in 2 Kgs 25:1 and Ezek 24:1). This difference accounts nicely for what appears to be an additional year

---

6. For a helpful summary of the three Babylonian incursions against Jerusalem (605, 598/97, and 588–586 BC), see Bodi, "Ezekiel," 476–77.

for the fugitive's travel.[7] The important point is that the fugitive's news vindicates the prophet's call and message (cf. Ezek 12:27; 33:33).

33:22 *no longer silent:* At the outset of his ministry, Ezekiel was prohibited from normal discourse with people. Every word proceeding from his mouth was a word from the LORD (see discussion at Ezek 3:26–27a and 24:27). Now that this phase of ministry dominated by warnings of doom is over, Ezekiel is free to engage in normal public discourse. His identity as a prophet of doom, marked by his harsh posture toward his compatriots, is taking a turn.

33:24 *Abraham . . . one man:* With the arrival of a refugee from Jerusalem, Ezekiel's attention turns to the attitude displayed by those who survived the city's destruction. As surviving heirs, they saw themselves as rightful owners of the whole promised land. And if it was rightfully claimed by one man, their ancestor Abraham, surely their collective numbers constituted an even stronger claim (cf. Gen 12:1, 7; 13:14–17; 15:18). In effect, this amounted to a land grab because it disenfranchised others of the "remnant" who at the time were still in exile.

33:25–26 *should you then possess the land?* The LORD's response undercuts their claim. While the land grant to Abraham was confirmed as an irrevocable promise after he demonstrated his faithfulness (cf. Gen 22:15–18), enjoyment of its blessing was conditioned upon obedience (see discussion at Ezek 33:15 above). These survivors remained steadfast in their hypocrisy. While recalling the Abrahamic tradition, they overlooked Abraham's example of walking blamelessly before God (Gen 17:1). Block stresses that they displayed no recognition of the religious dimensions of the covenant promises; their attitude was essentially secular.[8]

First, they failed in their cultic responsibilities for holiness. The phrase usually translated "eat meat with the blood" (NIV; ESV; NASB; NRSV) might refer to a failure to properly drain blood from meat, whether sacrificial animals or ordinary game animals (Lev 17:13–14; 19:26). Another possibility attends closely to the preposition translated "with" and renders the phrase "eat meat *over* the blood" (the Hebrew preposition ʿal frequently denotes a position above an object). Consequently, some commentators suggest this describes a type of divination practice where blood was poured into a pit in order to raise the dead and a communal

---

7. For more discussion, see Block, *Ezekiel 25–48*, 254–55.

8. Block, *Ezekiel 25–48*, 259–60. But perhaps his argument is stretched in ascribing to them a complete denial of the LORD's sovereignty over the land.

meal was shared with the deceased (see Lev 19:26b).⁹ However, in cultic contexts, eating "with" (*'al*) is an appropriate rendering. For example, Passover meat must not be eaten "with" leaven ("do not eat *with it* [*'al*] leaven; Deut 16:3), and when Saul's men slaughter animals to satisfy their hunger (not sacrifice), they do so in haste without properly draining the blood (i.e., eat the meat "with" [*'al*] the blood; 1 Sam 14:32-34). Therefore, the usual translation is most likely; the survivors were eating meat without properly draining the blood. Additional cultic infractions compounded their sin, specifically, they sacrificed before idols. Second, their violations of God's statutes involved murder ("shed blood"—"rely on your sword"), detestable things (see Ezek 7:3-4), and adultery. Their behavior showed no change from the type of sins denounced at the outset of Ezekiel's ministry (see Ezek 7-8). Unfortunately, Jerusalem's destruction resulted in no repentance.

33:27 *fall by the sword:* These survivors may think they have escaped judgment completely. However, as promised early in Ezekiel's message of doom, even those who survive the destruction of the city itself will fall victim to God's relentless judgment. The "sword," "devouring," and "plague" recall the prophet's warning in Ezek 5:10-17.

For those in Judah, any illusion that they are the privileged remnant is dashed by Ezekiel's persistent message of judgment. If forced to choose between the remnant in Judah and those in exile, Ezekiel clearly sides with the opinion of Jeremiah: those left in Judah are the "bad figs," and relative to them, the exiles are the "good figs" (Jer 24:1-10, esp. vv. 5 and 8).¹⁰

33:30 *your people:* The phrase "your people," qualified by a description that they are visiting Ezekiel, identifies them as the prophet's fellow exiles. So Ezekiel's attention has turned from the survivors in Judah to his compatriots in Babylonia. Perhaps not "bad figs," but the prophet's assessment of them is not particularly good either. They show an interest in Ezekiel's words, perhaps recalling the oracle of Ezek 11:14-17. Now that judgment against Jerusalem is complete (surprising their expectations; cf. Ezek 12:27), is their return imminent as well?

33:31 *hear your words:* The people are giving only lip service to Ezekiel's message, not showing deeds of repentance any more than the accused back in Judah. They are still greedy and unjust (cf. Ezek 7).

---

9. Greenberg, *Ezekiel 21-37*, 684; Bodi, "Ezekiel," 478.
10. Taylor, *Ezekiel*, 218.

33:32 *love songs:* No different than in popular culture today, love songs were a source of entertainment. Some ancient Egyptian love songs actually have in their title that it is a song "for entertainment."[11] While the language of these songs is rather delicate, like that found in the Song of Solomon, it nonetheless carries a sensuous tone. Set in the context of skillful living in the intimacy of marriage, such songs can appropriately be classified as "wisdom." This classification fits both Egypt and the Old Testament. But the solemn words of a prophetic oracle are not to be associated with love songs. Therefore, it is entirely inappropriate for Ezekiel's compatriots to treat his message as just another note of happy news and entertainment. They have not taken Ezekiel's words to heart.

33:33 *When all this comes:* Ezekiel's authority as a prophet and his message of doom has been vindicated. But even though Jerusalem's fate is complete, the warning of Ezek 33:11 still applies, whether one resides among the survivors or among those in exile.[12]

Theological Bridge to Application

The theology underlying this chapter is similar to that expounded in chapter 18. It is true that corporate responsibility operates at the community level, even inter-generationally in terms of consequences; but more important is the disposition of the *individual* toward God and his ways. God is not pleased to destroy anyone, and, in fact, is eager to relent from judgment when someone turns toward him. Underlying this passage as well is God's zeal to vindicate both his word and his messenger.

Focus of Application

It is important not to confuse the message of Ezek 33 with the gospel. "Life" in the Old Covenant meant flourishing in the land under covenant blessing. There are twin, complementary messages in this chapter. Both address the presumption of privileged status. First, God is consistent in his response to people's disposition toward him. If one has walked according to God's commands, the LORD does not regard this "track record" as having any value toward future blessing. No one can rest on his or her "laurels," and turning away from God's ways can have destructive

11. See, for example *COS* 1.51: 128.
12. Greenberg, *Ezekiel 21–37*, 692.

consequences. The New Testament speaks of temporal discipline for the Christian (e.g., Acts 5:1–11; 1 Cor 5:4–5; 11:30–32; Jas 5:15–16). Conversely, no pattern of wickedness is so great that God does not bless those who (re)turn to him.

Second, the message to the survivors of Jerusalem's destruction teaches that people cannot presume upon their identity with God's covenant people. One cannot lean on a "Christian heritage" to count for anything with God (cf. John 3:5–7). Generations of churches inherit beautiful buildings, but these mean nothing without community life characterized by the ways of God. Perhaps more common to church communities today is a culture that elevates the preaching of God's word but produces no fruit of the Spirit in people's the lives. Congregants listen week in and week out, enjoy the sermon, nod their heads approvingly, but stop short of receiving conviction. As James urges, we are to be people who do the word and not simply hear it, deluding ourselves that we have satisfied our religious duty (Jas 1:22). This is what we learn from Ezekiel's compatriots who sought entertainment from a good message. The preached word is not for amusement but for changing lives.

TWO KINDS OF SHEPHERDS
Ezekiel 34:1–31

Ezekiel's Message

The Lord condemns harsh, self-serving shepherds, but he pledges himself to lead as the gentle shepherd.

Key Themes

- The Lord condemns leaders who abuse people under their care or serve to satisfy their own needs or agendas.
- The Lord pledges his personal presence to gently nourish and bless those who are his.
- The Lord promises restoration to his covenant people Israel through the agency of a gentle shepherd-king.

Context in Ezekiel

Beginning in Ezek 34, Ezekiel's ministry transitions into a new season; the gloom of winter has turned to the promise of spring. In the first 33 chapters, Ezekiel functioned as a "watchman," warning his people of God's impending judgment and urging them to turn from their waywardness to the way of the Lord. In earlier oracles, Ezekiel offered hints of God's ultimate intention to save (e.g., Ezek 11:16–21), but the dominant mood was one of doom. In this new season, the prophet encourages the people with God's promise to save. Ezekiel glances back to earlier themes of judgment, but only to underscore the glorious nature of the changes promised by God to restore his people to himself and to the blessings of the covenant. These changes begin with the Lord's plan to replace Israel's failed leadership with his own gentle presence.

Interpretive Highlights

34:2 *shepherds of Israel*: Across the ancient Near East, including Israel, the various cultures applied the metaphor of "shepherd" to human kings, and the metaphor "flocks" to the people entrusted to their care. For example, in the prologue to his famous collection of laws, the Old Babylonian king, Hammurabi, bore the title "the shepherd, selected by the god Enlil."[1] In the legend of the Sumerian king, Etana, the poem describes how the goddess "Ishtar [was looking for] a shepherd, and searching high and low for a king."[2] In similar fashion, Israel's God called David from being a literal shepherd to being a shepherd-king of his people (2 Sam 5:1–3; Ps 78:70–71). In the absence of a king, people scatter like sheep without a shepherd (1 Kgs 22:17). The metaphor brings to mind important functions of a king to protect, to unify, and to provide for his people. Ezekiel employs this to good effect as he enumerates the manner in which self-serving shepherds seek their own benefit at the expense of the flock under their care. The question whether Ezekiel had in mind the wider group of leadership in Israel and Judah, or just the royal house, is unimportant. "Shepherds" likely refers to leaders more broadly in Jer 10:21; 23:1; 25:34. Either way, the important point of the accusation remains.

34:4 *you have ruled them harshly*: If it is not bad enough for Israel's kings to have served their own self-interest at the expense of their people, their rule went beyond neglect and selfishness and was actually abusive. The most powerful of Israel's elite class was the royal house; and in an earlier indictment, Ezekiel castigated the princes for tearing and devouring God's people like roaring lions (Ezek 22:25; cf. irresponsible leaders more generally, Ezek 8:12; 13:1–7; 22:26–28). This is consistent with the portrait of royalty recorded in the historical annals of Israel and Judah (1 Kgs 12:13–14; 17:13; 21:19; 2 Kgs 21:16; 24:3–4; cf. Isa 1:15; 59:3; Mic 3:1–10). But this was also true during the time of the last kings of Judah

---

1. The Laws of Hammurabi (*COS* 2.131: 336).

2. Etana (*COS* 1.131: 453). See also Block, *Ezekiel 25–48*, 280–81; Bodi, "Ezekiel," 478.

(Jehoiakim and Zedekiah), whom Ezekiel would have had foremost in mind. Ezekiel's prophetic contemporaries had the same opinion (Jer 2:34; 7:6; 19:4-5; 22:3; Hab 1:2; Zeph 1:8-9; 3:3-4). The royal houses of Israel and Judah too often followed the opposite policies from those God intended, as the biblical portrayal of ideal kings shows (Isa 11; Ps 72).

34:5-6 *scattered . . . every high hill:* The metaphor of injured sheep takes a different twist in the image of scattering. In addition to being victims of violent injustice at the hands of their leaders, failed leadership resulted in the trauma of exile (2 Kgs 17:21-23). The phrase "every high hill" might allude to religious apostasy lead by Israel's leadership. This began early and ran throughout Israel's history (1 Kgs 14:23; 2 Kgs 17:10; Jer 2:20; see comments at Ezek 6:13; 20:28), even among those in exile early in Ezekiel's ministry (Ezek 14:1-3). However, such temptations appear to decline among the exiles, particularly after the undeniable vindication of God's judgment against idolatry (Ezek 6:8-10; 12:16).

The similarity in thought and expression between Ezekiel and his contemporary, Jeremiah, is more than coincidental (cf. Jer 23:1-6). Letters were exchanged between Jeremiah and the exiles (Jer 29:1-3). It is not surprising that these two priestly-prophets were aware of each other's messages and backed up one another in their preaching.

34:10 **hold them accountable:** Judgment oracles contain an accusation for sin and an announcement of God's intention to judge. Usually the announcement of God's intervention contains a colorful description of the doom that awaits the accused. However, here Ezekiel merely notes that the Lord holds failed leaders to account, which results in their removal from oversight. Perhaps this understatement of the negative allows Ezekiel to emphasize more the positive message that the Lord himself will lead the people as their good shepherd.[3]

34:11 *my sheep:* The personal relationship between the Lord and his people is expressed by this phrase five times in this chapter. Additionally, one finds "my people" two times, which stresses the covenant relationship (see comments at Ezek 14:8). Not only were kings described as "shepherds" in the ancient Near East, but this was a common label for deities as well. For example, an Egyptian hymn to the sun-god hails him as "valiant Shepherd who drives his flock, their refuge, made to sustain them."[4] Hittite religion regarded the sun-god as the "Shepherd of

---

3. Block, *Ezekiel 25-48*, 285.
4. Two Hymns to the Sun-God (*COS* 1.27: 44).

the Lands."[5] The famous Babylonian account featuring the god, Marduk, as creator calls him the "Shepherd" of mankind.[6] Ancient Near Eastern kings boast how they collected scattered people at the behest of their gods.[7] The Old Testament extols the LORD as "Shepherd," not only of his people (as in this chapter) but also of the individual (Gen 48:15; Ps 23).

34:12 *clouds and darkness*: In ancient days, when God appeared to his people visibly, it often took the form of a thunderstorm, with lightening against the backdrop of dark clouds (for God as warrior, see comments at Ezek 1:4). The language of *darkness* helped convey the ominous danger of such an encounter (cf. Deut 4:11; Ps 97:2-3). Accordingly, the same imagery fits well with the prophetic expectations of God's powerful interventions at any time in the future (Isa 8:22; Amos 5:18; Joel 2:2; Zeph 1:15). When we consider how these prophecies find fulfillment, they show both near and distant future applications. Zephaniah, for example, speaks of the impending destruction of Jerusalem as well as the far distant end of the age (Zeph 1:12 and Zeph 1:2-3 respectively). Ezekiel anticipates the restoration of the LORD's people to their national homeland by a mighty intervention of God's hand; and near and distant applications should be expected.

34:13 *bring them out*: Ezekiel expands upon the good news announced only briefly in Ezek 11:17. The stress on intimacy of relationship between the LORD and his people continues with v. 15, where the language is emphatic: "I myself" appears twice.

34:17 *one sheep and another*: As noted already in this passage, the leaders of the community are called out for judgment. The phrase, "one sheep and another," is followed by the phrase "rams and [male] goats." These are the males in any flock who rank highest in the butting order. They represent Israel's leaders. The same word translated "rams" (*'ayil*) is used metaphorically of Judah's leaders in Ezek 17:13, and the word translated "goats" (*'attud*) refers to the lead goats of a flock in Jer 50:8.[8] The point is that there is a distinction within God's flock. In the context of Ezek 34, the prophet is contrasting those of God's people who are weaker with those who are abusive leaders among them (cf. Ezek 34:16 and Ezek 34:20-22). This image is not to be confused with the similar metaphor

---

5. *Appu and His Two Sons* (*COS* 1.58: 154).
6. *Epic of Creation* (*COS* 1.111: 402).
7. See texts cited by Block, *Ezekiel 25-48*, 290-91 and Bodi, "Ezekiel," 479.
8. Greenberg, *Ezekiel 21-37*, 701.

used by Jesus in Matt 25:31–46, which speaks of judgment in a different context altogether. Ezekiel announces that God tolerates no bullying among this people; and more to the point, God sides with the weak (v. 22).

34:23 *one shepherd, my servant David:* This is Ezekiel's first mention of a theme that he returns to in Ezek 37:24–25. While God promises to intervene personally as Shepherd on behalf of his people, this does not exclude human agency. The commentary on v. 2 above noted that the metaphor "shepherd" applied to kings and their function in the ancient world. In particular, David is described in these terms (2 Sam 5:1–3; Ps 78:70–71). Aside from his moral failure later in life, David showed himself faithful in his devotion to the LORD (1 Sam 13:14; 16:7). Consequently, God inaugurated a covenant with David in which he established David's dynasty as the sole, rightful heirs to the throne (2 Sam 7:5–16; Pss 89:19–37; 132:11–12; cf. 2 Kgs 8:19). As these passages indicate, individual generations descended from David might forfeit the right to the throne by virtue of their disloyalty, but the LORD would nevertheless remain committed to restoring a Davidic king to the throne at his appointed time. This promise underlies God's commitment in Ezek 34:23–24 to reinstate a faithful Davidic king as a human agent to shepherd God's people.

The emphasis on "one shepherd" recalls the division of Israel into a northern and southern kingdom after the failure of Solomon and his son (1 Kgs 11:26–12:20). The promise through Ezekiel assures the reunification of the covenant people as one nation with one king. Ezekiel's message mirrors that of his contemporary, Jeremiah (Jer 23:4; 30:8–9; 33:14–26).

34:24 *prince:* This might seem a curious expression for the Davidic king. Indeed, it is Ezekiel's preferred term for Israel's chief leader. As Block observes, this "is consistent, however, with [Ezekiel's] efforts elsewhere to downplay the roles of Israel's monarchs, and harks back to 1 Kgs 11:34 . . ."[9] Block notes the deliberate wording that this "prince" will be "among" the people, not simply a tyrant *over* them.

34:25 *covenant of peace:* What is best known from Jeremiah as the hope of a "New Covenant" (Jer 31:31) is described in other terms by other prophets. Hosea was first to speak of restoration of covenant between the nation and the LORD (Hos 2:18–23). Very much like Ezekiel's expectations in Ezek 34:25–31, Hosea spoke of the renewal of relationship and blessings enjoyed in the land, both with the animal kingdom as well as

---

9. Block, *Ezekiel 25–48*, 300. See Block's n. 147 for a list of verses illustrating Ezekiel's preference for the term "prince" over "king."

agriculturally. Isaiah also anticipated a renewed covenantal relationship. Like Hosea, he employed the metaphor of a restored marriage (Isa 54:4–8; cf. Ezek 16:60); and in the same context Isaiah calls this a "covenant of peace" (Isa 54:10), to which he applies the irrevocable nature of the Noahic covenant (Isa 54:10). The Noahic Covenant itself was an assurance of peace between God and the physical earth (Gen 9:8–17). In order to underscore the covenant blessings in the land, Ezekiel follows very closely the language of Lev 26:4–13 ("peace," Lev 26:6).[10] This section of Leviticus corresponds to the blessings of the covenant in contrast to covenant curses (Lev 26:14–39). Ezekiel's emphasis, then, is on fully restored spiritual relationship as well as enjoyment of all the physical blessings of the covenant.

34:31 *sheep of my pasture:* The Hebrew text has an unusual expression, with additional words not always translated in our English versions (NIV; NRSV). It was so awkward that it was left untranslated also by the Old Greek version. But the phrase "you are human" (*'adam*) appears after the phrase "sheep of my pasture" (literally, "you are my sheep, sheep of my pasture, you are human"). Hence the ESV translates the expression "human sheep of my pasture" (cf. NASB; NET). It is perhaps an emphatic way of restating the covenantal relationship: "you are my flock ... you are my *people*."[11]

Theological Bridge to Application

The faithfulness of God to his covenant promises undergirds this entire chapter. First, on account of his bountiful mercy he pledges himself to restoring relationship with his wayward children. In accord with the expectations of other prophets (Hosea, Isaiah, Jeremiah), Ezekiel graphically portrays the restoration of covenant blessings to Israel (and by extension, those joined in covenant through Israel's Davidic king). Inseparably related to this blessing is the agent of God's blessing, a future king in the line of David. The interesting paradox of Ezek 24 is how to integrate the fact that God *himself* promises to be the Shepherd, yet at the same time this gentle kingship comes through human agency. It would go too far on the basis of Ezekiel alone to posit a messianic God-man, but this dual

---

10. See the chart in Block, *Ezekiel 25–48*, 304.
11. Block, *Ezekiel 25–48*, 308.

expectation of both a divine *and* a human shepherd finds elegant satisfaction in the theology of the incarnation.

Focus of Application

The application of this chapter to Christian leaders is one of the most devastating in all the Bible. Jesus' ministry to the weak and poor was energized by his realization that all too often human leaders fail to care for the most needy (Matt 9:35–37). Jesus' parable of the lost sheep (Luke 15:3–7) was directed at indifferent and self-righteous leaders (cf. parable of the lost son; Luke 15:11–32). The apostles followed Jesus' example, caring for both spiritual and physical needs (cf. Gal 2:10; 2 Cor 8:6–15; spiritual shepherds in Acts 20:28–31).

It is all too easy, however, to point fingers at soft targets, like heretics or some televangelists. Both lead God's people astray from truth about God, and the latter "fleece the flock" (as the saying goes) to finance extravagant lifestyles. More insidious is the temptation for leaders to maneuver with the shrewdness of a serpent to protect their power or advance their agenda. The term "spiritual abuse" has come into use to describe the manner of leaders who control the details of people's lives, or who discipline behavior that is not in accordance with the particular expressions of faith characteristic of their local spiritual community. (This is referring to matters lying outside the consensus of the rule of life for God's people throughout church history). This chapter also warns anyone, not just leaders, who use their social power to gang up and bully others. "Mobbing" is the technical term being used for such dynamics.[12] See also the comments on application for Ezek 19:1–14.

But the key emphasis in Ezek 24 is not on the failure of human leaders. It is on the exaltation of the LORD's perfect leadership. While the Twenty-Third Psalm has encouraged individuals since time immemorial, the message of Ezekiel would direct our attention to the community-wide

---

12. The number of search hits on the key words, "bullying" "mobbing" "church" is shocking. For general introduction, see "Church Bullying: An Introduction," listed in the bibliography. "Mobbing" specifically involves church staff. It can occur *to* church staff members or in the context of volunteer programs. For mobbing among church staff, see the dissertation by Vensel, "Mobbing, Burnout, and Religious Coping," which is available online. A brief video summary can be viewed at https://youtu.be/4HpN34SSkhY. For academic treatment of the phenomenon more broadly, see Duffy and Sperry, *Mobbing*.

scope of the Lord's leadership. What kind of flock is he gathering? It is well to meditate on the Old Testament portrait of God as Shepherd, to allow this image to endear us to him, to move our hearts to follow his ways as individuals and as a flock. Ezekiel better prepares us for the next step, to consider our Great Shepherd, Jesus (1 Pet 5:4), who by his sacrificial service calls us to follow him (John 10:1–18, 25–30 [the fulfillment of Ezekiel's hope]).

RECLAIMING AND RENEWING THE LAND[1]

Ezekiel 35:1—36:15

Ezekiel's Message

The Lord zealously guards that which is his and prepares the way for fulfillment of his promises.

Key Themes

- The Lord zealously guards that which is his against the pretension of arrogant people.
- The Lord prepares the way for fulfillment of his promises to bless his people.
- The grant of fruitful land to the nation Israel remains a sworn commitment of the Lord.
- The Lord will reverse the shame of his people who suffer scorn.

Context in Ezekiel

The chapter-verse division between Ezek 35 and 36 is an unfortunate break. As noted by commentators, several considerations favor

---

1. Section title from Greenberg, *Ezekiel 21–37*, 710.

combining Ezek 35:1–15 with Ezek 36:1–15.2 A primary reason is that Ezekiel himself includes Ezek 36:1–15 within the same unit, introduced by the "word of the Lord" formula in Ezek 35:1 (the next use of this introduction is Ezek 36:16). Both Ezek 35:1–15 and 36:1–15 address the Lord's concern over who possesses his land (e.g., Ezek 35:10; 36:5, 8, 12), and both halves begin with the motif, "mountain(s)," to address the two people groups concerned (Edom and Israel). In addition, many other phrases mirror one another in the two sections; for example, "desolate/full towns" (Ezek 35:4, 9; 36:10–11); "hills, valleys, ravines" (Ezek 35:8; 36:4); reversal of fortune (Ezek 35:15; 36:7, 13–15). Therefore, these two sections are combined in this exposition.

If Ezek 34 concerns restoration of proper leadership of God's people for returning to the land, this unit concerns preparation of the land itself. Already in Ezek 25:12–14, the prophet delivered an oracle against Edom. But here, Edom's role is specifically related to possession of the land promised to Israel. God will first clear the land of enemies, and then change the land itself into a place of fruitful blessing.

Interpretive Highlights

35:2 *Mount Seir*: In the aftermath of Jacob and Esau's falling out, Esau settled in the high hills to the south of the Dead Sea, known as the "land of Seir" (Gen 32:3; 36:8). Esau's descendants became known as the Edomites (Gen 36:43; Ezek 35:15). Well before the Israelites settled the land, this region south of the Dead Sea was known as "Seir" in Egyptian records (fourteenth to twelfth-centuries BC), and it continued to be identified as such by Assyrians shortly before Israel's exile. A Judean inscription dating to the time of the Babylonian crisis refers to Edomite raids into southern Judah, and other artifacts discovered in the region bear the name of the Edomite god, Qaus.[3]

35:5 *ancient hostility*: Beginning with Israel's and Edom's forefathers, Jacob and Esau, there was dispute over the land ("blessing" involved inheritance rights; Gen 27:1–41). While Jacob and Esau were eventually reconciled (Gen 33:1–11), distrust remained in the memory of the Edomites, who blocked Israel's migration to the land of promise

---

2. The summaries by Cooper, *Ezekiel*, 306–7 and Block, *Ezekiel 25–48*, 309–10 are particularly helpful and more complete than offered here.

3. Bodi, "Ezekiel," 480.

(Num 20:14-21). Hostilities continued throughout the history of the two nations (1 Sam 14:47; 1 Kgs 11:14-22; 2 Kgs 8:20-22; 2 Chr 20:1-23; 28:17). Most relevant to Ezekiel's accusations is Edom's alliance with the Babylonians to destroy Judah and Jerusalem (Ps 137:7; Obad 10-14).[4] Edom itself fell prey to the Babylonian army some decades after Jerusalem's fall.[5]

35:6 *bloodshed*: The language of this verse bears close connection with the asylum provisions of Mosaic law (Deut 19:6; cf. Num 35:20-21). In the case of accidental homicide (i.e., manslaughter), the law provided refuge for one who might otherwise be killed by an avenging family member. "Manslaughter" was not penalized by death, as was premeditated murder, which was a more heinous crime. The echo of this legal language in Ezekiel portrays Edom's violence against Judah in terms of murderous intent, possibly even alluding to the slaughter of fugitives who were running from the Babylonians.[6]

35:10 *these two nations*: Even though Edom's actions involved only the southern kingdom of Judah, their aspirations for a land grab were perhaps more greedy, including hope of gaining territory in the former northern kingdom of Israel as well (for "two nations," see Ezek 37:22).

35:10 *I the* Lord *was there*: It was noted above that Edomite occupation of the land brought the presence of their god, Qaus (see comments at Ezek 35:2). This implies a claim that the territory was under this deity's ownership. Although the Lord did abandon his temple and holy city, Jerusalem, this abandonment involved only the special manifestation of his presence in the holy of holies (see comments at Ezek 10:18-19). But he did not abandon his land nor forfeit sovereign lordship. His continuing presence meant that the land remained his to dispose, and to restore to full blessing, as he wills (Ezek 48:35: "The Lord is there.")

35:11 *treat you in accordance*: This expresses the judicial principle that God's judgment measures in a balanced way the severity of the crime (*lex talionis*; cf. Ezek 35:15). It does not necessarily mean a literal recompense, rather a measured punishment or fair compensation (e.g., Exod 21:23-27). But in cases of premeditated murder, to which Edom's violent militarism is comparable, the judgment was death, with no recourse to paying a monetary ransom (Exod 21:12-14; Num 35:30-31).

---

4. Alexander, "Ezekiel," 838-39.
5. Bodi, "Ezekiel," 480.
6. Greenberg, *Ezekiel 21-37*, 713; Block, *Ezekiel 25-48*, 317-18.

35:13 *you boasted against me:* Because of a rare word in this verse, the translations vary slightly, but the point is clear. Edom was guilty not only for their merciless violence against the Lord's people in Judah, but they displayed arrogance against God himself. They acted as though the Lord were no longer present in the land (Ezek 35:10), and they taunted his reputation (cf. the fall of Belshazzar for similar *hubris*; Dan 5:22–31).

35:15 *inheritance of the house of Israel:* As Block notes, this is an underlying premise of the whole unit. God allotted the land of Abraham's sojourning to Israel (Edom also received its allotment; Deut 2:4–6), and it remained not only God's to give but Israel's to possess by promise.[7]

36:1 *Mountains of Israel:* Like the previous section, a geographical name associated with a people stands in for the people themselves (Mount Seir = Edom; Ezek 35:15). Here, Ezekiel addresses the "Mountains of Israel," but it is a figure of speech, indirectly encouraging the exiles in Babylon regarding the blessings that will be theirs upon return to the land of their inheritance (see comments at Ezek 6:3). Instead of "doom" for the "mountains of Israel," announced in Ezek 6:3, this is an oracle of salvation.

36:2 *ancient heights:* This oracle of encouragement first takes the form of an announcement of judgment against Israel's enemies, resumed from the previous section (Ezek 35:1–15). The expression "ancient heights" is a poetic designation for the "mountains of Israel" (Deut 33:15). The stress on antiquity in the mouth of Israel's enemies perhaps reflects their glee at possessing territory long occupied by Israel. The hills of Israel had been mountain shrines long before the Israelite occupation, and indeed had been the place of Israel's own idolatrous worship (Num 35:52; see comments at Ezek 6:3 and the **Special Topic: High Places and Sacred Trees**).

36:3 *rest of the nations:* The generic term "enemy" was used in the previous verse, and the mention of "the rest" here indicates that the oracle against Edom was at the same time an oracle against all of Israel's enemies who partnered in possessing Israel's "mountains." Edom was singled out in Ezek 35:1–15 because of its long-standing animosity, but its representative function is shown by the mention again of the "rest of the nations" together with "Edom" in Ezek 36:5.[8]

---

7. Block, *Ezekiel 25–48*, 321–22.
8. Block, *Ezekiel 25–48*, 330.

36:5 *burning zeal:* This is a strong description of the Lord's passionate jealousy on behalf of his people, used elsewhere only in Zeph 1:18 and 3:8 (cf. Ezek 36:6). The Hebrew text that the NIV translates "with glee and malice in their hearts" is captured more formally by Greenberg's rendering: "with wholehearted rejoicing, with wholesouled contempt" (cf. NASB).[9] This sort of malicious hatred finds reciprocal response from God (see comments at Ezek 25:6).

36:8 *you . . . will produce . . . for my people:* Although God speaks directly to the land here, the import of the promises is addressed indirectly to his people who will once again enjoy the abundant blessing of the land. Covenant blessing entails fruitfulness of plants (Lev 26:4–5, 10; Deut 28:4–5) and animals (Deut 28:4; cf. Ezek 36:11). The people who were once decimated on account of covenant curses (Ezek 5:1–4, 12–17) will multiply (Ezek 36:10–11).

36:8 *my people . . . they will soon come home:* The phrase "my people" is the standard covenant formula that asserts special relationship (Exod 3:7; 5:1; 6:7; Hos 2:23). With restoration of this relationship comes restoration of homeland as a permanent possession (Ezek 36:12).

36:13 *you devour your people:* If the land could figuratively "vomit" people out (Lev 28:25–28; 20:22), then the notion of "devouring" is understandable. Rather than expulsion from the land, this indicates the death of its occupants. There is nothing inherently "jinxed" (accursed) about the nature of the land; the Lord promises a reversal of any such appearances. It is a land God cares for and intends as a blessing (Deut 11:10). And so its inhabitants, Israel, will no longer suffer the taunts of other nations.

Theological Bridge to Application

Several truths about the character of God underlie this passage. First, God is sovereign owner and Lord of his good earth (Ps 24:1). The pretension of people to the contrary only rouses his anger, as does any arrogant posturing against him (Ezek 35:10, 13). Second, the Lord is true to his covenant promises. The promise of land to Abraham (Gen 12:1–3; 15:7–20; 17:8) comes to prominence in this passage; and throughout Ezek 36:8–15 is the language of covenant blessing as he restores his people to their inheritance. This was mentioned briefly in Ezek 11:16–17; but with

9. Greenberg, *Ezekiel 21–37*, 718.

the appearance of this theme in Ezek 35:1—36:15, it becomes central to the chapters of Ezekiel that follow. Third, as a corollary to this, he zealously intervenes to remove the shame of his people. The application of these truths is tricky, as discussed below.

Special Topic: Modern Israel in the Land

No one questions the relevance of the these oracles to the restoration of Israel after the exile. This began shortly after Cyrus's decree in 539 BC to allow deported peoples to return to their native homelands. But contemporary relevance of Ezek 35–37 is a more complicated question, especially in view of current political issues in the Middle East. Space only allows brief comment about ethnic Israel's future and the land after the destruction of Jerusalem and scattering of Jews during the Jewish-Roman wars (AD 66–136). One approach follows from a belief that ethnic Israel has been superseded as the special people of God by the church, who are now the heirs of Abraham by spiritual descent (e.g., Rom 9:8; Gal 6:16; 1 Pet 2:9). In the future expectations of this theological view, the physical land promises are no longer relevant. The Bible has no bearing on the question of modern Israel's right to a national homeland. Another view regarding Israel's future is that some sort of physical restoration of ethnic Israel to the land promised to Abraham is necessary in order to satisfy the covenantal and prophetic language in the Old Testament (e.g., Acts 1:6; 3:21; Rom 11:26). This makes the best sense of the grand narrative from Genesis to Revelation. The expectations of Ezekiel and other prophets cannot possibly be fulfilled by events in the postexilic period. More telling, the next unit in Ezekiel (Ezek 36:16–38) stresses just how important it is to God's reputation not to "give up" on the *nation* Israel. But even assuming the view that God will yet restore national Israel, the application to contemporary, international politics is much more complicated than typically assumed.

First, only a genuine prophet has the authority to declare what God is doing in current events. The United Nations authorization of a national homeland for Jews may or may not be a stage in the fulfillment of Old Testament promises (see commentary on Ezek 37:1–14). More important is the realization that modern-day Israel is a secular state, and from the standpoint of Christian theology, the people as a whole have no allegiance to Israel's Messiah, Jesus. Consequently, the nation is not following covenantal stipulations necessary to rightfully enjoy blessing (see commentary at Ezek 36:16–38). Those who advocate a permissive political posture toward modern-day Israel should be as eager to apply Old Testament legal and prophetic expectations of covenant faithfulness and justice as they are to declare blessing (see Focus of Application under Ezek 25:1–17). What of the prophetic pronouncement of covenant curses for faithlessness and injustice? Faithful Christian preaching requires application of God's word without respect to person or nation (e.g., Acts 7:1–53).

Consequently, without contemporary, prophetic authorization on how to configure political boundaries *today*, in the Middle East or on any continent, Christians must exercise caution before declaring what God is or is not doing on the geopolitical landscape. What is clear is the mandate to uphold in a consistent manner the Bible's message of righteousness and justice.

Focus of Application

Unless one is preaching specifically on the theology of *future* things, the application of this passage is not divine authorization regarding *contemporary* geopolitical boundaries (see **Special Topic: Modern Israel in the Land**). Ezekiel 35:1—36:15 is a powerful message about the sovereignty of God as LORD of his earth, who tolerates no rivals, especially *arrogant* challenges to his lordship. It is the modernist agenda to replace the Creator-LORD of the earth with gods of its own making (e.g., individualism, scientism), even as Edom set up its own tribal deity, Qaus, in the vacuum they thought was left by the departure of Israel's God, Yahweh.

Similar to the message of Ezek 25:1–17, God does not tolerate mocking scorn at the failure of others. Rather, he rises to vindicate his people (Ps 12:5). This passage in Ezekiel anticipates the *eventual* restoration of Israel to a *permanent* homeland (Ezek 36:12). It is a promise that is future, but assured. On analogy to this, because he is a covenant-keeping God, he will vindicate followers of Jesus; all who bear public or private shame in his name will one day be released to participate in the lavish blessing of our generous God.

SPIRITUAL TRANSFORMATION FOR GOD'S HONOR

Ezekiel 36:16–38

Ezekiel's Message

The Lord promises to defend his reputation by assuring fulfillment of his promises and restoring a people worthy to be called by his name.

Key Themes

- The Lord will vindicate his reputation, which is inseparably linked to his holy nature.
- The Lord will sovereignly fulfill his promises.
- By his Spirit, the Lord provides the internal impulse necessary for allegiance and faithful obedience to him.

Context in Ezekiel

The previous section of Ezekiel (Ezek 35:1—36:15) affirmed God's commitment to fulfill his covenant promise to Abraham that his descendants would indeed inherit a national homeland. A new unit begins in Ezek 36:16 ("Again, the word of the Lord came . . .") that takes up another problem created by the need for an exile in the first place, namely, the damage it inflicted on the reputation of Israel's God. Not only did the reality of exile raise a question about God's faithfulness to his promises, but an equally severe problem remained regarding the dishonor of God's name by the wayward behavior of his covenant people. The LORD commits himself to resolve both problems, and it is the spiritual transformation required by the covenant that Ezekiel takes up in this section.

Interpretive Highlights

36:17 *they defiled [the land] by their conduct:* Ezekiel draws on his priestly vocabulary to describe the consequences of Israel's immoral behavior in the land where God dwells in holiness. Both the verb translated "defiled" and its noun form ("uncleanness," or "impurity, also used in this verse) refer to actions or conditions that are incompatible with sacred space. There is nothing necessarily sinful in relation to the clean/unclean distinction. For example, sexual relations between a husband and wife, or the natural reproductive cycle of women who menstruate, rendered them "unclean" for a time (Lev 15:16–19). Even the process of childbirth rendered a woman temporarily "unclean" (Lev 12:1–8). This meant only that they were ineligible to enter the sacred space of the temple during their uncleanness. Similarly, abnormal conditions of the skin or clothing were also related to the condition of uncleanness (Lev 13:1–2, 47–49). For various reasons, these regulations pertained to what might contaminate sacred space. However, this purity language is also used *metaphorically* for the contamination that did result from sinful actions (as in this verse). Violence and idolatry were revolting to divine sanctity (see the commentary at Ezek 24:13). The result was the departure of God's glorious presence (see commentary at Ezek 10:18–19) and the expulsion of Israel from the sacred land (Ezek 36:19; cf. the necessity of driving out the Canaanite inhabitants who defiled the land; Lev 18:24–28).

36:20 *profaned my holy name:* The word translated "profaned" belongs to the same priestly vocabulary as "defile"/"unclean" and describes the polluting effect of sin (Lev 18:21; 19:12; 20:3; Ezek 20:39). This verse strikes the primary concern of this passage, the "name" of God (= "reputation"; Prov 22:1; 30:9 [of God]; Eccl 7:1). The concept of "holy" is that something is "set apart" as special. It could refer to priests (Lev 21:8), offerings (Lev 7:6), worship occasions (Neh 8:11), even God's people in a general sense of service (Exod 19:6; Deut 7:6). The word often has moral connotations (Lev 19:2, with following commandments), but is broader than ethical character. Because God is incomparable and transcends his creation, he is "holy" (set apart) in an absolute sense.

36:20 *they had to leave his land*: The behavior of the LORD's people brought defilement to God's land by violating even the sensibilities of the surrounding nations (Ezek 5:7; cf. Ezek 14:22-23). But with the exile, two new challenges to God's reputation arose. Not only did it appear that he was incapable of managing his people but he was also either (1) unwilling to protect them, or (2) incapable of protecting them. The Babylonian conquest could be interpreted as demonstrating the superiority of Babylon's god, Marduk, over Israel's God, Yahweh. As Block notes, "The first option challenges Yahweh's credibility and integrity; the second, his sovereignty."[1] A similar dilemma confronted the LORD in past episodes of the nation's history where he could justifiably have destroyed them (Exod 32:11-14; Ezek 20:8-22). In the verses that follow, the LORD declares his commitment to deal with all of the above (cf. Ezek 20:33, 41); not only with his people's displacement from their national homeland (Ezek 36:22-23), but also the problem of their behavior (Ezek 36:24-28).

36:23[2] *when I am proved holy*: The demonstration of God's transcendent sovereignty depends on his power to save his people. The

---

1. Block, *Ezekiel 25-48*, 348.

2. Because it is so theologically significant, this passage needs special comment due to a difficulty with the text. There is one important witness to the Old Greek translation of Ezekiel that does not contain the last part of Ezek 36:23 through Ezek 36:38. It is possible that a scribe's eye mistakenly jumped from "that I am the LORD" in Ezek 36:23 to the same phrase at the end of Ezek 36:38. This is a common mistake for scribes to make, and it could have occurred in the copying of a Hebrew manuscript, during translation of this passage into Greek, or in the transmission of the Greek translation itself. Some argue this is too large a block of text to be omitted by such a mistake (15 verses). But it is possible, depending on page layout. One can imagine, for example, a scribe taking a short break from transcription only to return to the same phrase but at the wrong location on the page. Alternatively, perhaps a full page of a manuscript was skipped over or lost. There are also stylistic features in the wording of Ezek 36:24-38 that lead some scholars to suspect that these are not original to Ezekiel; but this type of argumentation is very subjective. It is also pointed out that this particular Greek manuscript even contains differences in the order of complete chapters in this part of the book (Ezek 36:23 > chapters 38-39 > chapter 37 > chapters 40-48). Such considerations lead some scholars to conclude there was in existence another Hebrew version of Ezekiel with these major differences. It is interesting that the chapter rearrangement and missing passage (Ezek 36:23b-38) are both in the same manuscript. However, the chapter rearrangement is not *necessarily* related to the absence of Ezek 36:23b-38. For a helpful summary, see Lyons, *Introduction to the Study of Ezekiel*, 75-77. With caution and good reason all English translations include Ezek 36:23b-38, not allowing evidence of only one Greek manuscript to weigh so heavily. All other Greek manuscripts

covenant established Israel as a priestly nation, that is, a people whose mission it is to mediate a relationship between God and the other nations (Exod 19:5–6; cf. Gen 12:3). This is the active responsibility of the people. However, even in their passive role as recipients of grace, the Lord's dealings with his people demonstrates his unique character as the one true God. The nations would view him not just as a tribal deity, but "Lord of the whole earth."[3] This mission is fundamental to the narrative arc of the whole Bible (see discussion at Ezek 36:36).

36:25 *sprinkle clean water*: Water served to symbolize cleansing from ceremonial defilement where no sin was involved (Exod 30:17–21; Lev 14:2, 8–9, 51–52; cf. above discussion about "unclean"). But metaphorically, water was also an image for cleansing from sin (Ps 51:7). The spiritual cleansing mentioned in this verse is bracketed by the same comment in v. 29. Inside this bracket (Ezek 36:26–27), Ezekiel describes the means by which God will accomplish an internal renewal that corresponds to this outward, ritual symbol of cleansing.

36:26 *new heart . . . new spirit*: Ezekiel used this language in Ezek 18:31 to challenge individuals to turn to God and his ways. But the inward transformation necessary for *the nation as a whole* to be faithful to the Lord was only anticipated in the Old Covenant and not part of its provisions (see **Special Topic: Transformation of Heart in the Old Covenant**). Several prophets announce the day when such faithfulness would characterize the nation, and they describe the corresponding blessings (see discussion at Ezek 34:25). Jeremiah gave this promise its most commonly know designation, "the New Covenant" (Jer 31:31), in which the desire for allegiance and faithful service would become an internal instinct (Jer 31:33–34). Ezekiel describes this promise in his own terms, with his characteristic emphasis on God's Spirit. The contrasting metaphors, "stone" and "flesh," correspond to spiritual sensibilities that are either dead or living.

---

include the passage, as does all the evidence from Hebrew manuscripts. Every ancient authority considered the passage in question to be canonical, and these verses seem necessary to make good sense of the flow of thought in the context. Several major, technical commentaries from a variety of traditions argue in favor of the originality of these verses (notably Zimmerli, *Ezekiel 25–48*, 242, 245, Greenberg, *Ezekiel 21–37*, 739–40, and Block, *Ezekiel 25–48*, 337–43). Because of the importance of this passage and the fact that some scholars prefer to view it as a secondary insertion, it is wise to be aware of this difficulty, but also to appreciate the authority in support of its authenticity.

3. Taylor, *Ezekiel*, 231.

Special Topic: Transformation of Heart in the Old Covenant

The book of Deuteronomy records Moses' farewell address to the nation in which he restates the terms of the covenant relationship between God and Israel. The Old Covenant was a legal treaty, but it called for more than a contractual conformity to covenant stipulations. The essence of the covenant is a relationship of affectionate allegiance to the LORD that is characterized by obedience—a life that is fundamentally a matter of the "heart" (Deut 4:9, 39; 6:4–6 [Israel's creed]; 8:2; 10:12; 11:13; 13:3; 26:16; 29:18). But there was nothing in the stipulations of the covenant itself that provided for compliance—for walking faithfully with the LORD. Indeed, Moses warned Israel that their *natural* inclination was *not* toward such faithful commitment (Deut 5:29). Nevertheless, an inward turning of desire toward the LORD was necessary; and Moses used the outward symbol of circumcision as the metaphor for the call to inward covenant fidelity (Deut 10:15–16; humans should mirror the LORD's affection). Such inward transformation is the work of God. This is stressed, for example, in Deut 29:4, where the word translated "mind" (NIV; NRSV) is the same Hebrew word usually translated "heart" (ESV). While God's Spirit worked this inward transformation in the lives of *individuals* in the Old Testament (Ps 51:12, "willing spirit"; Ps 40:8, "your law is within my inner self"; cf. Jer 31:33), this was not part of the Old Covenant experienced by *all* members of the covenant community (i.e., the nation as a whole). With prophetic foresight, Moses announced that a day would come when God would extend this inward grace to the nation as a whole (Deut 30:6; in the context of a promised return from exile). It is this movement of God's Spirit that Ezekiel eagerly anticipates.

36:27 *move you to follow:* The NIV nicely nuances the Hebrew text, which the NASB and ESV render "cause you to walk." The result of inward transformation is outward faithfulness (Ezek 36:27). The promise that God's Spirit would cause his people to walk in his ways should not be over interpreted in a mechanistic, deterministic fashion. It is true that the inward impulse to spiritual life comes from God's Spirit (see Ezek 37:1–14), but nothing in the image necessitates a puppet-like control of individual decisions. Greenberg notes how Jeremiah carefully balances the sovereign work of God with the human impulse side (Jer 24:7; 31:18–20; Lam 5:21).[4] This is a delicate mystery that calls for sensitivity regardless of one's theological tradition.

4. Greenberg, *Ezekiel 21–37*, 736.

36:30 *increase the fruit* . . . Beginning in Ezek 36:29, the prophet describes the result of spiritual and physical restoration (see comments at Ezek 36:8 for realization of covenant blessings).

36:31 *loath yourselves* . . . One result of spiritual renewal is the sensitivity of heart to grieve over personal sin (see comments at Ezek 6:9; cf. 20:43). Lament psalms (e.g., Pss 38 and 51; cf. Isa 59:12–15; Dan 9:4–19; Ezra 9:5–15) illustrate the emotional anguish that appropriately accompanies realization of how one's actions have offended God or injured others.

36:35 *the garden of Eden:* There could be no more vivid portrait of what life might be like without the curse than the image of Eden's garden in Gen 2 (cf. Ezek 47, with allusion to the rivers). With this mention of Eden, Ezekiel describes lavish fruit in a well-cultivated land that has been planted by the LORD himself (Ezek 36:29–30, 34, 36).

36:36 *the nations . . . will know:* The missional heart of God shows forth in this passage, coming to climactic expression in this verse. Not only is God concerned for his holiness, but underlying this is his desire to make clear to all people that the LORD is the true God who is worthy of relationship.[5] The passage ends on the same note of concern for God's special covenant nation (Ezek 36:38).

Theological Bridge to Application

God's holiness is arguably the most important attribute in answering the question, "Who is God"? Holiness implicates his transcendence over creation and, in the moral sphere, assures that he is indeed a good God. Proper understanding of this is important for appreciating what is at stake in this passage. Failure of God's promises might suggest that he is either unable or unwilling to save. If either is true, it threatens the truthfulness of the gospel itself and the credibility of the mission of God.

Focus of Application

In order to clarify the meaning of this passage, it is important to help people understand the difference between what God promised under the Old Covenant and what he provides in the New Covenant. In Moses' preaching of the Old Covenant, he emphasized that a proper relationship

---

5. Wright, *Ezekiel*, 292.

with God is always a matter of affection in the heart, the desire for whole relationship with him. This understanding may have become perverted in some Israelite and Jewish circles, but no differently than it is perverted today in some Christian circles. A "heart" relationship is what God has *always* demanded, and many within the Old Covenant community were enlivened by God's Spirit and understood this. But the Old Covenant stipulations did not provide inward "circumcision" for the community *as a whole*. In contrast, the New Covenant promises that God's Spirit creates a *community* in which everyone within that community is characterized by the Spirit's work (Rom 8:1–4, 14; Gal 5:16–25).

The physical blessings described in this passage were linked to stipulations for the nation Israel under the Old Covenant, not for the church. But the more difficult part of this passage is not explaining why faithful Christians are not always materially prosperous, but why Christians frequently fail to walk in the ways of the Lord. We are complicated creatures, and until the redemption of our bodies we continue to suffer weaknesses. Sin is both complicated and relentless. It is important to recognize that we live in a "now but not yet" expression of God's kingdom. Blessings of the New Covenant are realized by God's people today (e.g., Eph 1:3). But the full experience of God's promises, both materially and spiritually (Eph 1:13–14), await the coming of Jesus Messiah.

This passage impresses on us the importance of the Lord's reputation for his mission in the world. How we live can glorify his name or tarnish it; we can either advance his kingdom or diminish it.

A WHOLE COVENANT PACKAGE
Ezekiel 37:1–28

Ezekiel's Message

The LORD brings to consummation all his covenant promises on behalf of his helpless people.

Key Themes

- Humans are spiritually helpless apart from the intervention of God's Spirit.
- God commits to permanent restoration of his people Israel, both physically and spiritually.
- The fullness of covenant blessing entails restoration of wholeness ("peace") under God's Davidic king and in God's presence.

Context in Ezekiel

With chapter 37 of Ezekiel, the prophet's announcement of restoration for the people reaches a crescendo in the graphic vision of a resurrected nation. But the break as a new preaching unit is somewhat artificial. The vision of breathing new life by the Spirit into dead bones illustrates the promise of inward spiritual restoration announced in the previous oracle; and so Ezek 37:1–14 is a continuation of chapter 36.[1] In addition, Eze-

---

1. Alexander, "Ezekiel," 848.

kiel's use of the introduction formula, "The word of of the LORD came," in Ezek 37:15 marks the second half of the chapter as a distinct unit. Therefore a word is in order for holding the two halves together.

The justification is in part a pragmatic choice, since the depth and complexity of the message in Ezek 36:16-38 merits individual attention in its own right, without the added time necessary to expound the vision of dry bones. Also, in several respects, the message of Ezek 37:15-38 repeats what Ezekiel has already announced in Ezek 34:20-31, allowing briefer treatment. From a positive perspective, retaining Ezek 37 as a single unit makes good rhetorical sense. First, Ezek 37:15-38 summarizes everything Ezekiel has announced regarding the fulfillment of God's covenant promises to Israel. Second, the vision of resurrection graphically portrays the work of God's Spirit to bring it all to reality. Hence, combining together the two sub-units of Ezek 37 together makes good sense as a climactic summary of these promises.

Interpretive Highlights

37:1 *The hand of the LORD was on me:* Visionary experiences were a notable means by which Ezekiel sometimes received the divine message (Ezek 1:1—3:15; 8:1—11:25; 40:1—48:35). This particular experience includes a symbolic vision (Ezek 37:1-10) and its interpretation (Ezek 37:11 14). The Spirit's agency in creating such revelatory experiences through ecstatic (not physical) transport is made more clear in Ezek 11:24.[2] The Hebrew text specifies "*the* valley," hence a place recognizable to Ezekiel. The same word is translated "plain" in Ezek 3:22-23 (NIV; NASB; but "valley," ESV); perhaps the broad river valley (or canals) in the vicinity of Ezekiel and the exiles.

37:3 *can these bones live?* The emphasis that the bones are very dry points to the severity of the problem; a state of extreme deterioration.[3] The scene recalls what a battle field would look like long after the carnage, perhaps alluding to one of the covenant curses (Deut 28:25-26).[4] The question, then, is rhetorical. It solicits a humble response from the prophet, who knows full well the hopeless condition of these former bodies. An intact corpse might be revived (cf. 1 Kgs 17:17-23; 2 Kgs 4:17-37);

---

2. Block, *Ezekiel 25-48*, 373.
3. Greenberg, *Ezekiel 21-37*, 742.
4. Greenberg, *Ezekiel 21-37*, 748; Block, *Ezekiel 25-48*, 378.

but what of this desperate scenario? Yet Ezekiel leaves the assessment to the sovereign determination of God.

37:4 Prophesy to these bones: As Block astutely observes, the hypothetical audience is the bones, but the real audience is the exilic community to whom Ezekiel announces God's plan. The intent is to encourage the hearts of God's people and revitalize their spiritual faith, as noted by the acknowledgement formula in v. 6.[5]

37:5 *I will make breath enter you:* The word translated "breath" here and in vv. 6, 8, 9, and 10 (NIV; ESV; NASB) is the same word that is translated "Spirit" (*ruah*) in Ezek 37:1, 14. While overlapping in meaning with another word for "breath" (*nishmah*, in Gen 2:7) the word *ruah* is more flexible in its usage. It refers to the breath necessary for life (Gen 6:17; Ps 146:4), as in these verses; and by extension, one's vitality (Judg 15:19; 1 Sam 30:12). Often it denotes the "wind" (Gen 8:1; Ps 135:7), as in Ezek 37:9. And as a force that is both powerful and invisible, it is an appropriate metaphor for God's "Spirit" (Gen 41:38; Exod 31:3; Ps 139:7; Ezek 11:5); and so is used this way in Ezek 37:1 and 14. Ezekiel plays on the variety of meanings for this word throughout the context. It refers to the "breath" given to lifeless bodies, but its ultimate source is strongly identified as God's Spirit.

37:8 *there was no breath in them:* This phrase marks the end of a first stage in what is described as a two-stage process. Physical reassembly does not constitute "life." A dead corpse needs animation, which this phrase underscores. On the question of two stages in the historical outworking of the prophecy, see Ezek 37:14 below.

37:9 *the four winds:* The phrase, "four winds," is the equivalent of our modern four compass points, i.e., from all directions (e.g., Jer 49:36; Zech 2:6). Once again, the Hebrew word *ruah* performs double duty as it denotes the meteorological wind yet at the same time is a metaphor describing the action of God's Spirit to give life to the reconstituted bodies. Consistent with the idea that the scattered bones were the result of a massive battle-field slaughter, the reversal of the process results in the raising of a large "army" (v. 10, *hayil*; Deut 11:4; Ezek 38:15).

37:11 *whole house of Israel:* Verse 11 begins the interpretation of the vision. The "bones" are the "whole house of Israel." This phrase refers specifically to Ezekiel's contemporaries, since God cites their words of despair in exile. It is rather limited, then, by context and does not include

---

5. Block, *Ezekiel 25–48*, 376.

ethnic Israel, universally speaking. However, the expression "whole house" incorporates not just the Judean exiles in Babylon but also those from the northern tribes who were deported by the Assyrians. This can be inferred from the following context in which both north and south are united as "one stick" (Ezek 37:15–17).

37:11 *dried up . . . cut off*: The dryness of the bones refers to the expired hope of Ezekiel's contemporaries who are waiting for God to intervene. One could use word pictures of withered flowers, where the same word is used for "dried" (Isa 40:24; Ezek 17:9). But the graphic vision should be sufficient to convey their felt condition. The word for "cut off" is unusual, but has parallels in the image of Isaiah's servant separated from life and community (Isa 53:8), or the psalmist feeling alienated from God (Ps 31:22). The result is a complete loss of hope in God.

37:12 *open your graves:* There is some discussion as to whether this refers to bodily resurrection of individuals at the end of the age. The answer is a little more complicated than usually perceived. It is important to separate two distinct questions: (1) Apart from this particular text, did Israel's orthodox faith anticipate a bodily resurrection, and (2) did Ezekiel intend to promise bodily resurrection in Ezek 37? It is possible that a truth is implicit in the background of a passage without being implicated in the communicative intent of that passage. So, it is true that ancient Israelites expected bodily resurrection. But that expectation is not the topic of Ezekiel's vision. Rather, the vision utilizes the idea of bodily resurrection to illustrate something else. Ezekiel's audience was concerned about the end of exile ("our hope is gone"), not whether they would enjoy embodied life with the LORD at some point after death. So while Ezekiel and his audience would have believed in bodily resurrection (see **Special Topic: Sheol** at Ezek 31:15–16), in the context of Ezek 37 the prophet only uses this assumption metaphorically to speak about restoration from exile ("death") to life in the land ("bring you up from [the graves]" means "back to the land").

37:14 *I will put my Spirit in you and you will live:* In Ezek 37:6, the prophet spoke of dead bodies animated by "breath" (*ruah*). Here, the prophet uses the same word, *ruah*, in the technical sense of God's Spirit, to highlight the Agent who gives spiritual life (Ezek 36:27, "my Spirit").

There is discussion about the historical outworking of this vision, and whether there is a specified chronological order between physical restoration to the land and spiritual restoration to covenant faithfulness (Ezek 37:8–9). On the one hand, some emphasize that a first-stage physical restoration chronologically precedes a second-stage spiritual restoration.[6] A similar order might be assumed from Ezek 36:24–28. But others note that in the interpretation of the vision, the two stages are ignored completely.[7] A crucial text outside Ezekiel, Deut 30:1–5, places spiritual restoration *before* restoration to blessing in the land (Deut 30:6–9 repeats the same sequence). Since there is ambiguity as to the order in Ezek 37:13–14, which is the actual interpretation of the vision of dry bones, care should be taken not to emphasize any chronological outworking of the promise based on Ezekiel's vision. Ezekiel 37:8 underscored the necessity of *both* physical restoration *and* spiritual restoration, which the interpretation reinforces, without any necessary chronological sequencing. Ezekiel simply addresses two problems, one being physical exile and the other being spiritual alienation. The LORD's promise addresses both problems (see discussion at Ezek 36:20).

Special Topic: Ezekiel 37 and Future Hope

It is important to distinguish between the historical outworking of Ezekiel's vision at the end of the exile (Ezekiel's immediate concern) and a possible distant-future fulfillment at the end of the age. In the historical outworking, the communities in exile did return to the land and appear also to have returned with more faithful hearts (i.e., both physical and spiritual restoration). Neither Ezra–Nehemiah nor the postexilic prophets castigate the people for idolatry. But some Jews, in Egypt for example, worshipped with a mixture of Jewish beliefs, local Egyptian beliefs, and a carryover of Canaanite beliefs. Furthermore, the religious history of Second Temple Judaism is hardly a story of faithfulness to God's Torah.[8] Along with this, kingship was never restored (Ezek 37:24), and physical-spiritual restoration was neither universal for the nation nor permanent (cf. Ezek 37:25–26). It would appear that faithful Israelites continued to live with the tension of a partial restoration of promises (a "now but not yet"). In this sense, then, the exile was not completely over.

Daniel Block offers a brief summary of the "afterlife" of Ezekiel's vision in the history of interpretation and art.[9] Jewish rabbis understood

---

6. Alexander, "Ezekiel," 848–49.
7. Taylor, *Ezekiel*, 235.
8. See the discussion in Lynch, "Monotheism," 346–48.
9. Block, *Ezekiel 25–48*, 388–91.

that Ezekiel spoke about the end of Babylonian exile; yet, in recognition of the incomplete nature of restoration, some looked to bodily resurrection in the messianic age. There are scant allusions to Ezek 37 in the New Testament (possibly Matt 27:51–54; John 20:22; 14:8; Rev 11:11). The most credible links refer to the promise of the indwelling Spirit, which makes sense in view of the inauguration of the New Covenant at the Cross and Pentecost. In view of this, Christians today live a "now but not yet" life of faith. Ezekiel's promise of the Spirit has been realized in part, but who does not groan under the weight of sin with longing for full realization of the promise (Rom 8)?

37:16 *a stick of wood and write on it*: As noted above, Ezek 37:15–28 pulls together in climactic summary the expected fulfillment of God's covenantal promises. Ezekiel frequently used physical object lessons (see **Special Topic: Prophetic Signs in the Ancient Near East** at Ezek 4:1–3), and this one expands on the promise of physical restoration just highlighted in the vision: "the whole house of Israel" would be brought together as one nation with one king (Ezek 37:21–22). The tribal designation "Joseph" (as well as the dominant half-tribe within Joseph, "Ephraim") was used as metonymy (part for the whole) to designate the whole northern kingdom (Ps 78:67; Hos 4:16–17). The Israelites associated with Judah, the southern kingdom, would include Benjamin and Simeon (Josh 19:1; 21:9; 1 Kgs 12:20–21).

It has been suggested that the two sticks in this passage refer to the two halves of a wooden writing tablet (wax covering provided the writing surface).[10] Indeed, the word translated "sticks" often means any sort of wood (e.g., Deut 19:5). However, such tablets were permanently hinged and never became "one" in a way that illustrates the full integration of two kingdoms. Simply holding two sticks with the join in the palm of the hand gives the appearance of one stick appropriate to this illustration.

37:23 *sinful backsliding*: There is a translation difficulty in this verse. Some translations read "from all their sinful backsliding" (NIV; cf. ESV; NET) whereas others render the Hebrew text as "from all their dwelling places in which they have sinned" (NASB). Until about AD 600, scribes wrote Hebrew without vowels. So, Ezekiel would have written in consonants only, and problems could arise when vowels were later assigned. Different vowels can be assigned to the same Hebrew consonants depending on the way the original consonants are understood (*meshubotehem*,

---

10. Block, *Ezekiel 25–48*, 399–401; Bodi, "Ezekiel," 483.

"their falling away" or *moshbotehem*, "their dwelling places"). With support of the Old Greek translation, "from their falling away" is probably correct. The covenant formula: "my people" underscores the restoration to relationship (cf. Lev 23:30; "my people," Exod 3:7; 5:1; 6:7; Hos 2:23).

37:24 ***My servant David:*** See comments at Ezek 34:23.

37:25 ***forever:*** Stress on the *permanence* of restoration is one of two additional elements Ezekiel adds to this passage in comparison to the parallel message in Ezek 34:20–31 (repeated five times in Ezek 37:24–28). Since the restoration envisioned in this passage was never close to fully realized, Cooper correctly notes that the emphasis on permanence begs for fulfillment in a future consummation of the present age.[11]

37:26 ***covenant of peace:*** See comments at Ezek 34:25.

37:26 ***my sanctuary among them:*** This is a second additional element to the parallel in Ezek 34:20–31. The word translated "sanctuary" recalls the promise of covenant blessing in Lev 26:11. This text refers to God's glorious presence with his people as he dwelt first in the wilderness tabernacle (Exod 40:34) and then in the Jerusalem temple (Ps 26:8; 46:4). This theme is crucial to Ezekiel's message. Reemerging here after brief mention in Ezek 11:16, it anticipates the extensive vision of temple restoration in Ezek 40–48. Earlier in Ezekiel's ministry, he contrasted the departure of God's glory from the Jerusalem temple with assurance of God's "sanctuary" with those in exile, even if only for "a little while" (or perhaps "diminished"; see comments at Ezek 11:16). The promise of a *permanent* sanctuary in Ezek 37:26–28 contrasts strongly with this and is underscored by the final words in the book (Ezek 48:35).

Theological Bridge to Application

No passage in Ezekiel underscores the helplessness of humanity in contrast to the sovereign power of God's Spirit as much as the vision of dry bones in Ezekiel. Both the visual image of degraded bones and its interpretation ("hope is gone") point to human need that only God's Spirit can remedy through the inbreathing of spiritual life.

---

11. Cooper, *Ezekiel*, 327.

Focus of Application

This passage is arguably the most visually dramatic and thematically climactic message of hope in all of Ezekiel. The image of human carnage reduced to a field of desiccated bones is both frightful and sobering, especially when we realize that it describes not only the spiritual state of Israel at a particular moment in history but also the natural, spiritual state of every human. Jesus would state the need succinctly to Nicodemus: you must be born to life by the blowing of God's Spirit (John 3:3-8).

The covenant promises to national Israel have been discussed at length in other units (e.g., Ezek 35:1—36:15 / Reclaiming and Renewing the Land). The promise of a unified people of God under David's son may not be realized for ethnic Israel *as yet*. But the promises in this passage have much relevance for the church today. First, God's Spirit calls people from every language and nation to unify under the kingship of Jesus (Rev 5:9-14), who is their prince forever. Second, God took up permanent residence in the incarnation (he "tabernacled among us" John 1:14). Third, through the indwelling of God's Spirit, the church is a permanent temple of God (John 20:22, "breathed"; Acts 2:1-4, "wind"; 1 Cor 3:16, "you all [corporately] are God's temple"; Eph 2:19-22, "a dwelling of God by his Spirit"). In fact, Paul directly applies the promise of Ezek 37:27 to the church as God's temple (2 Cor 6:16). Fourth, in spite of temporary affliction (2 Cor 4:16-18), we have peace now and for eternity (Rom 5:1; Phil 4:4-9). The message of Ezekiel stands on its own and applies in all these ways, so these New Testament texts should not become the focus of exposition. But they do serve to validate the application of Ezekiel's theology to us today.

THE PERMANENCE OF GOD'S CARE

Ezekiel 38:1—39:29

Ezekiel's Message

The Lord will defeat his enemies in order to give peace to his people forever.

Key Themes

- The Lord assures the ultimate defeat of all enemies of his people to assure their permanent security in blessing.
- God's people will enjoy the favor of his glorious presence.
- In the end, no questions will remain regarding the integrity of God's holiness and glory.

Context in Ezekiel

The placement of yet another oracle against foreign nations after Ezekiel's message of Israel's restoration (Ezek 33:1—37:28) might seem odd. Ezekiels' oracles against the nations already preceded this part of Ezekiel (Ezek 25:1—32:32). But, as Cooper notes, Ezek 38–39 demonstrates "just how secure Israel will be in their land."[1] Without these chapters, Ezekiel's prophecies about Israel's suffering and restoration would revolve mainly

---

1. Cooper, *Ezekiel*, 334.

around the crisis of the exile. But their inclusion provides a view into the distant future and a decisive victory.[2] These chapters function, then, as an "end bracket," complementing the similar use of oracles against the nations that precede Ezekiel's announcements of salvation:

(A) The LORD will clear the way for restoration by removing Israel's enemies (Ezek 25–32). (B) Jerusalem's destruction clears the way for restoration (Ezek 33)—for leadership (Ezek 34), for flourishing in the land (Ezek 35:1—36:15), for spiritual renewal (Ezek 36:16-38), and for consummation of all covenant blessing (Ezek 37). (A') The LORD will maintain Israel's peace by destroying future enemies (Ezek 38–39).

Interpretive Highlights

38:2 *Gog . . . chief prince:* There is no consensus of opinion on the identity of "Gog," since this individual is otherwise unattested.[3] The other names in this context are reasonably secure, and that forms the best starting point for discussion. The name "Magog" is listed in Gen 10:2–3 (cf. 1 Chr 1:5), together with Meshek, Tubal, and Gomer with Beth Togarmah, who are both mentioned in Ezek 38:5. These are descendants from Noah's son, Japhet. As early as Josephus, these have been identified as people inhabiting Asia Minor (modern-day Turkey) and the mountainous regions to the north.[4] The name "Magog" could be a Hebrew form of the Sumerian/Akkadian equivalent, which means "land of Gog." If so, Ezekiel is merely extracting the proper name from the regional designation, "land of Gog," in order to make the addressee of the oracle personal (i.e., "Gog").[5] One common suggestion is that "Gog" is a form of the name of a famous, seventh-century king of western Asia Minor, Gyges of Lydia. The name

---

2. Clements, *Ezekiel*, 171, 173.

3. The Reubenite, Gog, of 1 Chr 5:4 cannot be the same as the foreigner in Ezek 38:1.

4. Josephus, *Antiquities of the Jews* 1.6.1 §§123–25 (Feldman, *Josephus*, 43–44). Cf. Bodi, "Ezekiel," 484.

5. There is a suggestion that the name "Magog" is a cryptic form of "Babel" (i.e., Babylon). In the broader context of Ezek 25–39, this provides an oracle against the one enemy of Israel that is not mentioned in Ezekiel's other oracles against the nations, their Babylonian captors. The encryption involves reversing the letters *m-g-g* to *g-g-m* and selecting the letter in the Hebrew alphabet that immediately precedes it: *b-b-l* (see Cooper, *Ezekiel*, 331–33; Bodi, "Ezekiel," 484.). However, while later rabbis played on words in such fanciful ways, this is foreign to the composition strategies of Old Testament authors.

would be chosen simply as a well-known representative of the rulers of this region.

The word translated "chief" in the phrase, "chief prince," is the common word for "head, beginning, source, chief, leader" (*rosh*). It was translated by the Old Greek (followed by NASB) as a proper name, "Rosh." By mere coincidence, this Hebrew word for "head" sounds similar to the word "Russia." This similarity attracted the imagination of some interpreters and became popularized in the Scofield Reference Bible as the identification for the Hebrew word, *rosh*.[6] This suggestion failed to convince later scholars even within the interpretive tradition of Scofield.[7] In addition to the lack of any accepted linguistic method that could link *rosh* with the state of Russia, alternative identifications for *rosh* as a proper name have never gained wide acceptance; and the Hebrew word order naturally allows reading *rosh* in its normal sense of "head" or "chief."[8]

38:4 *hooks in your jaws:* This metaphor stresses the sovereign control that the LORD exercises over this powerful war lord (cf. Ezek 29:4). Similar imagery describes God's sovereign call on Assyria (Isa 7:17–18). The description of Gog's army is filled with words that underscore the formidability of this enemy in size and equipment: "whole," "fully," "great," "large and small."

38:5 *Persia, Cush and Put:* The army of Gog represents foes from the north of Israel. Persia lies to the far east, while Cush (the region of modern-day Ethiopia) is to the southwest and Put (the region of modern-day Lybia) is as close to the west as the Mediterranean Sea barrier allows. Alternatively, the word translated "Persia" could refer to the region of Upper Egypt, in which case the emphasis is on the northern-southern axis of the coalition (viewing Lybia as part of the armies approaching from the south).[9] Since Israel is bounded on the west by sea and on the east by desert, this "pincher" action leaves Israel surrounded. The point is that Gog marshals allies from every compass direction to attack Israel.

38:8 *After many days . . . In future years:* The first expression appears only in Josh 23:1 and refers to a long period of time (in Joshua's case, on the order of a lifespan). The second expression (lit. "in latter

---

6. The same sort of popular etymologizing linked "Meshek" with "Moscow" and "Tubal" with "Tobolsk," similarly ignoring the letters that fail to align.

7. For example, see the corresponding note in the *The Ryrie Study Bible*.

8. For further discussion, see Block, *Ezekiel 25-48*, 434–35, Alexander, "Ezekiel," 853, and Cook, *Ezekiel 38-48*, 74–75.

9. Block, *Ezekiel 25-48*, 439–40; Cook, *Ezekiel 38-48*, 75.

years") is a variant of a similar phrase, "in latter days," used in Ezek 38:16.[10] The phrase, "latter days," is frequently used to refer to the remote future (e.g., Gen 49:1; Isa 2:2; Jer 23:20; Mic 4:1; Dan 10:14; and the Aramaic equivalent in Dan 2:28). With these two expressions, then, Ezekiel places the events of chapters 39 and 39 in the undisclosed future. Like in other prophetic contexts, the events of Ezek 38-39 have yet to unfold even in essential fulfillment; so a convergence at the end of the age (the "eschaton") is an appropriate expectation (see below regarding Rev 20:8). The use of the phrase "in that day" (Ezek 38:14) further reinforces the eschatological (end times) framework for Ezekiel's thought here. On the one hand, the phrase, "in that day," can refer to any event when God intervenes for war (see comments at Ezek 7:7); however, it is common in prophetic language to refer to future events that are not realized until the final consummation of God's kingdom (e.g., Isa 11:10; 27:1; Joel 3:18; Zech 3:10; 12:8-9; 14:9).

38:8 *recovered from war:* While the expected time of this oracle is undisclosed, the circumstances are repeated several times with different wording: Israel is back in the land and enjoying "safety." The people's sense of security is so certain that, practically speaking, they no longer feel the need for the ordinary precautions of building city walls or gates (Ezek 38:11; cf. Ezek 38:14; 39:26). Cook notes that the description could be figurative, since Ezek 36:35 describes the cities of Israel after restoration as well fortified.[11] The portrait is one of full blessing under the covenant (see comments about covenant peace at Ezek 34:25 and blessing at Ezek 37:25-26). Ezekiel's implication is that an attack under such conditions, against an unsuspecting people, is hideously evil.

38:10 *thoughts will come into your mind:* Ezekiel is mindful of the dual reality of divine sovereignty (Ezek 38:4) and human responsibility (cf. Gen 50:20; Exod 7:3; 8:15, 32; 9:34-35; 10:20, 27).

38:12 *center of the land:* Some commentators, in the tradition of the Old Greek and Latin versions, understand the word "center" (*tabbur*) as "navel" or "umbilical cord" [of the earth]. The ancients conceived of sacred places as nexus points connecting heaven and earth; and a people might imagine *their* city as *the* focal point of the universe.[12] Block is probably correct, however, to doubt that this concept is expressed here in

---

10. Block, *Ezekiel 25-48*, 443.
11. Cook, *Ezekiel 38-48*, 76.
12. Bodi, "Ezekiel," 485-86.

connection with *tabbur*. He notes that the word *tabbur* is used only here and in Judg 9:37, where its meaning is unclear—possibly an elevated plateau. Hebrew has an undisputed word for "umbilical cord" (*shor*) that Ezekiel himself uses in Ezek 16:4, and the prophet could easily have used it here if he intended "umbilical cord." The meaning, "elevated plateau," makes sense in this context as a secure location, even without walls.[13]

38:13 *Sheba and Dedan:* In anticipation of the plunder to be gained by Gog and his allies, nearby peoples eagerly await fruitful trading opportunities (cf. Ezek 27:20, 22 and discussion about commercial greed in that context).

38:13 *villages:* The translations differ here on whether the Hebrew consonants should be read "villages" (NIV; NASB; with Old Greek) or "lions" (a metaphor for "leaders," ESV; or "young warriors," NRSV and NET). The reading "lions" is the traditional reading of the Hebrew vowels and is perhaps more likely. It refers to those who benefit most from plunder.[14]

38:14–16 *In that day . . . days to come:* See comments at Ezek 38:8.

38:16 *I am proved holy:* In Ezek 36:23 (see comments), it was the LORD's dealings with his own people that would serve as an object lesson to the nations. Here, the LORD's enemy, Gog, unwittingly serves the same function.

38:17 *You are the one I spoke of:* The Hebrew text has a consonant at the beginning of this sentence that indicates it is a question. But the NIV, perhaps following the Old Greek, assumes this letter is mistakenly written a second time from the previous word, which ends with the same letter. The ESV, NASB, NRSV, NET, NKJV differ from the NIV and are all likely correct in leaving the Hebrew text as written. They translate this verse as a question: "Are you the one I spoke of . . . ?" The difference is significant. The NIV translation makes the affirmation that Gog is the fulfillment of earlier prophecy. The other translations indicate that this is a presumptuous attitude on the part of Gog. He thinks he is acting as an agent to fulfill prophecy (in a manner similar to Cyrus; Isa 45:1–3, 13). But he is mistaken. The question, then, is rhetorical—it is an implicit accusation against such arrogance. As Cook observes, this matches the rhetorical questions in vv. 13 and 14.[15]

---

13. Block, *Ezekiel 25–48*, 448.
14. For more discussion, see Cook, *Ezekiel 38–48*, 76.
15. Cook, *Ezekiel 38–48*, 78.

38:19–22 *earthquake . . . hailstones:* Ezekiel's announcement of intervention against Gog uses language common of divine warfare. This is consistent with Ezekiel's opening vision of God's glory, which incorporated divine warrior imagery (see comments at Ezek 1:4, 15). The image of hail is familiar from the war of conquest (Josh 10:11). When David recollected the manner with which the Lord fought against his enemies, he used earthquake and fire imagery as figures of speech (2 Sam 22:8–9, 12). Similarly, divine earthquakes are associated with mountains collapsing (Hab 3:6, 10; Isa 13:13; Nah 1:5). Confusion of the enemy, so that they self-destruct, is another divine tactic (Judg 7:22; 1 Sam 14:20). Only one with divine attributes can unleash this sort of devastating power. Ezekiel utilizes the basic categories of all animals (fish, birds, beasts, creeping things; Gen 1) to underscore the extent to which fear of the divine warrior's wrath will spread (cf. Zeph 1:3).

39:1–2 *Gog:* A second cycle of announcements against Gog begins with words similar to the opening of chapter 38. Chapter 39 expands in more detail the destruction of Gog, thereby expressing the same ideas as chapter 38, but from the perspective of the aftermath of battle.

39:4 *food to . . . birds . . . animals:* A common motif in descriptions of ancient warfare is the total annihilation of the enemy army and abandonment of their bodies on the open field of battle to be scavenged by birds and wild animals (cf. 1 Sam 17:44). An example is from the Assyrian king, Shalmaneser III, who boasted, "I filled the extensive plain with the corpses of their warriors . . . I dyed the mountain with their blood."[16] Another Assyrian official describes how he left the road full of corpses "visible to the eagles and vultures."[17]

39:6 *fire on Magog . . . in safety in the coastlands:* The army of Magog and its allies attacked God's people who dwelt in safety (same Hebrew expression as in Ezek 38:8). Now their treacherous assault reaps a comparable judgment (cf. Pss 57:6; 64:3–4 with 7–8). As discussed in Ezek 38:1, the location of Magog was likely western Asia Minor, which incorporates many Mediterranean islands and coastlands.

39:7 *I will make known my holy name:* See comments at Ezek 36:23 and 38:16.

39:9–10 *weapons for fuel . . . for seven years:* The old adage that "we should interpret a text in a literal sense unless it makes no sense" is not

---

16. Shalmaneser III's Kurkh Monolith (*COS* 2.113A: 262).
17. Ninurta-kudurri-usur's Suhu Annals (*COS* 2.115B: 280).

a valid principle based on how normal communication actually operates (see **Special Topic: Literal or Literalism?**). Hence, it is unnecessary to resort to explanations as to how ancient weapons find correspondence to modern weapons of war in order to fulfill this prophecy. Nor is it necessary to calculate the fuel needs of a nation for seven years. Both interpretive moves miss Ezekiel's point. The number seven is extremely common in biblical and ancient Near Eastern literature to express completeness (e.g., Lev 8:33; Job 2:13; 5:19; Prov 26:25) or the extreme degree of something (e.g., Ps 12:6; Prov 6:16; Dan 3:19). Elsewhere, Ezekiel uses the number seven for symbolic or rhetorical purposes, and it serves the same purpose here.[18] Perhaps more immediate in the mind of Israelites reading this text would be the symbolic significance of "seven years" as it relates to the sabbath cycles (Lev 25:1–7; 26:34, 43). The nation will enjoy its rest.[19] In Ezek 38:4, the prophet described a massive army brimming with an abundant arsenal. Viewing this from the perspective of the aftermath of the battle magnifies the colossal scale and complete decisiveness of the LORD's victory (cf. similar imagery in Isa 9:3–5). Ezekiel used the theme of "punishment fits the crime" in Ezek 39:6. Here the same motif is in operation: the plunderer will himself be plundered.

Special Topic: Literal or Literalism?

The goal of interpretation, whether it is listening to someone speak or reading a text, is to understand what the speaker or author communicates. Virtuous readers will strive to respect the communicative intent of an author. How does the communication exchange work in practice? In communication theory, it is common to hear that we all assume the most literal meaning of words, and from that basis we consider figurative meanings when the literal makes no sense. However, modern linguistics

---

18. For example: (1) Ezek 3:15–16 (seven-days distress); (2) Ezek 9:2 (seven angels); (3) the introductory discussions for Ezek 20:1–44 (seven phases of Israel's history) and 29:1–30:26 (seven oracles against the nations, the seventh of which consists of seven oracles); (4) the structure of Ezek 38–39 itself is divided into seven oracles (opening "word" formula in Ezek 38:1 and the phrase "This is what the sovereign LORD says" in Ezek 38:10, 14, 17; 39:1, 17, 25). Block observes that this very verse contains seven terms for weapons, beginning with the word for "armor" that is generically translated "weapons" (Block, *Ezekiel 25–48*, 465).

19. Cook, *Ezekiel 38–48*, 98.

has shown that this is not correct.[20] Instead of processing words in a "linear" fashion, starting from literal and then working toward more "remote" figurative meanings only when necessary, we actually process all communication in "parallel" fashion. That is, when we hear speech or read words on a page, our brains are capable of processing all possible meanings simultaneously, whether they be literal options or figurative ones. Based on context, not initial dictionary entries, our brains narrow the meaning to the one that best fits the context and optimizes the relevance of the message. In fact, some studies have shown that people actually adopt metaphorical meanings over literal when possible, because figurative language conveys more relevant meaning than mere dictionary meaning.

However, figurative meanings do not rule out real-world references. A clear example is Daniel's vision of four beasts rising from the sea. All agree that this is highly figurative; however, these four beasts reveal something about four real world empires, and ultimately convey truth about fallen, human kingdoms in general, in contrast to God's kingdom. Therefore, the question is not so simple as "literal" or "figurative." Each case must be considered in its context to determine what the text is talking about (the referent) and what the author is saying about it.

Related to this issue of literal and figurative is the question of the *type* of text. People recognize that poetry, for example, contains a high concentration of figurative language. But this is also not the end of consideration. Straight narrative can employ figurative language, and poetry refers to real people and events. The narrative of Judg 4:15 states that Sisera's army died from sword wounds; but surely some died from arrows, spears, and clubs (a figure called "metonymy"). By contrast, Judg 5 is a poetic rendition of this battle, employing very stylized language, yet it refers to real events.

Throughout Ezekiel, the prophet has written in poetry and elevated prose. At times, the language is highly figurative (e.g., see commentary on Ezek 28). Some of Ezekiel's oracles display a type of style similar to apocalyptic. This sort of prophetic speech frequently uses hyperbolic

20. The following references are technical, scholarly discussions in linguistics, but I include them to justify my argument, which departs from the popular assumption even among many Bible scholars: see Rumelhart, "Some Problems With Literal Meanings," 75–76; Sperber, and Wilson, *Relevance*, 233; Wilson, and Sperber, "Relevance Theory," 615–20; Wilson, and Sperber, "Truthfulness and Relevance," 50, 79–80; Glucksberg, *Understanding Figurative Language*, 10–28; Stemmer, "Neuropragmatics," 2013; Carston, "Word Meaning," 190–91.

language (exaggeration) as well as symbolic images (Daniel's visions are a good example). One can compare such speech to impressionist paintings in contrast to a photograph. Both convey information about literal objects in the real world, but they express it differently.[21] Impressionistic art is more interested in broad ideas that are graphically conveyed. One might well recognize the object (e.g., Monet's garden) but would not want to press the details.

This is the best way to approach much of the language of judgment in Ezekiel. The key question is not, how do I make this fit in detail into real world events; rather, what truths would first come to mind for the original audience and how would *they* weigh what is most relevant to *their* interests? It is *possible* that Ezekiel intends us to understand "seven years" and "seven months" as actual chronological details. However, the reflexes of an audience attuned to the symbolic number "seven" might not even consider this possibility. A context marked by a high concentration of stylistic language, which borders on apocalyptic, reinforces this reflex for symbolic relevance. A literal battle in the real world is not thereby excluded; but the mental processing of the original audience would optimize much of the detailed language of the passage with figurative meaning rather than literal.[22]

39:11 *burial place . . . Hamon Gog:* The most likely geographical location for the burial place is the Jezreel Valley, which is the only valley that completely bisects the land of Israel west to east and so provides the major thoroughfare from the Mediterranean Sea in the west to the Jordan River valley in the east. The Hebrew word translated "those who travel" can also be rendered "those who pass by" (NASB), or simply "those who pass." Based on the similarity of this expression to a phrase used in Ugaritic legend, some commentators of good authority understand this as an allusion to deceased enemy warriors (similarly, "pass on" in the English idiom can mean "to die").[23] In other words, the name of the valley takes on the identity of those who died in this colossal conflict between the LORD and Gog's armies: "the Valley of the Travelers" (ESV; NRSV; i.e.,

---

21. For a very helpful discussion, including this analogy from impressionistic art, see Sandy, *Plowshares & Pruning Hooks*, esp. 101–28.

22. Efforts to work out the literal details of these oracles can be found in Alexander, "Ezekiel," 862–66 or Cooper, *Ezekiel*, 328–48. However, while I agree there is a real battle in view, finding a chronological outworking over-reads what Ezekiel intends to communicate.

23. Block, *Ezekiel 25–48*, 469; Cook, *Ezekiel 38–48*, 87–88, 91.

"those who have passed on"). Further support might come from the banquet feast described later in this passage, which could allude to a known practice of feasting with deceased ancestors through necromancy, particularly in Ugaritic religion. However, all this is overly subtle for this context. The decision rides on whether the original audience would have naturally made the link to the idea of deceased heroes of Ugaritic legend (comparing this to Gog's dead army). In my opinion, more immediate to the original audience was the simple geographical description. The name of the burial place, "Hamon Gog," means "the multitude (*hamon*) of Gog" (cf. the same word as in "multitude of nations" in Gen 17:4). The point of this whole description is the massive body count resulting from Gog's defeat—annihilation is decisive and complete.

39:12 *seven months . . . to cleanse the land:* As a priest, Ezekiel would be particularly sensitive to the contaminating effects of such a large number of dead bodies on the holy land (Num 19:11–21). As a priest, he also was very attuned to how the number seven relates to issues of purification (e.g., atonement [Lev 4:6, 17], consecration [Lev 8:11], and purification [Lev 12:2; 13:4, 33; 14:7–8, 39]). Particularly relevant in this context is the seven-day purification period needed for cleansing after contact with a *single* corpse (Num 19:11–21). Such a multitude of dead bodies, as in this battle, takes seven *months* to cleanse the land, not just seven *days*. As in vv. 9 and 10 above, the point is not the literalism of a purification ritual; rather, Ezekiel emphasizes the massive carnage of enemy combatants.

39:14 *more detailed search:* The physical cleansing of God's holy land is as important as the cleansing of his people who will inhabit it (cf. Ezek 36:22–25, 33). Purification will be so thorough as to continue beyond "seven" months (cf. "seven + eight," Eccl 11:2; Mic 5:5). The subunit concludes in v. 16 with the emphatic statement: "and so they will cleanse the land."

39:17 *great sacrifice:* Victory banquets were important occasions in ancient culture (cf. Ps 23:5), and thanksgiving sacrifices to God for deliverance from enemies was a part (cf. Ps 22:22–29). In this passage, the prophet combines these two images in a gruesome portrait: scavenger beasts and birds are invited to a "sacrificial banquet" (cf. Zeph 1:7; Isa 34:6). In ironic reversal, it is the beasts who feed on the bodies of humans instead of humans on sacrificial animals (see comments at Ezek 39:4).

39:21 *I will display my glory . . .* This statement begins a summary of the entire unit dealing with Israel's restoration (Ezek 33–39), transitioning from the eschatological battle to Israel's present need.[24] The phrase "from that day forward" likely looks back to "that day" of victory over Gog (Ezek 39:11). Hence, the "punishment" referred to in v. 21 recaps the oracle of final victory over God's enemies. But Ezek 39:21–29 also rehearses the necessity of the Lord's dealings with Israel, both in judgment as well as restoration. The effect of all these divine actions is the vindication of God's reputation, which is related to the display of his glory and echoes back to the very beginning of the book of Ezekiel ("proved holy," v. 27; see comments at Ezek 36:23, 36).

39:23–24 *I hid my face:* The notion of "seeing the face" in the Old Testament involves enjoying the presence of someone and finding favor (cf. Gen 32:20; 33:10; Job 33:26; Ps 11:7). Consequently, someone hiding their face is a sign of displeasure toward the other (Exod 10:28; 2 Sam 3:13), and so it describes God's disposition toward Israel when it is under covenant curse (Deut 32:20).[25] To say that God no longer hides his face signals the permanent end of his displeasure. Indeed, the chapter ends on this note and restates the promise of restoration by God's Spirit promised in Ezek 36:26–27. Instead of an outpouring of God's wrath (e.g., Ezek 7:8; 20:8; eleven times in the book altogether), he will pour out his Spirit.[26] Covenant curses are lifted with full blessing in the land (see comments at Ezek 34:25 and 37:24–28).

Theological Bridge to Application

Ezek 38–39 is Ezekiel's equivalent to Isaiah's image of God's climactic defeat over the chaos-monster, the ultimate force behind all who oppose God's kingdom (Isa 27:1; 51:9–10; see comments at Ezek 29:3). Cook observes that as soon as Israel is restored to the central place in world order, chaos makes a final futile effort, only to be decisively destroyed by the Divine Warrior.[27] The thought world is similar to what Ezekiel himself expresses in the defeat of Tyre (Ezek 27–28). This important message undergirds all hope that evil will be defeated once and for all, thereby assuring the eternal enjoyment of God's blessing.

---

24. Cooper, *Ezekiel*, 345–46; Cook, *Ezekiel 38–48*, 108.
25. For the many ancient Near Eastern parallels, see Bodi, "Ezekiel," 488.
26. Block, *Ezekiel 25–48*, 488.
27. Cook, *Ezekiel 38–48*, 5.

Focus of Application

As noted in previous discussion, these chapters of Ezekiel are not designed to offer a blow by blow description of how the eschatological battle between God and the enemies of his kingdom will play out. Rather, this passage is an assurance of restoration for national Israel; and fulfillment of these chapters of Ezekiel cannot simply be transferred to the church. The geographical promises of land are too prominent, and any failure in God's covenantal responsibilities to the nation is inconceivable. Indeed, his faithfulness to these promises are inseparably tied with the vindication of his holiness, which is the central message of the text. God's and his people's enemies, both cosmic and earthly, will one day be defeated in visible fashion. But beyond these broad brushstrokes, applying these chapters in literalistic fashion to detail the future is hazardous.

The central message of this unit is the unassailable power of God to defeat all opposition to his kingdom purposes. The heinous villainy of Gog and his allies (to consider crushing peaceful people) finds a hideous mirror in the individuals or nations that persecute God's people today. Within the same week of completing this commentary, I read of a pastor and wife in one country who were run over by a bulldozer that was proceeding to knock down their church building. Meanwhile in another country, a monument was erected to the recent massacre of 500 Christians on that spot by a religious group who hated them. Even as Ezek 38–39 indicated a distant, future realization for national Israel, so the hope of God's people today is in the eschatological victory of Jesus. That is John's explicit application of this text in Rev 20:8. Satan (the driving force of chaos) and his remaining followers are destroyed once and for all. John may also have drawn on the language of the "banquet" scene in Ezek 39:4, 17–20 for his description of the "supper of God" in Rev 19:17–21 (a different "invitation" than to the Lamb's wedding banquet; Rev 19:9!).

In Rev 19:17–21, the powers behind the persecution of God's people are eliminated. But imagining only those who launch physical attacks against God's people is too narrow. Appropriate applications also include economic and social forces, which implicates corporations as well as media power. The former are committed to the seduction and subordination of the masses to pure commercial interest (i.e., commercialism). The latter are often ideologically bent on subverting values of human dignity (e.g., violence or objectification of women), or twisting truth in the public square (e.g., "spin"). These are manifestations of chaos; systemic forces driven by what the Apostle Paul calls "principalities and powers." Strategically defeated on the cross (Col 2:15), their final destruction awaits the Divine Warrior's return.

RETURN OF GOD'S GLORY
Ezekiel 40:1—43:12

Ezekiel's Message

The LORD permanently indwells his temple, demanding holiness in those who are attached to him.

Key Themes

- The LORD promises his permanent presence with his restored people.
- The LORD's perfections stand in contrast to the chaos of life in this world.
- The LORD demands that his people conform to his ways, ordering life according to what befits a holy people who mirror God's holiness.

Context in Ezekiel

The book of Ezekiel opens with a vision of God's glory arriving in the land of exile, and in chapter 10, the prophet records his vision of God's glory departing the Jerusalem temple. In Ezek 40–48, the oracles of restoration (Ezek 33–48) reach another climax with a vision of God's glory returning to a new temple in the midst of his people, who have been reunited in their homeland. These chapters form a complete literary unit that announces the new residence of God, comprised of a city-like temple-complex (Ezek 40:2) as well as a surrounding "metroplex" that serves God's sacred space (Ezek 48:35).

The description of the new temple contains a large number of technical architectural terms and verbal descriptions that are no longer clearly understood.[1] So we find a higher concentration of translation differences in these chapters than normally expected. However, the basic contours are clear enough, and the main point of each passage does not differ among the various English versions. For interest in architectural details of the temple vision, technical commentaries can be consulted.

Interpretive Highlights

40:1 *In the twenty-fifth year:* While this is the last vision reported in the book of Ezekiel, it is not the last revelatory experience that Ezekiel would have in his life from a chronological standpoint (see comments at Ezek 29:19). The temple vision occurs 13 years after the previous date notice in Ezek 33:21. In the flow of thought in the book, the temple vision brings to climax the message of hope for Israel's restoration, both spiritually to the LORD and physically to the land.

Why twenty-five years? It may be appropriate because twenty-five years is the turning point in a Jubilee cycle, the end of which marks the restoration to "normal," a "reset" if you will, of all land and relational obligations (Lev 25:8–55). The concept of Jubilee is not absent from this context (Ezek 46:17), and many times the vision employs the number twenty-five or its multiples.[2] The month and day point in similar fashion to the release from bondage, since this exact day is either (1) the Jubilee release on Day of Atonement (Lev 25:9; if the first month of the political calendar) or (2) the Passover day (Exod 12:2; if the first month of the religious calendar) that recalls Israel's release from bondage in Egypt. Even Ezekiel's age at the time of this vision reflects this symbolism. His ministry commenced at age thirty in the fifth year of exile (Ezek 1:1–2), so twenty-five years into the exile would be his fiftieth year, when priests retire from service (Num 4:3; 8:23–25). At the "big picture" level, then, the vision of Ezek 40–48 envisions restoration of the God-nation-land relationship, which was fundamental to the life of Israel.[3]

---

1. Cook, *Ezekiel 38–48*, 26.
2. Block, *Ezekiel 25–48*, 495–96; Cook, *Ezekiel 38–48*, 124, 126.
3. Block, *Ezekiel 25–48*, 506; Cook, *Ezekiel 38–48*, 126.

Numerous commentators are attracted to the observation that this day is also the day in the Babylonian religious calendar when their patron-god, Marduk, was reinstalled in his renewed temple. This date notice in Ezekiel, then, coupled with the promise of the Lord's return to his temple, would be an implicit counter-narrative to this Babylonian Akitu festival.[4] However, this may be too subtle, since Ezekiel seems unconcerned with polemical attacks on Babylonian religion (contrast Isaiah; cf. Isa 46:1). Indeed, Babylon is missing from Ezekiel's oracles against the nations, unless, by chance, Gog is a code name for Babylon—again, overly subtle (see comments at 38:1 and notes there, as well Theological Bridge to Application for Ezek 25:1–17).

40:2 *In visions of God*: This is the same expression used to introduce other experiences by the prophet that involve the glory of the Lord and the temple (Ezek 1:1; 8:3 with 9:3). The vantage point, a "very high mountain," reinforces the surreal nature of the experience, since a temple would normally be located at the top of a mountain, not viewed at a distance to the south, as in this vision. The identification of the city-like structure is the elaborate temple-complex soon to be described (cf.Ezek 48:35).

40:3 *a man . . . cord . . . measuring rod*: Visionary experiences often incorporate a heavenly guide (cf. Dan 8:15–16; 9:21; 12:5–6; Zech 1:8). This guide holds two recognizable building tools, a measuring cord and rod (cf. Zech 2:1–2). These two measuring tools are often depicted in ancient Near Eastern iconography associated with temple construction (see fig. 2).[5]

40:4 *Tell the house of Israel*: The message is in the *telling* of the vision for purposes of spiritual conviction (Ezek 43:10; 44:5–6; 45:9). In contrast to emphatic commands in other temple contexts to actually build a physical structure, the ethical application of the visual imagery is stressed here (note the explicit command with Moses' tabernacle [Exod 25:8–9, 40] and Solomon's temple [1 Chr 22:6–10; 28:11]). This contrast stands out, especially since the wording in the verse exactly parallels Exod 25:9 ("everything I show you").[6] It is as though Ezekiel intentionally *avoids* the command to build. The wording in Ezek 43:10–12 likewise turns the readers expectations elsewhere than literal construction (see comments there). Other clues in these chapters reinforce the interpretation that the

---

4. Block, *Ezekiel 25–48*, 513; Cook, *Ezekiel 38–48*, 124–25.
5. Bodi, "Ezekiel," 490.
6. Bodi, "Ezekiel," 510; Cook, *Ezekiel 38–48*, 113.

message requires a spiritual response to the vision, not actualization of a building project (see **Special Topic: A Future Temple?**).

Special Topic: A Future Temple?

Some interpret Ezekiel's vision as exact design specifications for an actual temple to be built.[7] If Ezekiel and his contemporaries understood the purpose of the vision to guide construction of a temple, there is no hint that the restoration community exerted any effort to replicate Ezekiel's design specifications. The second temple was not as glorious as the first (Ezra 3:12; Hag 2:3; Zech 4:10), and Herod's grand expansions did not approximate Ezekiel's specifications. So either this constitutes gross disobedience, or the vision was understood by Ezekiel and his contemporaries in some other way. Their expectations could have been eschatological (for the undisclosed, distant future). But as Block observes, there is a striking absence of terms throughout these chapters that are typically found in prophetic oracles with an eschatological time horizon.[8] For example, Ezekiel uses phrases like "the day" (Ezek 7:10) or "in that day" (Ezek 30:2–3; 38:14, 18–19) to signal to readers that he has multiple future events or a distant horizon in mind. Granted, resources for such an elaborate construction project were beyond the means of the impoverished postexilic community; but one would expect *some* attempt to replicate features of the vision, with at least *some* attention to innovations. This would represent a good faith effort on the part of the postexilic community for a "now but not yet" expression of hope. All this raises doubt that the original audience considered the physical aspects of Ezekiel's design to be relevant for actual construction. Several other lines of thought support this.

First, as noted in the commentary on Ezek 40:4, the absence of a command to actually build the temple is significant. In contrast, the intention of the vision is revealed in the applications that appear in Ezek 43:6–11; 44:5–16; and 45:9–12 (see discussion at Ezek 43:10–11).

Second, Moses' tabernacle and Solomon's temple are given specific height dimensions (Exod 26:16; 1 Kgs 6:2). For Ezekiel's temple, vertical dimensions are sparse, only the outer wall (Ezek 40:5), the alcove wall (Ezek 40:12), the preparation tables (Ezek 40:42), the wooden altar in the

---

7. For a responsible effort in this regard, see the commentaries by Cooper, *Ezekiel*, or Alexander, "Ezekiel."

8. Block, *Ezekiel 25–48*, 504–5, 510.

holy place (Ezek 41:22), and *possibly* the gate height (Ezek 40:14).[9] The text states that the priests rooms all have the "same length and width" (Ezek 42:11) . . . no mention of height. In the light of this contrast to other biblical temple designs, omission of vertical specifications for core structures in Ezekiel's temple is inexplicable if it were intended for actual construction. Rather, Ezekiel offers a very stylized design that focuses on geometric perfection, employing multiples of 25 and its square.

Third, literal actualization of the Edenic river might be imaginable (Ezek 47); however, the cosmic symbolism of such a life-giving source lends itself more naturally to a symbolic interpretation for Ezekiel's original audience, whose assumptions were instinctively attuned to such symbolic meanings (see comments at Ezek 47:1).

Fourth, both the design description (e.g., altar) and many of the liturgical practices described in Ezek 43:12—46:31 contradict the Mosaic prescriptions. But more difficult is a canonical reading (e.g., Heb 10:14, 18) in which future sacrificial practices are no longer relevant. These are not memorial sacrifices, rather they effect atonement (see comments at Ezek 40:38-47). It is granted that Paul supported sacrifices when he sponsored the fulfillment of a vow (Acts 21:24; 24:17). However, the narrative presents Paul's behavior as a concession to his Jewish kinsmen so as not to create a stumbling block to the gospel during this transition time (Acts 21:25; cf. Acts 15:29, strangled meat). Some Christian gatherings continued in the temple, perhaps with evangelistic intention, but thanksgiving for atonement remained focused on the LORD's Table (Acts 2:46-47). So, imagining the reestablishment of atonement sacrifices millennia after Jesus' "once for all" sacrifice remains problematic (see further discussion at Ezek 40:38-47). This is especially because, in Ezekiel's vision, there is the persistent need for sacrifice in order for people to be accepted before God (Ezek 43:27).

Fifth, perhaps even more difficult than atoning sacrifices, the strict boundaries of sacred space in Ezekiel's vision are in conflict with New Testament teaching regarding Jesus as the new temple (e.g., Mark 15:38; John 2:19-22; Heb 12:22-24) and the Holy Spirit indwelling the people of God as his temple (1 Cor 3:16-17; Eph 2:19-22). While this does not require replacement theology, where the church supersedes ethnic Israel, it recognizes that the future hope of redeemed Israel is not an inferior experience, impeded by all the physical boundaries of sacred space. God

---

9. On this last item, contrast Block, *Ezekiel 25-48*, 518 nn. 24-26 with Cook, *Ezekiel 38-48*, 120-21.

will dwell among all his people in a most perfect way—that is the message of Ezekiel's vision, described in the most optimal language that would make sense to Ezekiel's contemporaries but fulfilled in a way that would have been unimaginable to them at the time.

In the person of Jesus, God inhabits a human body for all eternity; and when he returns to earth, his residence presumably would be a physical structure. In the conceptual world of the Bible, that structure will by definition be a temple. Will Jesus' home replicate the rigid boundaries of sacred space, blocking access, along with attending sacrifices described in Ezekiel's vision? This is unlikely.

40:5–37 *gate . . . court*: The most immediate impression of the gate and court system of the temple is its perfect symmetry: squares and rectangles with a two-to-one aspect ratio (see fig. 1). What might escape first impressions, however, is the nature of Ezekiel's description as he walks his audience through the temple. Cook offers the important observation that Ezekiel is drawing his audience in as closely as possible to replicate *his experience* of the temple excursion. In Cook's words, like Ezekiel's vision of the valley of dry bones, "This approach of deliberate sensory and emotive rehearsal profoundly affects readers. It pushes them to relive Ezekiel's experience. As we accompany the prophet we begin connecting dots and reaching theological and spiritual conclusions along with him."[10] As noted above, the perfect geometric plan is the antithesis of chaos or disorder, whether it be personal state of mind or perception of the disturbed world all around us. Temples in the ancient world were microcosms, displaying the ideals of created order.[11] The palm-tree artwork is significant in this regard (repeated in Ezek 40:16, 22, 26, 31, 34, 37). In temples across the ancient world, trees often marked transition zones between ordinary life and sacred space. Trees connote life and strength (cf. Ps 92:12).[12] Passing through the gate structures would be like passing through a long tunnel, what Cook calls a "wormhole effect."[13] The resulting impression is that access to God is a carefully controlled affair; one does not approach the holy without experiencing a transition into another realm.

---

10. Cook, *Ezekiel 38–48*, 127; cf. Block, *Ezekiel 25–48*, 505–06.
11. Cook, *Ezekiel 38–48*, 6, 149–50; Walton, "The Temple in Context," 349–54.
12. Cook, *Ezekiel 38–48*, 131.
13. Cook, *Ezekiel 38–48*, 129.

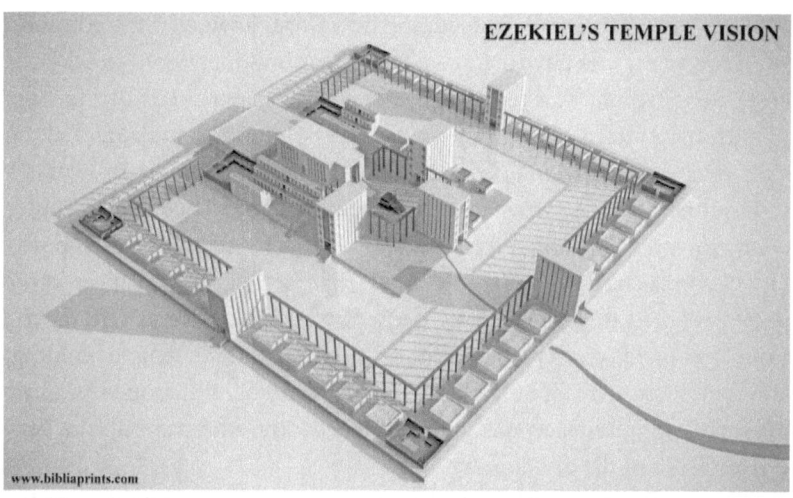

Figure 1: Ezekiel's Temple Vision (http://www.bibliaprints.com).
Used with permission.

40:38–47 offerings . . . slaughtered: In conjunction with the gate system, Ezekiel describes preparation places for sacrificial offerings. This passage names thanksgiving sacrifices, perhaps assumed under "other offerings" in Ezek 40:42. This type of offering ("peace" or "fellowship offering," *shelamim*) commemorated some gracious act of God by celebration of a communal meal and did *not* make atonement (Lev 3:1–17; 7:11–22). However, the sacrifices listed in Ezek 40:39 include all three types of *atonement* sacrifices: the whole burnt offering (*'olah*, Lev 1:3–4), the sin offering (*hatta't*, Lev 4:3, 20, 31), and the guilt offering (*'asham*, Lev 5:5–6).

These three offerings do not fit a post-crucifixion worship context. It is not satisfactory to deny any efficacy for Old Testament sacrifices. Had Israelites *not* performed the prescribed sacrifices in Old Testament days, there would have been no atonement. Hebrews 10:4 should be read in context, which stresses the temporary nature, but not the inherent worthlessness, of animal sacrifice (cf. Heb 9:13). It is difficult to imagine how animal sacrifices in a post-crucifixion kingdom could function as mere memorial offerings (see **Special Topic: A Future Temple?**).

40:48—41:26 the temple: In the Hebrew language, as well as other ancient Near Eastern languages, the words for a "temple" were the same words used for a human king's palace (*bayit*, God's [1 Kgs 7:12; Ezek 40:48] and Solomon's [1 Kgs 9:1]; *hekal*, God's [2 Kgs 18:6; Ezek 42:8] and Ahab's [1 Kgs 21:1]). Indeed, the first word, *bayit*, was the common word for a house of any sort, whether tent or building (Gen 27:15; Deut 8:12). So a "temple" was regarded as the palace residence of a divine king.

In the pattern of the Tabernacle and Solomon's temple, and along with most other ancient Near Eastern temples, the temple in Ezekiel's vision consisted of a two-chambered structure approached from an outer court, sometimes through a pillared porch (court [40:47]; pillared porch [40:48]; first chamber [41:1-2]; inner chamber [41:3-4]). These three parts occupied three, increasing degrees of sacred space as one moved from the outside courtyard into the first chamber of the temple building, and then into the most holy place. The first chamber functioned as a sort of reception hall that would prepare a visitor for entrance into the very throne room of the divine-king.

Inside the temple building, the artwork also featured palm trees together with cherubim (Ezek 41:18-26). The palm decorations have been discussed in conjunction with the gates; and for cherubim, see comments at Ezek 1. This imagery is similar to Moses' tabernacle and Solomon's temple (Exod 26:1, 31; 36:8, 35; 1 Kgs 6:29, 32; 7:29, 36). However, unlike these previous temples, both of which were furnished with a light stand, a table of showbread, an incense altar, and the ark of the covenant, Ezekiel sees only a wooden altar which the heavenly guide calls "the table that is before the LORD" (Ezek 41:22). In the absence of the other furnishings, the symbolism of this table is all the more important. Because it is pure wood construction, it can hardly be an altar for burning incense. Rather, it is a "table," and this word alludes to the table holding the bread of presence (Lev 24:5-9). As an offering to God and a portion shared with priests, the bread on this table symbolizes the fellowship enjoyed between God and humanity.[14] Cook reasonably speculates that the absence of other furnishings indicates they have been replaced by a more perfect presence of the LORD.[15] Much of the imagery in Ezekiel's temple vision is similar to that found in palace and temple architecture in Mesopotamia. A good illustration is a carved panel found in the palace of a Mesopotamian king to commemorate temple construction (see fig. 2)—a man holds a measuring rod; cherubim guard the sacred precinct; palm trees (together with other stylized, sacred trees) flank the building along with cosmic mountains; two sources of water flow from within provide

---

14. Cook, *Ezekiel 38-48*, 167.
15. Cook, *Ezekiel 38-48*, 165.

life-giving streams to fish and sprouting trees. Every feature does not need to map over to Ezekiel's vision to make the point that such features communicate symbolic meaning to the ancient viewer.

Figure 2: Investiture panel at Mari's royal palace of King Zimri-Lin (a contemporary of the Babylonian king Hammurabi), Syria, 1778–1758 BCE. Present location: Musée du Louvre, Paris. Drawing by Margaret Wohler. Key: A = Cosmic mountain symbols; B = Guardian composite creatures; C = Paired river goddesses; D = Rod and ring symbols; 1 = Guardian palm trees; 2 = Stylized "cosmic" trees; 3 = Seedling trees of life. From Cook, *Ezekiel*, 126. Used with permission from Stephen Cook.

42:1–20 *outer court . . . rooms:* These special rooms are reserved for priests who share in certain offerings that are exclusively set aside for priestly consumption, i.e., "most holy" (cf. Lev 6:16, 26; 7:6). Proper boundaries of sacred space are thereby preserved (Ezek 42:13).

43:1–5 *the glory of the LORD filled the temple:* When the LORD filled former temples with his glory, it signaled his dwelling among his people (Exod 40:34–35; 1 Kgs 8:10–11). After viewing the perfections of God's new dwelling place, Ezekiel's excursion comes to a climax with the vision of the LORD returning to take up *permanent* residence among his people (cf. Ezek 37:26)—reversing the vision of God's temple departure (cf. Ezek 10:18–19; "a little while," 11:16). This significance is explicit in Ezek 43:7.

43:6–9 *Israel will never again defile:* Corresponding to the permanent presence of God, the demands of his holiness must and will be met.

Such idolatrous practices as described in Ezek 6, 8 and 16 cannot continue (see comments in those chapters, and especially Ezek 36:17, 20 for the concept of defilement). Here, specific reference is made to a type of ancestral worship that mixed necromancy (calling back the dead; cf. Ezek 13:17–18) and ritual feasting with the deceased.[16] The boundaries of sacred space were also violated when kings built palace structures directly connected to the temple perimeter (cf. Jer 26:10?). All these practices polluted God's abode. The application of Ezekiel's temple vision begins to take shape with this command to put away such deeds (Ezek 43:9).

43:10–12 *describe . . . perfection . . . ashamed:* The description of the temple (telling and writing; see comments at Ezek 40:4) is intended to move the heart of Israelites to put away sinful behavior that violates the perfection of God's ordered world, symbolized by Ezekiel's vision. The word translated "perfection" (*taknit*, NIV) is sometimes rendered "plan" (ESV; NASB) or "pattern" (NET; NKJV; NRSV). However, the only other time this word occurs in the Old Testament is Ezek 28:12, where it stresses the perfection of the cherub in Eden. In this verse, all these translations agree with the NIV to translate the word "perfection." It is significant that a different, but similar sounding word, is used for the architectural design of Moses' tabernacle and Solomon's temple (*tabnit*, "structure"; Exod 25:19; 1 Chr 28:19). Ezekiel avoided this technical architectural term in preference for a word that stresses the perfect proportions of his vision.[17] This word "perfection" (*taknit*) is repeated in v. 11 (NIV translates it "arrangement" there). Observing the geometric perfection of God's holy space in contrast to one's own failures stirs shame, which is an appropriate emotion when it energizes repentance (cf. Ezek 16:54, 61).

The Hebrew for these verses is difficult. The Old Greek translation seems to stress the obligation to carefully observe the moral instructions of God's law: "you shall describe [this house] before them, and they shall keep all my statutes and all my ordinances and shall perform them" (*New English Translation of the Septuagint*).[18] Block's translation expresses the same force: "Write them down in their sight so that they may observe all my rulings and all my ordinances by executing them."[19] The NIV transla-

16. See Bodi, "Ezekiel," 495.

17. See Cook, *Ezekiel 38–48*, 129. A related noun, *matkonet*, denotes things that exist in exact proportions, such as correctly measured grain (Ezek 45:11), a liturgical recipe (Exod 30:32), or building qualities (2 Chr 24:13).

18. Pietersma and Wright, eds., *A New English Translation*.

19. Block, *Ezekiel 25–48*, 587.

tion, "that they may be faithful," captures this sense for the Hebrew text as well, which uses a common word in Scripture for complying with ethical instruction (*shamar*, "observe," ESV; NASB; sometimes translated "keep"; e.g., Deut 4:6; 16:12; 1 Kgs 11:1). This is evasive language, if the intention were to command Israel to actually "build" something. Most weighty is the sense of moral duty that the perfect design instills (cf. Pss 19:7; 119:1–8)—failure to follow this exhortation means continuing in shameful behavior, not disobedience to construct the design. Everything about this temple presses the need for holiness (v. 12).

Theological Bridge to Application

The temple vision is the climax of Ezekiel's oracles of restoration for Israel. The immediately preceding chapters (Ezek 38–39) describe the final eschatological battle against Gog and his forces, which join with the other oracles against the nations (Ezek 25–32) to form bookends around the oracles of restoration. When Israel's king, the Lord, rests from subduing all his enemies, he takes up permanent residence once again in his temple. This pattern of victory followed by temple dwelling is similar to other ancient Near Eastern accounts. Major deities take up temple residence after conquering their enemies who threaten world order.[20] Ezek 40:1–43:12, then, presents Israel's God as the sovereign king over all forces that might challenge the peace of his kingdom.

Focus of Application

Even if Ezekiel's intention was that his visionary temple would one day be built, these chapters do not license anyone to begin construction of a new temple. Throughout the ancient Near East, including Israel, not even divinely appointed kings dared undertake temple construction or remodeling without explicit command from the deity *in their present context* (cf. 2 Sam 7:1–17; 1 Chr 22:6–10; Hag 1:8; Zech 4:9). But as argued above (see **Special Topic: A New Temple?**), it is not Ezekiel's intention for Israel to model a building after his visionary experience. Rather, the effect lies in the moral impact the vision would have on his audience. Both in their lives and in their approach to sacred space in worship, the postexilic (second temple) community of Jews still functioned as priests

---

20. Block, *Ezekiel 25–48*, 510; Bodi, "Ezekiel," 491.

to the nations. So they continued to attend to the ways of the LORD and to the outward expression of purity laws. But in a post-crucifixion context, in which God's Spirit indwells his people as temple, the lesson of Ezekiel is directed toward the attitudes and ethical behavior of our lives.

The geometric perfection of the temple's design stands in contrast to forces operating in this world that bring chaos, both within our souls as well as in the physical turmoil around us. The strict boundaries with varying degrees of holiness serve to warn us that God is not one to be trifled with. Massive gate structures feature guarded alcoves, and fierce (lion-headed) cherubim guard God's chambers. What if our contemporary worship embraced greater awareness of the transcendent majesty of God? . . . a few coffee cups, casually sipped in worship, might drop from shaking hands. More important is that this vision of perfection directs our hearts to examine our own imperfections, which in turn, motivates us to follow the ways of our LORD. As bearers of the divine image, renewed individually and corporately in conformity to Jesus' image, we ourselves are sacred space, reflecting the holiness of the Spirit who indwells. Although Ezekiel has presented a vision that humiliates us for our own failures, he has already paved the path of redemption from our shame through the promise of a New Covenant (Ezek 35:1—36:15).

RETURN TO ORDER IN WORSHIP AND THE LAND

Ezekiel 43:13—48:35

Ezekiel's Message

The LORD establishes the boundaries of holiness and restores justice and fullness of life to his creation.

Key Themes

- The presence of the LORD establishes boundaries of respect for his holiness.
- The presence of the LORD demands just and equitable relationships among his covenant people.
- The presence of the LORD transforms his creation for the vitality of his people.

Context in Ezekiel

The temple description in Ezek 40:1—43:12 addressed the problem of God's absence from among his people. The glory of God will return to Israel in perfection and permanence. The rest of Ezekiel's vision (Ezek 43:13—48:35) focuses on the restoration of worship and life in the land, correcting the defilements that corrupted worship and the injustices that marred Israelite relationships between one another and with their land.

In Block's words, the vision of Ezek 40–48 offers "a glimpse of the spiritual possibilities for Israel based on the reality revealed in chapter 1 and answering the abuses expressed in chapters 8–11 and the inadequacies of the... 'sanctuary in small measure' (11:16)."[1]

Interpretive Highlights

43:13–27 altar ... dedicate ... I will accept you: An altar is essentially a table upon which sacrifices are burned, symbolically consumed by God in the fire. Of course, in orthodox Israelite religion, the notion that God needed food was explicitly denied (Ps 50:9–13). But the "acceptance" of the sacrifice meant acceptance of the worshipper(s) for whom the animal was a substitute (Lev 1:4, 9). It is important to understand the significance of "atonement." Even objects, such as the altar in this passage, can be ritually cleansed (that is "atoned") through the application of sacrificial blood that functions as a detergent to remove the contamination of sin (Ezek 43:20; see **Special Topic: Atonement**).

The altar ceremony described here is not for ongoing instructions about its use, rather it is a ritual of dedication (cf. Exod 29:37, "sanctify it"). The Hebrew in Ezekiel, however, is literally "fill its [the altar's] hands," which is a phrase normally connected with investiture of a priest (Exod 28:41; Lev 8:33, literally "fill your hands"). Cook observes that the altar is personified here, as something that both dispenses holiness and absorbs impurity (Exod 29:37; Ezek 42:14; 44:19; 46:20).[2] The most important effect of the entire dedication ritual, however, is expressed in Ezek 43:27. As a result of properly initiating the altar for sacrifices, God will accept his people into fellowship because their sin will have been removed.

Special Topic: Atonement

Several aspects of atonement are usually involved in sacrificial contexts. First, atonement meant the removal of sin. The basic meaning of this form of the Hebrew verb, "atone," means to wipe away or remove (Deut 21:8–9; note especially the poetic parallelism in Jer 18:23). This is best illustrated on the Day of Atonement when the sins of the people were removed to the wilderness by the substitute scapegoat (Lev 16:10, 20–22).

1. Block, *Ezekiel 25–48*, 497.
2. Cook, *Ezekiel 38–48*, 197.

The popular misunderstanding that the verb means "to cover" arises from looking at the example in Gen 6:14 ("cover" the ark), but this is a significantly different form of the verb than is used in context involving sacrifice.[3]

The second component is related to the first. If the verb means to wipe away, then it appropriately expresses the idea that blood acts like a detergent that cleanses things that are ritually unclean or have become contaminated by sin (see the important comments at Ezek 36:17). If sin is removed, and its contamination, then the object or person is approved to occupy sacred space. This was the primary significance for application of blood to temple objects. Inanimate objects do not sin, necessitating atonement in the same sense as a human. Rather, objects become contaminated by the sins of the people around the sacred architecture.

Third, if sin is removed, then God's wrath toward the sinful offenses (or the contaminating effects of sin) is averted. The poetic parallelism in Prov 16:14 offers a good illustration of this use of the word (A king's wrath is a messenger of death // but a wise man atones for it). The reunion between Jacob and Esau further illustrates this when Jacob declares his hope to "atone" the face of his brother Esau (Gen 32:20 with 33:10). The word translated "pacify" (NIV) or "appease" (ESV) is the same Hebrew word for "atone."

A fourth component is the idea of "ransom." If someone is angry, a ransom can be paid to "remove" (i.e., "atone") their anger (Exod 30:16; see also Num 35:31, 33; Lev 17:11, blood [=life] is the payment price).

44:1-3 *gate the LORD . . . entered through it*: Because the eastern gate was the entrance through which the glory of God returned, it was retired from use in Ezekiel's vision. Perhaps the reason is that God's renewed presence with his people is permanent, hence the eastern direction toward which the glory once departed (Ezek 11:23) is now permanently sealed off. The LORD has no intention of ever leaving again.[4] A rather enigmatic figure is introduced at this point in the vision, "the prince" (see comments Ezek 45:7). The prince has the unique privilege to celebrate

---

3. In technical terms, the verb *kpr* in the Qal stem (used in Gen 6:14) means to "cover," but the Piel form of the verb (which is always used in contexts of sacrifice) means the opposite, to "remove." The Old Testament examples cited above validate this. This difference is observed in other Semitic languages as well that share this same word with Hebrew.

4. Cook, *Ezekiel 38–48*, 203.

fellowship meals with the LORD in this gatehouse; but access *through* this gate is sealed off even from his use.

How does the brief mention of this topic contribute to the message of this vision? In Ezek 11:1–13, the prophet also experienced a vision of the eastern gate as the glory *departed*; and in that context, there was a judgment oracle against corrupt leaders who were sitting in the eastern gate. In Ezek 44:1–3, the vision of the glory's *return* is reported and there is anticipation of fellowship between God and a *faithful* leader ("the prince"). In a way parallel to Ezek 11:1–13, this sets the context for the following admonition to leaders in Ezekiel's day to carefully observe God's instructions, especially protecting access to sacred space (Ezek 44:5, 9).[5]

44:4–8 *glory . . . rebellious house of Israel*: As Ezekiel lies facedown before the glory of God (cf. Ezek 43:3), he receives a message of rebuke for the leaders of his day. The fact that this vision once again moves into an ethical warning points to the significance of these visionary experiences (cf. Ezek 43:6–11). This application opens and closes with stress on qualifications for entrance (Ezek 44:5 and 9).

Specifically, the "detestable practices" (Ezek 44:6) involved allowing "foreigners", who were neither internally nor externally qualified, to enter the sanctuary and manage temple objects (Ezek 44:7–9). Any foreigners simply *participating* in Israel's temple worship had to proselytize and were required to observe the same regulations for entrance as covenanted Israelites (Num 15:14–16; Isa 56:3–8). In view of the requirement that Levites are to guard and serve in the temple (Num 18:1–7), it seems these foreigners were employed in place of the Levites for safekeeping boundaries and objects of sacred space (contrast Ezek 44:8 with v. 11).[6] Circumcision was an outward sign, but its absence betrayed a lack of inward faith (Gen 17:9–14; Deut 10:16; cf. Exod 12:41–51). Such carelessness cut the heart out of the covenant relationship (Ezek 44:7).

44:9–16 *Levites who went far from me*: The NIV omits an important connecting link in Hebrew between Ezek 44:9 and 10. A phrase meaning "except" or "but" in Hebrew (cf. ESV; NASB; NET; NRSV; NJPS; Old Greek) contrasts the prohibition of foreigners and the responsibility of Levites to help implement worship. Yet, in addition to the above admonition regarding foreigners, another boundary concerning the Levites and sacred space needed to be set in order.

---

5. See parallel wording between the two passages detailed by Block, *Ezekiel 25–48*, 619–20.

6. Block, *Ezekiel 25–48*, 623. But see next footnote for Cook's alternative view.

When the sacrificial system was first instituted, the descendants of the tribe of Levi were set apart to serve various needs of worship (Num 1:47–50; 3:1–10; Deut 18:1–8; 21:5). From this tribe, Aaron's family was designated as priests in a narrower sense, that is, only they were permitted to handle blood, place sacrifices on the altar, and bring incense into the temple (Num 3:1–10). When certain Levites attempted to usurp this right to serve at the altar, they were judged severely (Num 16:10, 31–35). This was not the last Levitical failure. Guilt for idolatry and misconduct in worship ultimately fell on the shoulders of the priests and the Levites, whose responsibility it was to guard such matters (cf. Num 18:1–4, 23). The history of Israel's failure rested on them. But the instruction in Ezek 44:11 should not be construed as a penalty assessed against the Levites; rather, it reestablishes the proper boundaries of rights and responsibilities in worship. In other words, history reinforced the wisdom of limiting full priestly rights to the family that showed itself faithful, the Zadokites who descended from Aaron (Ezek 44:15–16; cf. 1 Chr 6:3–8). The Zadokites evidently remained loyal to the LORD from the time that Zadok found special favor under David and Solomon (2 Sam 8:17; 1 Kgs 2:35). This passage, then, reaffirms the boundaries of old. Only the Zadokite (Aaronite) priests could preside at the altar or in the temple building, but the Levitical priests would serve more broadly to assist worshippers in the slaughter of animals and to guard the sacred precincts from unlawful transgression by non-priestly laity.[7]

44:17–31 *the holy and the common . . . unclean and the clean:* After reasserting the proper role of Levites, Ezekiel rehearses regulations that protect the important lifestyle example of the priests. They taught the difference between things set apart in a special way for the service of God ("holy"; see commentary at Ezek 26:20), and things that were an ordinary part of every day life ("common"). These two terms define the status of people or objects. For example, priests are "holy" with regard to special temple service, and the nation itself is "holy" with regard to its missiological purpose (see comments at Ezek 36:23). "Holy" and "common" described the *status* of something; a person or object was either specially appointed for service to God or they were just ordinary. This

---

7. Block, *Ezekiel 25–48*, 631–32. Cook agrees with the assessment that Ezekiel's instructions are not punitive against Levites. However, he sees a more simple intertextual link with the original failure of Levites in Num 16:10. He regards the prohibition against foreigners to refer to non-Levitical, Israelite laity rather than non-Israelites. See Cook, *Ezekiel 38–48*, 214–17.

status remained independent of their *condition*. So alongside the category of *status* are categories that describe the *condition* of people or things as either "clean" or "unclean" (see comments at Ezek 18:6; 36:17). For example, priests can defile themselves by contact with something dead (see comments at Ezek 6:5). They still possess holy status, but their condition becomes unclean for a time. By these regulations, the priests taught the people about the special status of God as well as certain conditions that are not compatible with his holiness. Sweat (hence linen, because it breathes, versus wool) and other bodily emissions were not ritually compatible with the most holy spaces (cf. Lev 15; Deut 23:11–14). Head shaving perhaps imitated pagan mourning practices (cf. Lev 21:5–6). Self control, hence sobriety, was necessary in priestly service (cf. Lev 10:1–3, 8–9). The priests' uncommon status was best symbolized through observance of special marriage requirements (cf. Lev 21:7–8, 13–15). Death is the ultimate antithesis of God's essential nature (he *is* life); so specific instructions in Ezek 44:25–31 revolve around this lesson.

45:1–6 *belong to the whole house of Israel:* The temple compound is holy, and certain people are holy, but the surrounding land also has special status in Ezekiel's vision. This sacred district provides for the Levitical families, but a city within this district is for all Israelites. Since the nation itself is set apart as "priestly" (see comments at Ezek 20:41), they can participate in the sacred residence of God in a manner comparable to the priests.

45:7 *prince:* The word translated "prince" is a common word for males of the royal family (1 Kgs 11:34; Ezek 7:27; 19:1) or other important leaders in society (Gen 25:16; Exod 22:28; Num 7:84; Josh 9:15). It is sometimes translated "chief, "leader," or "ruler," as context demands. In other places in Ezekiel, the prophet avoids the term "king," and substitutes "prince" instead (e.g., Ezek 12:10). Even the future, ideal, Davidic king received this title (see comments at Ezek 34:24). It is important to observe, however, that Ezekiel does not make reference to the Davidic line in his temple vision, even though the restoration of Israel under the Davidic dynasty is an important theme (see commentary at Ezek 34:23–24; 37:24–28). Ezekiel's prince resides outside the borders of sacred space designated for Levites (Ezek 45:7), yet at the same time he enjoys a very privileged status in worship (Ezek 44:3). The "prince" in the temple vision offers sacrifice for his own sin and bears children (Ezek 45:22; 46:16). Ezekiel is ambiguous regarding the prince's identity. But in the light of these descriptions, any temptation to read messianic significance into the identity and role of this prince is nullified by our understanding of Jesus as Messiah.

It is hazardous to project into the future Ezekiel's ideas about his temple personnel, just as it is hazardous to project the literalness of his temple buildings. In the postexilic period, there was no king in Israel, yet civil authorities like Zerubbabel, Ezra, and Nehemiah took responsibility to oversee aspects of temple restoration and worship (cf. Ezra 2:2, 8:24–36; Neh 8:18; 12:47). So the spirit of Ezekiel's instructions regarding the prince would have application to such leaders, but we lack evidence of how this worked out in actual practice during the early second-temple period.

45:8–12 *my princes . . . no longer oppress:* The importance of Ezekiel's instructions regarding the prince becomes clear when he announces that other "princes" (i.e., civil leaders over Israel) will no longer oppress. Beginning in chapter 45, ownership of land becomes a crucial issue in Ezekiel's vision. Violation of Mosaic laws that protected God's distribution of land was in the background of earlier accusations against violent leadership (see comments at Ezek 11:3, 15; 34:17), and this prohibition extended even to the prince (Ezek 46:18). The special prince observes proper boundaries, and this would impel the other princes to respect just land allocation as well. Economic justice lies at the heart of Ezekiel's vision of restoration, and it should not escape the reader that the prophet applies words like "violence" and "oppression" to actions that do not comply with justice. The emphatic command to leaders of Ezekiel's day to stop sinful behavior ("Enough!" ESV; NASB; JPS, Ezek 45:9) underscores the point.

45:16–17 *special offering to the prince:* Ezekiel 43:18–27 described the atonement for *dedication* of the altar. In Ezek 44:13–24, the prophet's vision characterizes the *ongoing* rituals of atonement for the temple. The naming of the "prince" as recipient of offerings underscores the important role he plays in the administration of worship, not dissimilar from the role played by kings in the past who were responsible to provide for temple needs (e.g., 1 Kgs 8:62–63; 2 Chr 24:4; 29:20–36; compare also the role of postexilic, civil leaders noted above).

45:18–25 *first month on the first day:* The date that commences the festival calendar for Israel is noteworthy. According to the Mosaic calendar, the religious festivals begin with Passover on the fourteenth day of the first month and included three major pilgrimages: (1) Passover; (2) Weeks/Harvest/First Fruits; and (3) Ingathering/Tabernacles, which included Trumpets and Day of Atonement (Exod 23:14–16; Lev 23:4–44; Num 28:16–40; Deut 16:1–17 [esp. v. 16]). Comparing these passages with Ezekiel, some have stressed the differences, particularly the absence of any mention of Feast of Weeks or Day of Atonement. But rehearsal of the entire worship calendar does not serve Ezekiel's purpose. Rather, he punctuates the innovation that his instruction introduces to the beginning of the festive calendar (first day of first month—*before* Passover begins). This explains the prophet's particular discussion of Passover by name, because his new instruction augments this existing festival. There is no need to labor the absence of other events by name, such as Day of Atonement. It is true that this new observance of atonement on the first day of the first month *functions* in a way similar to Day of Atonement in that it purges contamination from the altar and temple.[8] But this does not mean it replaces the Day of Atonement. The main point of the passage is to emphasize the atoning benefits and purification of sacred space that is provided in Ezekiel's vision.[9]

46:1 *the gate . . . is to be opened*: Issues of access to sacred space continue to dominate Ezekiel's vision. The regulations concerning entrance through the eastern, inner gate reinforce the tightly controlled boundaries of sacred space (this is not the eastern, outer gate, which remains permanently closed; see comments at Ezek 44:1–3).

46:12 *freewill offering*: These sacrifices arose from contexts where a worshipper simply wished to express affection to the LORD, not out of any obligation other than an adoring heart (cf. Exod 35:29). On occasions of such displays of love, there is an exception to the normal gate keeping—in such circumstances, access to God's presence is always to be opened. Note that this is the gate inside the temple compound leading to the altar (Ezek 40:32), not the gate on the outside wall that remained closed perpetually (Ezek 40:5, 10; 44:1–2).

---

8. Cook is correct to view the "you" throughout these instructions as general, not specific to the prophet Ezekiel as though he himself would implement them. In addition, against those who think that Ezekiel has no high priest in his vision, the word "priest" with the definite article (Ezek 45:19) presumes this to be the high priest. Confirming this is his function to apply blood to the altar, similar to the High Priest's duty on Day of Atonement (Cook, *Ezekiel 38–48*, 237).

9. It is possible, as Block argues, that the rituals described in this chapter pertain only to dedication of the new temple during the first calendar year (Block, *Ezekiel 25–48*, 662–64). But instructions that follow (Ezek 46:1–24) apply to the ongoing maintenance of the temple. So, apart from a specific indication of "dedication" in this passage (as appeared in Ezek 43:26), these festival offerings seem normative.

46:18 *inheritance of the people*: This verse was cited in comments on Ezek 45:8–12 and it deserves mention again. The repetition of this theme shows what is central to Ezekiel's concern in these chapters. The people have rights to God's gifts to them, and Israel's land allotment is a primary token of this.

47:1 *water . . . from the threshold of the temple*: It is unnecessary to ask exactly how the course of the river(s) emerges from within the architecture of the temple buildings, or how the river deepens without the inflow of tributaries. As discussed in **Special Topic: A Future Temple?**, seeking literalism in the vision misses the point. Instead, this part of Ezekiel's vision draws from familiar imagery relating to temples in the ancient world. Various texts and pictures from the ancient Near East depict deities in their temples holding vessels from which flow streams of water, and often incorporated into these portraits are trees springing forth in all their fullness, as well as abundant fish (see fig. 2 and discussion at Ezek 40:5–37). In Ezekiel 47:9, the prophet uses a special form of the word translated "river" (*nahalayim*, a "dual" form) that indicates *two* rivers (a pairing of some sort). This corresponds to these ancient images that frequently show *two* streams flowing forth.[10] The Old Testament shows familiarity with the link between temples and life-giving waters (Pss 36:8–9; 46:4). Ezekiel drew upon images from the Garden of Eden in Ezek 28:12–19, and the life-giving properties of rivers flowing from God's Edenic temple perhaps also influenced this vision in Ezek 47 (cf. Gen 2:8–10 and see discussion at Ezek 40:48—41:26). With corresponding imagery, Isaiah anticipates the same transformation from lifeless desert to a well-watered paradise (Isa 35:6–7). The prophets Joel (Joel 3:17–18) and Zechariah (Zech 14:6–11) reflect similar theology to that of Ezekiel—from the holy city or its temple (literalistic details do not matter when expressing theology in impressionistic language) will flow abundant, life-giving waters.[11] The final verse of the chapter provides the main point—the water nurtures the trees whose fruit brings healing. An ancient prayer for healing, found in the library of the Assyrian king, Assurbanipal, brings together the image of trees growing by two rivers that flow forth from the sanctuaries of two deities: "In Eridu [Mesopotamia's oldest temple city] there is a black *kiškanu*-tree, growing in a pure place. Its appearance is lapis-lazuli, erected on the primeval waters-*apsû* . . . In

---

10. Bodi, "Ezekiel," 497–98.
11. Block, *Ezekiel 25–48*, 697–98.

the midst (of the sanctuary) are (the sun-god) Šamaš and (the vegetation god) Tammuz at the mouth [i.e., the source] of two rivers."¹²

Cook notes the balance in Ezekiel between boundaries protecting sacred space and the blessing that emanates from the presence of God: "Walls and gates limit access to the holy; well-being offerings [i.e., those eaten by all worshippers] and the sacred river distribute the benefits to all Israel."¹³

47:13–14 *boundaries of the land . . . equally among them:* The original distribution of land to the tribes of Israel followed various topographical features and corresponded partially to tribal size. The important difference stressed in Ezekiel's vision is the *equal* distribution of land promised to Israel's ancestors. This supports the applications found elsewhere in the vision that rightful access to the promised land and sacred space are to be protected (see comments at Ezek 45:6, 8; 46:18). Of unusual interest is the place granted to foreigners, who are also allowed a stake in the land, assuming their commitment is shown by establishing family roots (Ezek 47:22–23). The participation of God's people in the mission of God to bless the nations appears in such provisions (cf. Gen 12:3; Isa 56:3–8; Zech 8:20–23).

48:30 *the exits of the city:* All twelve tribes participate in restoration to the land ("resurrection," Ezek 37:15–28), all twelve tribes receive a fair allocation of that land (Ezek 47:13—48:29), and all twelve tribes have equal access to the city that is near the temple in the sacred district (cf. Ezek 45:6; 48:15–20).¹⁴ The most significant feature of this city is its name: "The LORD is there." The sound of the name in Hebrew, *yahweh shammah*, is similar to the name of Jerusalem, *yerushalayim*. In a break from the past history associated with the name Jerusalem, which is tainted with centuries of violence and idolatry, this new name signals a new start with new significance, the LORD's permanent dwelling a few miles north of this city.¹⁵ Cook suggests that the name is spoken from a viewpoint *within* the city, meaning that the name is a pointer to the LORD's presence close by to the north ("the LORD is just over there!").¹⁶ In either case, the point remains the same. The book of Ezekiel closes with

---

12. Bodi, "Ezekiel," 498.
13. Cook, *Ezekiel 38–48*, 273.
14. The discussion and diagram in Block, *Ezekiel 25–48*, 732–33 is particularly helpful to visualize the sacred reserve.
15. Block, *Ezekiel 25–48*, 739; Bodi, "Ezekiel," 499.
16. Cook, *Ezekiel 38–48*, 296–97.

the answer to the central problem facing the exiles and underscored in Ezekiel's opening vision—where is their God? He speaks his promise in Ezek 48:35; he will live permanently in their midst!

Theological Bridge to Application

Standing out from the detailed treatment of purity laws and description of carefully allocated land is the vision of the sacred river. Cook registers the insightful observation that the river runs through a temple court that no longer features the bronze sea (cf. 1 Kgs 7:23–26).[17] The sea symbolized the LORD's control over the cosmic waters that threaten life with their chaos.[18] In Ezekiel's temple, chaos is not even visibly represented. Rather, life-giving power radiates from God's presence, renewing his creation. Chaos is not simply subdued, it is eradicated. The cosmos is once again well ordered and life-giving. The validation of this comes in the vision of Rev 21:1; 22:1–3—"and there is no longer a sea" . . . (each side of the river is the tree of life bearing fruit) . . . "no longer will anything be cursed."

Focus of Application

The details of these chapters can be overwhelming; but the essential message emerges in basic simplicity. First, Ezek 43:13—44:31 depicts the restoration of proper respect for sacred space created by God's presence. Atonement means removal of sin and purging of its contaminating effects. For believers today, Ezekiel's instructions remind us that sin has consequences beyond the individual. It defiles others, since together believers constitute God's holy temple, which is the corporate body in Christ. There is a balance between the holy and the familiar. Access to God is open, but this does not ignore the necessity of submission to his demands for holiness in manner of life. When the work of Christ's atonement becomes fully realized in the new creation, not only is sin removed but also its contaminating effects.

A second lesson from this passage emerges from the meticulous details of land allocation, together with the emphatic warning against exploitation and injustice. God's people are treated with equity in the inheritance they enjoy. Granted, in the world of Ezekiel and ancient

---

17. Cook, *Ezekiel 38–48*, 271.
18. Monson, "1 Kings," 35, 39.

Israel and the Old Covenant, access to sacred space was regulated for the purpose of maintaining the purity of God's presence. But such distinctions are no longer applicable among Christians who share equally in the responsibilities and blessings of the New Covenant. What was true for ancient Israel, where Ezekiel envisioned the restoration of relationships between God–People–Land, is all the more true in the church, where we practice in the present, as much as possible, the ideals of the future.

God promises restoration of physical life, in all its fullness. This is graphically portrayed in the vision of the river, which causes the trees to flourish, which in turn gives healing to all that is broken. As Block outlines, it is no surprise that Ezekiel's temple vision provided ample imagery to John's vision of the new heavens and new earth: (1) a visionary transport to a high mountain (Rev 21:10); (2) a new world with a new city at its center (Rev 21:1–2, 10); (3) God in the midst of his people (Rev 21:3–4); (4) God's glory in the city (Rev 21:11); (5) a heavenly interpreter with a measuring rod (Rev 21:15–17); (6) a symmetrical city plan with walls and twelve gates for the twelve tribes (Rev 21:11–21); (7) purity and holiness abide (Rev 21:27); (8) a river of life with flourishing trees (Rev 22:1–2). We can add to his list the absence of chaos and curse (Rev 21:1; 22:3) and the healing of all suffering (Rev 21:4; 22:2).[19] Even so, Lord-Jesus, come (Rev 22:20)!

---

19. Block, *Ezekiel 25–48*, 502–03.

BIBLIOGRAPHY

Alexander, Ralph H. "Ezekiel." In *The Expositor's Bible Commentary*, edited by Tremper Longman III and David E. Garland, 421–924. Grand Rapids: Zondervan, 2010.
Allen, Leslie C. *Ezekiel 1–19*. Word Biblical Commentary 28. Dallas: Word, 1994.
———. *Ezekiel 20–48*. Word Biblical Commentary 29. Dallas: Word, 1990.
Barker, Paul A. "Sabbath, Sabbatical Year, Jubilee." In *Dictionary of the Old Testament: Pentateuch*, edited by T. Desmond Alexander and David W. Baker, 695–706. Downers Grove, IL: InterVarsity, 2003.
Beale, G. K. *A New Testament Biblical Theology: The Unfolding of the Old Testament in the New*. Grand Rapids: Baker, 2011.
Block, Daniel I. *The Book of Ezekiel: Chapters 1–24*. New International Commentary on the Old Testament. Grand Rapids: Eerdmans, 1997.
———. *The Book of Ezekiel: Chapters 25–48*. New International Commentary on the Old Testament. Grand Rapids: Eerdmans, 1998.
———. "Preaching Ezekiel." In *Reclaiming the Old Testament for Christian Preaching*, edited by Grenville J. R. Kent et al., 157–78. Downers Grove, IL: InterVarsity, 2010.
———. *By the River Chebar: Historical, Literary, and Theological Studies in the Book of Ezekiel*. Eugene, OR: Cascade Books, 2013.
———. "Divine Abandonment: Ezekiel's Adaptation of an Ancient Near Eastern Motif." In *By the River Chebar: Historical, Literary, and Theological Studies in the Book of Ezekiel*, 73–107. Eugene, OR: Cascade Books, 2013.
———. "The Prophet of the Spirit: The Use of רוח in the Book of Ezekiel." In *By the River Chebar: Historical, Literary, and Theological Studies in the Book of Ezekiel*, 27–50. Eugene, OR: Cascade Books, 2013.
Bock, Darrell L. "Son of Man." In *Dictionary of Jesus and the Gospels*, edited by Joel B. Green et al., 894–900. Downers Grove, IL: InterVarsity, 2013.
Bodi, Daniel. "Ezekiel." In *Zondervan Illustrated Bible Backgrounds Commentary*, edited by John H. Walton, 400–517. Grand Rapids: Zondervan, 2009.
Calvin, John. *Commentary on the Book of the Prophet Isaiah*. Translated by William Pringle. Grand Rapids: Eerdmans, 1948.
Carston, Robyn. "Word Meaning, What Is Said and Explicature." In *What Is Said and What Is Not*, edited by Carlo Penco and Filippo Domaneschi, 175–203. Standford: CSLI Publications, 2013.
Chisholm, Robert B., Jr. "When Prophecy Appears to Fail, Check Your Hermeneutic." *Journal of the Evangelical Theological Society* 53 (2010) 561–77.
Church Bullying: An Introduction. http://churchbullying.org/introduction/

Clements, Ronald E. *Ezekiel*. Westminster Bible Companion. Louisville: Westminster John Knox, 1996.
Cook, Stephen L. *Ezekiel 38–48: A New Translation with Introduction and Commentary*. Anchor Yale Bible 22B. New Haven: Yale University Press, 2018.
Cooper, Lamar Eugene, Sr. *Ezekiel*. New American Commentary 17. Nashville: Broadman & Holman, 1994.
Copan, Paul, and Matthew Flannagan. "The Ethics of 'Holy War' for Christian Morality and Theology." In *Holy War in the Bible: Christian Morality and an Old Testament Problem*, edited by Heath A. Thomas et al., 201–39. Downers Grove, IL: InterVarsity, 2013.
Curtis, A. H. W. "Canaanite Gods and Religion." In *Dictionary of the Old Testament: Historical Books*, edited by Bill T. Arnold and H. G. M. Williamson, 132–42. Downers Grove, IL: InterVarsity, 2005.
Dillard, Raymond B. *2 Chronicles*. Word Biblical Commentary 15. Waco, TX: Word, 1987.
Duffy, Maureen, and Len Sperry. *Mobbing: Causes, Consequences, and Solutions*. Oxford: Oxford University Press, 2012.
Durand, J.-M. *Archives épistolaires de Mari I/1*. Archives royales de Mari 26. Paris: Editions recherche sur les civilisations, 1988.
Farber, Walter. "Witchcraft, Magic, and Diviniation in Ancient Mesopotamia." In *Civilizations of the Ancient Near East*, edited by Jack M. Sasson, 1895–909. Peabody, MA: Hendrickson, 2000.
Feldman, Louis H. *Flavius Josephus: Judean Antiquities 1–4*. Flavius Josephus: Translation and Commentary 3. Leiden: Brill, 2000.
Fulton, Deirdre N. "The Exile and the Exilic Communities." In *Behind the Scenes of the Old Testament: Cultural, Social, and Historical Contexts*, edited by Jonathan S. Greer et al., 230–35. Grand Rapids: Baker, 2018.
Galambush, Julie. *Jerusalem in the Book of Ezekiel: The City as Yahweh's Wife*. SBL Dissertation Series 130. Atlanta: Scholars, 1992.
Gelb, Ignace J., et al., eds. *The Assyrian Dictionary of the Oriental Institute of the University of Chicago*. Chicago: The Oriental Institute, 1964–99.
Glucksberg, Sam. *Understanding Figurative Language: From Metaphor to Idioms*. Oxford: Oxford University Press, 2001.
Grayson, A. Kirk. *Assyrian and Babylonian Chronicles*. Winona Lake, IN: Eisenbrauns, 2000.
———. *The Royal Inscriptions of Sennacherib, King of Assyria (704–681 BC), Part 1*. Royal Inscriptions of the Neo-Assyrian Period 3/1. Winona Lake, IN: Eisenbrauns, 2012.
Green, Gene L. "Relevance Theory and Biblical Interpretation." In *The Oxford Encyclopedia of Biblical Interpretation*, edited by Steven L. McKenzie, 266–73. Oxford: Oxford University Press, 2013.
———. "Relevance Theory and Theological Interpretation: Thoughts on Metarepresentation." *Journal of Theological Interpretation* 4 (2010) 75–90.
Greenberg, Moshe. *Ezekiel 1–20*. Anchor Bible 22. Garden City, NY: Doubleday, 1983.
———. *Ezekiel 21–37*. Anchor Bible 22A. Garden City, NY: Doubleday, 1997.
Grenz, Stanley J. *Prayer: The Cry for the Kingdom*. Peabody, MA: Hendrickson, 1988.

Hallo, William W., and K. Lawson Younger, Jr., eds. *The Context of Scripture: Canonical Inscriptions, Monumental Inscriptions, and Archival Documents from the Biblical World*. Leiden: Brill, 2003.

Hamori, Esther J. *Women's Divination in Biblical Literature: Prophecy, Necromancy, and Other Arts of Knowledge*. Anchor Yale Bible Reference Library. New Haven: Yale University Press, 2015.

Herodotus. *The History*. Translated by David Grene. Chicago: University of Chicago Press, 1987.

Heiser, Michael S. *The Unseen Realm: Recovering the Supernatural Worldview of the Bible*. Bellingham, WA: Lexham, 2015.

Hilber, John W. "The Culture of Prophecy and Writing in the Ancient Near East." In *Do Historical Matters Matter to Faith?*, edited by James K. Hoffmeier and Dennis Magary, 219–41. Wheaton, IL: Crossway, 2012.

———. "Diversity of OT Prophetic Phenomena and NT Prophecy." *Westminster Theological Journal* 56 (1994) 243–58.

———. "Prophecy, Divination, and Magic in the Ancient Near East." In *Behind the Scenes of the Old Testament: Cultural, Social, and Historical Contexts*, edited by Jonathan S. Greer et al., 368–74. Grand Rapids: Baker, 2018.

———. "Psalms." In *Zondervan Illustrated Bible Backgrounds Commentary*, vol. 5, edited by John H. Walton, 316–463. Grand Rapids: Zondervan, 2009.

Homer. *The Odyssey*. Translated by A. T. Murray and George E. Dimock. Cambridge: Harvard University Press, 1995.

Johnston, Philip S. *Shades of Sheol: Death and Afterlife in the Old Testament*. Downers Grove, IL: InterVarsity, 2002.

King, Philip J., and Lawrence E. Stager. *Life in Biblical Israel*. Library of Ancient Israel. Louisville: Westminster John Knox, 2001.

Kitchen, K. A. *On the Reliability of the Old Testament*. Grand Rapids: Eerdmans, 2003.

———. *Poetry of Ancient Egypt*. Jonsered: Åströms, 1999.

Kuruvilla, Abraham. *Privilege the Text!*. Chicago: Moody, 2013.

Livingstone, Alasdair. *Court Poetry and Literary Miscellanea*. State Archives of Assryia 3. Helsinki: University of Helsinki Press, 1989.

Lynch, Matthew J. "Monotheism in Ancient Israel." In *Behind the Scenes of the Old Testament: Cultural, Social, and Historical Contexts*, edited by Jonathan S. Greer et al., 340–48. Grand Rapids: Baker, 2018.

Lyons, Michael A. *An Introduction to the Study of Ezekiel*. T. & T. Clark Approaches to Biblical Studies. London: Bloomsbury T. & T. Clark, 2015.

Monson, John. "1 Kings." In *Zondervan Illustrated Bible Backgrounds Commentary*, edited by John H. Walton, 3:2–109. Grand Rapids: Zondervan, 2009.

Nissinen, Martti, et al. *Prophets and Prophecy in the Ancient Near East*. Writings from the Ancient World 12. Atlanta: Society of Biblical Literature, 2003.

Petter, Donna L. "High Places." In *Dictionary of the Old Testament: Historical Books*, edited by Bill T. Arnold and H. G. M. Williamson, 413–18. Downers Grove, IL: InterVarsity, 2005.

Pietersma, Albert, and Benjamin G. Wright, eds. *A New English Translation of the Septuagint*. Oxford: Oxford University Press, 2007.

Pratt, Richard L., Jr. "Historical Contingencies and Biblical Predictions." In *The Way of Wisdom: Essays in Honor of Bruce K. Waltke*, edited by J. I. Packer and Sven K. Soderland, 180–203. Grand Rapids: Zondervan, 2000.

Pritchard, James B., ed. *Ancient Near Eastern Texts Relating to the Old Testament*. 3rd ed. Princeton: Princeton University Press, 1969.

Rumelhart, David E. "Some Problems With the Notion of Literal Meanings." In *Metaphor and Thought*, edited by Andrew Ortony, 71–82. 2nd ed. Cambridge: Cambridge University Press, 1993.

Sandy, D. Brent. *Plowshares & Pruning Hooks: Rethinking the Language of Biblical Prophecy and Apocalyptic*. Downers Grove, IL: InterVarsity, 2002.

Sperber, Dan, and Deirdre Wilson. *Relevance: Communication and Cognition*. Cambridge: Harvard University Press, 1995.

Steinmann, Andrew E. "Cherubim." In *Dictionary of the Old Testament: Pentateuch*, edited by T. Desmond Alexander and David W. Baker, 112–13. Downers Grove, IL: InterVarsity, 2003.

Stemmer, Brigitte. "Neuropragmatics." In *The Oxford Handbook of Pragmatics*, edited by Yan Huang, 1–30. Oxford Handbooks in Linguistics. Oxford: Oxford University Press, 2013.

Taylor, John B. *Ezekiel: An Introduction and Commentary*. Tyndale Old Testament Commentaries. Downers Grove, IL: InterVarsity, 1969.

Van Dam, C. "Divination, Magic." In *Dictionary of the Old Testament: Prophets*, edited by Mark J. Boda and J. Gordon McConville, 159–62. Downers Grove, IL: InterVarsity, 2012.

Vensel, Steven R. "Mobbing, Burnout, and Religious Coping Styles among Protestant Clergy: A Structural Equation Model and Its Implications for Counselors." Ph.D. diss., Florida Atlantic University, 2012. Available at https://fau.digital.flvc.org/islandora/object/fau%3A3989/datastream/OBJ/view/Mobbing__burnout__and_religious_coping_styles_among_Protestant_clergy.pdf.

Walton, John H. "Genesis." In *Zondervan Illustrated Bible Backgrounds Commentary*, edited by John H. Walton, 1:1–159. Grand Rapids: Zondervan, 2009.

———. "The Temple in Context." In *Behind the Scenes of the Old Testament: Cultural, Social, and Historical Contexts*, edited by Jonathan S. Greer et al., 349–54. Grand Rapids: Baker, 2018.

Wilson, Deirdre, and Dan Sperber. "Relevance Theory." In *The Handbook of Pragmatics*, edited by Laurence R. Horn and Gregory L. Ward, 607–32. Blackwell Handbooks in Linguistics 16. Oxford: Blackwell, 2004.

Wilson, Deirdre, and Dan Sperber. "Truthfulness and Relevance." In *Meaning and Relevance*, 47–83. Cambridge: Cambridge University Press, 2012.

Wright, Christopher J. H. *The Message of Ezekiel: A New Heart and a New Spirit*. The Bible Speaks Today. Downers Grove, IL: InterVarsity, 2001.

———. *The Mission of God's People*. Grand Rapids: Zondervan, 2010.

Zimmerli, Walther. *Ezekiel 2: A Commentary on the Book of the Prophet Ezekiel, Chapters 25–48*. Translated by James D. Martin. Hermeneia. Philadelphia: Fortress, 1983.

www.ingramcontent.com/pod-product-compliance
Lightning Source LLC
Chambersburg PA
CBHW022001220426
43663CB00007B/915